NEWSPAPER DESIGN TODAY

1. Award winners. Top left, *The Observer*, winner of the news pages award in the 1988 UK Newspaper Design Awards. Top right, *The Independent*, winner of the main award for national dailies in 1987 and 1988. Bottom left, *The Northamptonshire Evening Telegraph*, overall winner among evening papers. The citation said: 'Everything about it, from story count to story shape, choice of type to use of space, was exemplary.' Bottom right, *Eastern Daily Press*. Overall winner in the Regional Mornings section of the 1988 UK Newspaper Design Awards and winner of the award for news pages in that section. The paper won praise for its traditional Bodoni headlines.

NEWSPAPER DESIGN TODAY
A MANUAL FOR PROFESSIONALS

Allen Hutt and Bob James

LUND HUMPHRIES LONDON

First edition 1989
Published by Lund Humphries Publishers Ltd,
16 Pembridge Road, London W11

British Library Cataloguing in Publication Data:
Hutt, Allen, *1901–1973*
Newspaper design today.
1. Newspapers. Layout
I. Title   II. James, Bob   III. Hutt, Allen. Newspaper design
686.2'252
ISBN 0-85331-533-7

21033109

Designed and edited by DAG Publications Ltd
Designed by David Gibbons; layout by Anthony A. Evans;
typeset by Nene Phototypesetters Ltd in Sabon. Made and
printed in Great Britain by The Bath Press, Bath

While the quality of the originals sometimes renders the
reproduction of the illustrations in this book less than
perfect, every effort has been made to reproduce them as
clearly and legibly as possible.

CONTENTS

ALLEN HUTT

by Bob James

YOUNG JAMES, he used to call me. There was usually a pause, the merest hint of a twinkle in his eye promising more to follow, and when it came it was almost invariably a mock scolding. 'Young James, haven't I taught you anything?' was a favourite opening as he corrected some assertion about perhaps a headline typeface and then went on to thrill all who were listening with a masterly appraisal not only of the typeface and its designer but also of its uses and misuses. We shared many platforms at newspaper design courses, he the master and I an apprentice, although truly he would not see it that way for what we called our song-and-dance act was all in the cause of teaching.

Allen Hutt was an outstanding journalist, typographer and designer, equally at home in crafting a headline, a new titlepiece or a scholarly treatise. His achievements were many, although maybe he was most proud of being designated Royal Designer for Industry in 1970.

He was a man of causes, all of them pursued with a fervour that was infectious. Those who listened to his lectures on typography would often be imbued with the determination to spread his message — that newspaper typography and make-up can never be divorced from the journalism of which they are only the vehicle. It happened to me, and I am delighted to promote that gospel: it is as vital today as it was then.

INTRODUCTION

ALLEN HUTT died in 1973, but his kind of newspaper design lives on, based on the belief that 'newspaper typography and make-up can never be divorced from the journalism of which they are only the vehicle'. The quoted words are pure Hutt, taken from the preface of the first edition of *Newspaper Design,* a book written by a journalist for journalists and promoting the philosophy that the general principles of newspaper typography must march together with its daily practice.

This togetherness of theory and practice has always posed problems for those newspaper people whose natural inclinations, for one reason or another, have been to divorce the journalism from its presentation. Hutt's belief was that packaging was important but no more so than the content. His advice to editors was constant: the firmly expressed view that a product packaged well could be sold well, provided that it consistently satisfied the consumer. This is as true today as ever it was, and we must continue to press the cause – newspaper design has no future apart from the future of newspapers.

The natural evolution of a newspaper is one of changing content to meet the changing needs and interests of readers, and of changing methods of presentation to accommodate changing reading habits. The two matters are nevertheless entwined, inextricably so, in a marriage of content and form, message and medium, that allows newspapers to pursue their different markets. There are obvious dangers when the marketing process spawns a kind of newspaper design that sells lookalike newspapers in which content is neutralised so as to fit a pattern. Allen Hutt was early in recognising these dangers and pressed the case for the training of journalists in the theory and practice of typography and design rather than subordinate that life-blood of newspapers, the journalism, to the whims of those whose prime aim would be the making of pretty patterns.

Bob James was a young sub-editor when he first read Hutt's great standard work, *Newspaper Design,* and fell under its influence not only in his day-to-day work but in his own growing belief in training as an essential combination of theory with practice, in which aim and understanding would dictate the techniques to be employed. The two men were to meet and share ideas as well as many platforms at the design seminars and training courses for senior journalists that sprang up in the 1960s.

This book is itself the product of an evolutionary process. In updating Allen Hutt's *Newspaper Design,* Bob James acknowledges the important influence of others who shared many of Hutt's aims, beliefs, and platforms too; notably Harold Evans and Leslie Sellers, whose works have contributed so much to the cause of journalism training.

ACKNOWLEDGEMENTS

THIS book has a long history, dating back to 1947 when the late Stanley Morison first vetted a synopsis prepared by Allen Hutt for what was to become, many years later, the first edition of *Newspaper Design*. Morison was a great influence on Hutt in an association that lasted for more than thirty years, and Hutt went to great lengths to acknowledge this in his book.

We are all of us influenced by our teachers and colleagues, the journalists, printers and publishers we have worked with and those whose work and works we admire. Everything we read and experience is likely to play a part in the evolutionary process that determines what we come to regard as being our style, although in truth it owes most to the sources of the knowledge and skills so necessary in any craft. Just as Hutt owed much to Morison, so the present author owes much to Hutt and, through him, to that earlier generation of influence. This would be a long list indeed were it to attempt to offer recognition to all of those people, in many countries, who have given support, advice, encouragement, and inspiration, and it may be safer and comprehensive to offer due thanks to all who have been of influence in this book's production, from Morison onwards.

Names must be named, of course, and chief among the present author's debts are those owed to the many fine journalists who have been friends and colleagues through the years. First among these must be his first editor, W. H. Hopper, of the *Northern Despatch* at Darlington, who urged him to do every job in journalism in preparation for editorship, only to find instead that he was grooming not an editor but a teacher. Harold Evans and Leslie Sellers, like Allen Hutt, were of later and continuing inspiration.

Practical acknowledgment must be made to all the newspapers mentioned and illustrated in this book and also to some organisations who have played important parts in a perhaps indirect way. Among these are the Pacific Area Newspaper Publishers Association and the Commonwealth Press Union, who, by inviting the author to conduct so many seminars and lecture tours, have afforded him the valuable opportunity to study newspapers in many countries. Type manufacturers and their designers have provided much information over the years, and specific mention must be made of the Monotype Corporation, who were painstaking in setting so many examples and generous in their praise of the efforts of others. Mention must also be made of the publishers of the book, especially the always-patient and supportive John Taylor, the designers of DAG Publications Ltd, David Gibbons and Tony Evans, and also the typesetters and printers.

2. Broadsheets have become narrower over the years for a variety of reasons, including ease of reading, newsprint saving, and perhaps also because it has been the fashionable thing to do. As recently as 1965 the *Wigan Observer* (Figure 2) had a page 119 pica ems wide.
It may appear old-fashioned but from a typographical standpoint there was a high degree of readability in that 8pt text set in ten 11½em columns, the slugs indented by an en at each side to increase the whiting beside column rules with a 6pt base-width. Modern newspapers, often with half that spacing, might take note!

8

FORM AND CONTENT

THE graphic design of a newspaper is not a thing in itself ... Those were the opening words in the first edition of *Newspaper Design*, published in 1960; and the message is the same today and will be reflected throughout this book. The content of a successful newspaper is the most important factor in its success, and presentation is an integral part of that element. Just as what we say and the way we say it are bound together inextricably in communicating by word of mouth, so too are the same elements combined in communicating through print. Words are the content; the typography is the way we express them.

Communicating by means of the printed word to a mass audience of third parties through the columns of a newspaper is a complicated process. It is not so much a question of deciding what should be said and then saying it, but more a matter of anticipating what the readers will understand from what is written. That can be done only when we begin at the beginning and consider the way in which people read, so that we can all the more effectively communicate our message. Writing, it might be said, has more to do with reading than with the physical process of putting words on to paper. The more we think on this plane the more importance we may place upon presentation as being the factor that decides whether a story is read or is not.

However, there is as much danger in overestimating the value of packaging as there is in undervaluing it. Those who would produce a pattern and fit the content to it are just as wrong as those who subscribe to the discredited view that if the story is good enough people will read it no matter how poor the presentation. The two are as one. There is a bond between form and content, a marriage of equals in which we take first the content and then give it the presentation it deserves.

This is surely the common inference to be drawn from the views of those who have this century most influenced the world of newspaper design. Stanley Morison put the point forcibly in the last sentence of his great work on the evolution of English newspaper typography, *The English Newspaper, 1622–1932:*

The community would unquestionably benefit if men of learning would extend their interest to the end that the

tranquillity, exactitude, clarity and ease of reading, which have been secured in the English book, may also be obtained in that other category of printing, the fundamental economic character of which is more fully developed, and which is in consequence more widely distributed – the English newspaper.

More than half a century has passed since those words were written, and we can only question whether a Morison of today would be satisfied that the men of learning have exercised due influence over the typographical presentation of newspapers. Our newspapers have certainly changed, and substantially so, but that is to be expected, for they are documents of the age they chronicle and must inevitably reflect its fashions and values. The coming of the computer has also caused enormous change, altering for all time the very techniques of printing newspapers. The modern Morison, however, would question whether we have improved that quality perhaps most accurately described as the process of communication by means of the printed word.

Herbert Spencer in *The Visible Word: Problems of Legibility* is succinct with this two-sentence comment on that process:

No matter how vital the message, or how great the author's wisdom, or how remarkable the printer's skill, unread print is merely a little paper and a little ink. The true economics of printing must be measured by how much is read and understood and not by how much is produced.

Even blunter, Edmund C. Arnold, in *Modern Newspaper Design*, opens a chapter on functional typography:

The newspaper typographer is a communicator. His sole job is to use type as a tool for quick, accurate transmission of information.
'Designers' who work with type may use the handsome forms of the Latin alphabet as decoration or may arrange the lines and blocks of type as elements of abstract composition. Whether the type is – or even can be – read is immaterial to them. Not to the typographer, though; he considers unread type as a waste of costly materials, equipment, and manpower.

Beatrice Warde wrote of it more eloquently, perhaps, in her wonderful essay *The Crystal Goblet*, with its appropriate alternative sub-title *Printing Should Be Invisible*:

The most important thing about printing is that it conveys thought, ideas, images, from one mind to other minds. This statement is what you might call the front door of the

3

3 and 4. There are a great many brash tabloids but few broadsheets would rival Berlin's *Bild* for the kind of razzmatazz shown in Figure 3. The flags above the Princess Diana story are in full colour while the underscore shows lines of crowns on a blue background. It's much the same on the back page (Figure 4) and most of the pages inside.

science of typography. Within lie hundreds of rooms but unless you start by assuming that *printing is meant to convey specific and coherent ideas*, it is very easy to find yourself in the wrong house altogether.

Harold Evans, journalist first and typographer second, in Book V of his manual *Editing and Design*, offers this message:

What is important for the future of newspaper design – indeed of newspapers – is that we should understand what we are trying to do. If we can, we will be able energetically to exploit the favourable influences, minimise the adverse, and discount the transitory. And the very first essential is to realise that design is part of journalism. Design is not decoration. It is communication.

Yes, we could go on with more quotations from men and women of learning who, since Morison, have sought to influence and improve the process of communication between newspapers and their readers. It has been a long and continuing campaign to impress upon newspapers a grasp of the essential principles of typography that we are apt to take for granted in other publishing houses.

Some considerable hope lies in the new era of electronic editing. There is a growing realisation that the present and future generations of journalists need to know more about typography than any previous generation could have been expected to know no matter how desirable such knowledge might have been. The journalist at the keyboard has more control of the communication process than ever before, controlling both what is said and the way it is to be said. He or she is more of a composer than the compositor ever was.

A good deal depends on this marriage of content and form. There have always been those who for one reason or another have wished to separate the two in some demarcation between writers and printers, and there are those who would have it continue but in a different form with journalists on the one hand and designers on the other.

In the United States, particularly, the influence of the graphic designer has been increasingly noticeable. At best it results in more technical excellence in the application of general typographical principles to project the journalism of words and pictures. At worst it takes over, the content being subordinated to the often pre-determined layout that may look good but not project the story. In between is the vast no man's land where constant battles are fought between the camps that represent form and content, where the strongest wins – and so often the reader loses.

It should be a relatively easy matter to join two forces in a common aid, that in which everything is done with the needs of the reader in mind. Take a journalist and teach him design, or teach journalism to designers, and we should develop the same joint talent. If we do not, newspapers will become (as so many magazines have become) publications that appear at first consideration to be more appetising than they turn out to be. The most successful magazines, and clearly the most successful newspapers, will be those that react to the news and reflect it, ever capable of instant adaptation to changes in it.

The formula page of unchanging shapes, where the content is massaged into modules as inflexible and boring as the child's building block, has undoubted value in such areas of information journalism as television guides, city prices, sporting statistics, horoscopes and the like; but news is news and should take the space and shape it needs.

This is another marriage, that of providing for what we may call 'reader appeal', grabbing the attention of passers-by as they flick through our pages, and 'reader comfort' needed by those of us who wish to curl up on the sofa for the unmistakeable pleasure of a good read.

Typography and layout are the tools the editor uses to do this. According to Edmund C. Arnold, the four purposes of layout are:

1. to increase readability and to attract the reader into the news
2. to sort the news so that the reader knows at a glance which are the most important stories
3. to create attractive and interesting pages
4. to create recognition, to make the reader identify and want your paper as soon as he sees it.

This broad approach, however, takes for granted the basic physical characteristics of a newspaper page, which is unlike any other printed page. A newspaper page combines text and display over a large area – too large to take in at one glance – and, unlike the book or magazine page, it is likely to contain a variety of separate and unrelated items, each with different appeal to the likely readers. Such a page needs a guide to the readers, directing them through the relative priorities of each element so that they can see what is on offer and make a selection. The design of a newspaper page, especially a news page, is its own menu.

The page is divided usually into columns, the number and width of which are traditionally decided by the economics of advertising. The trend over several decades has been to improve advertising yields by increasing the number of columns and reducing their width or measure, an effect heightened even further by the ever-decreasing width of newspaper pages to achieve often huge savings in newsprint by almost subliminal means. The 96-em broadsheet is a thing of the past; *The Times* of London is but 81.5 ems while *USA Today*, typical of the North American broadsheet, is 77.5 ems. Editorially, the width of a page is of more significance than the width of its columns. Column widths, increasingly, are of concern only as regards advertising, which is sold on the basis of a column grid, perhaps sixths, sevenths, eighths, or ninths of a page width. Once the advertisements are planned into a page that grid disappears. What is left is space, measured in pica ems, for the editorial planners to design as best they can for the benefit of the reader.

This in itself requires an increased understanding by the page-planner of the relationship of type size and measure to ensure good reading. The column that is

5. An unusual format of four columns to the page for a special supplement in *The Times*. It is a delightful read in 12pt Times New Roman with generous whiting between lines and columns.

6 and 7. There could be few slabs of type containing more words than in this page of a famous printing issue of *The Times* in 1912 but it was still very readable in six 16-em legs set full-out to the column rules. Figure 7 shows another page from the 64-page in-paper supplement, a history of private printing presses and a wonderful illustration from the Kelmscott Chaucer.

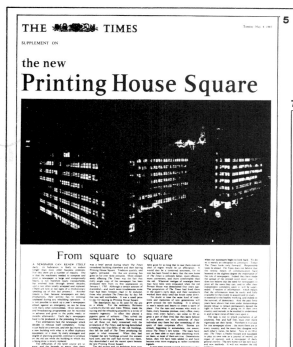

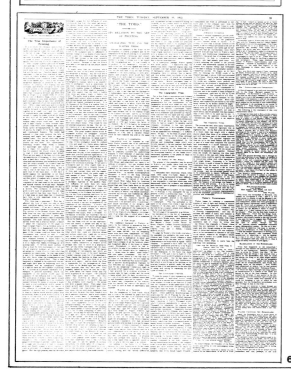

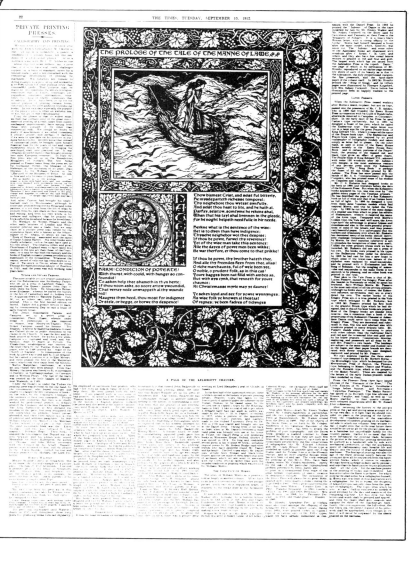

too narrow or too wide will be too demanding of its readers. There are newspapers with advertising columns of six- and seven-pica ems, which are quite effective in their way; but to inflict that kind of measure on the editorial part of a page is to misunderstand the needs of the reader. These days, spatial awareness is the name of the game.

We face an additional problem in that newspapers are expected to look like newspapers. The way they look is part of their 'newsiness' as though evidence of being produced in a hurry is in some way a measure of quality. Readers grow accustomed to newspaper style and then expect their newspaper to conform to an idea of style that they have consciously or subconsciously formed. When *The Times* of London split into two sections some of its readers were irritated, for they were used to their all-in-one package, which they found comfortable as well as familiar. They did not know their way around the strange two-section paper that fell apart in their hands. New readers, on the other hand, perhaps including many well used to the handling of newspapers in two, three, or even more sections, felt no such irritation – but may have felt some when, after technical readjustment, *The Times* returned (albeit temporarily) to its one-section form some months later. Some of the old readers were undoubtedly delighted, but there were some who, having come to terms with the change, were even more irritated by all this to-ing and fro-ing.

Yet style must not be static. It has its evolutions and sometimes even its revolutions, although these last are rare and only successful if they are the result of deliberate and careful planning. In Britain through the 1980s there has been an enormous swing from broadsheet format to tabloid, a change undertaken best by those newspapers planning the move in detail and preparing not only themselves but also their readers with a programme of promotion designed to anticipate reaction and arouse in its place an air of expectancy. It was the same for the many American newspapers changing from evening publication to morning. It will be the same for all major changes of style; that element of surprise for which newspapers sometimes strive, springing great changes without warning, may have the slight benefit of surprising competitors, but it will be at the expense of creating shock among readers.

History will record the achievements of Harold Evans as Editor of *The Sunday Times* and *The Times* but the newspaper historian is also likely to record his notable re-design of *The Northern Echo*, the impor-

tant north of England morning paper he edited for five years in the early 1960s. His changes were physical in changing the look of the paper and philosophical in changing its stance to focus on the likely reader rather than just the current readership. Just as important, they were planned and put into effect over the whole period of his editorship and in that respect were probably unfinished when he left for Fleet Street. Those who are impatient for change might use *The Northern Echo* for case study.

8. One of the few remaining elements of *The Northern Echo* from its Harold Evans era is the elegant Clarendon titlepiece, here a trifle lop-sided with a single earpiece where once it had none. That slight criticism apart, it is a superb front page demonstrating the marriage of strong journalism and strong display, the inseparable components of newspaper design. All major news headlines are in Century Schoolbook Bold, with Century Schoolbook text to match. Headings in the tightly-packed digest (17 items!) are in Helios Triumvirate.

9. Another happy marriage, this time of long stories and wordy headlines, which together help give *The Sunday Times* the look and feel of a writer's paper.

9

A22   ★★★★   THE SUNDAY TIMES 14 FEBRUARY 1988

Why it's only fair to reward professionalism in rugby

by David Kirk

Bath power and confidence leave Tigers floundering

by Stephen Jones

| Leicester | 0pts |
| Bath | 13pts |

Hint to selectors: John Hall of Bath in the thick of the muddy action

Close-run thing for Waterloo

by David Lawrenson

Sale take the lead out of their boots to end Coventry cup run

by Norman Harris

| Coventry | 0pts |
| Sale | 13pts |

Fieldhouse edges Saints home

by Peter Jones

| Warrington | 20pts |
| St Helens | 24pts |

RUGBY RESULTS

FOR THE RECORD

BOWLS

ATHLETICS

ICE SPEEDWAY

HANG GLIDING

SQUASH

GOLF

DARTS

CRICKET

RUNNING

RACING RESULTS

JULIAN'S SELECTIONS

In an entirely different field, the tiny weekly *Bexhill-on-Sea Observer*, an old-fashioned and ailing broadsheet, turned tabloid in 1985, but did so by first re-designing the broadsheet using a form of modular make-up that would suit the tabloid when scaled down. *The Buckinghamshire Advertiser* consulted its readers and campaigned among them for many weeks before making a similar change. Both conversions were successful, and of course there have been many others. The important point is concerned with the conservatism of readers. A casual or aimless departure from accepted convention strikes the reader as a solecism and provokes unfavourable reaction. Convention, however, is not mere conservatism. A proper regard for the conventions of newspaper style should not be allowed to degenerate into the perpetuation of outmoded methods of presentation. Morison wrote authoritatively on this matter in *The English Newspaper, 1622–1932*:

> The physical act of reading can only become tolerable when the deciphering of alphabetical symbols is performed without effort, when it has become, so far as may be, inherent in the mental constitution – in one word, *habit*. The reading habits of the people are based on physical, ocular laws; and, within those laws, upon the printed matter they experience. A considerable degree of similarity in the typography of newspapers argues originally a partial and, ultimately, a complete consent of readers. First a new idea in layout is tried by an innovator, and competing papers follow when success rewards the new display with increased circulation or prestige . . . An old-fashioned layout acts like a tariff against the new readers who must be secured if the wastage of circulation by death of old readers is to be repaired.
>
> Such 'new' readers have to be detached from other papers. In the final analysis, therefore, these young or new readers, with reading habits based upon the typography of the majority of papers, must ultimately prevail over the more rigidly conservative journal – or that journal will slowly but surely lose ground to its rivals.

There is some evidence that Morison was engaged upon a propaganda exercise when he wrote that particular chapter in his famous work. He was commenting upon the fact that there had never been a double-column heading in *The Times*, a point at which, he said, the paper was 'out of step with the entire London press without being out of step with right reason' for the use of such a device inevitably introduced the habit of artificial display, dressing the paper with the air of news when there was none. Interestingly, this wonderful line so aptly describing what today we might call 'tonking up the news', was quoted from *The Daily Courant* of 1702. But Mori-

10   11

10, 11, 12 and 13. From broadsheet to tabloid the Bexhill-on-Sea way. The old-fashioned broadsheet (Figure 10) was transformed by adopting a form of modular make-up (Figure 12) which would suit the coming of a tabloid version (Figures 11 and 13).

14 and 15. The *Daily Mail* is a seven-column tabloid but with little trace of it in pages like these one-subject spreads.

12

14

13

15

son went further. If *The Times* ever accepted double-column headings, he said, it would not be because they were necessary but because a generation of readers had been habituated to them by reading journals less scrupulously conducted.

It is axiomatic that no journal, other than a gazette enjoying a privileged and uncompetitive status, can for any length of time isolate itself from the reading habits of prospective readers. When, therefore, *The Times* of the future accepts double-column headings it will indicate its conviction that such headlines have become permanently incorporated into the reading experience of the general public, and into its own particular public's idea of a newspaper.

Morison clearly knew something, for on 2 December 1932, eight months after his book was published, the first double-column heading appeared in *The Times*.

Whatever his motives, Morison made an important point in directing our attention to the prospective or likely reader who comes to a newspaper with reading habits formed elsewhere. There is a direct parallel in the predicament of the black-and-white newspaper, which increasingly will be regarded as old-fashioned by readers grown accustomed to colour elsewhere, on television, in magazines, holiday brochures and, of course, other newspapers.

As we said at the outset, newspaper design is certainly not a thing in itself. It is a part of the process of communication, impossible to isolate and difficult to define, but we will understand it all the better for a brief study of those visual laws already mentioned. It is remarkable that, although their very function is concerned with the provision of reading matter, few journalists seem to have learned much about the physical act of reading in the mechanics of communication.

Writing and reading, as the principal forms of communication by non-oral means, involve the transfer of mental images from source to recipient. It has always been so, as witness the pictograms of early times, passing on the news of the day in pictures drawn on the walls of caves, right through the ages. See a word like 'man' and the reader gets a mental picture of a man, but journalistically 'man' is a poor communicating word, for it leaves the reader to picture the man involved – which is where communication begins to break down. A mass audience of individuals will 'see' different characters. Had the word been 'prince' or 'poet', 'bartender' or 'banker', there would have been a more consistent picture in the minds of readers. Add a few describing words – a

'penniless prince', 'starving poet', 'talkative bartender', 'balding banker', and the mental pictures become sharper, more precise.

Our earliest language-teachers taught us about the simple sentence, as in 'the cat sat on the mat'. Journalistically that is bad communication, however, for the recipients of the message will see different cats, sitting in different ways on different mats. Say that it is a 'long cat', a 'red cat', a 'hungry cat', and the true picture will be implanted into the reader's comprehension. Say that 'the cat yawned on its mistress's hearthrug', and we can all begin to be confident that communication is taking place without risk of ambiguity or obscurity. If only more newspaper writers were conscious of their responsibility to draw precise mental pictures for their readers there would be fewer complaints of misrepresentation, misquoting, etc.

The journalist can and should develop this further. Hemingway wrote for Hemingway readers, Jane Austen for Austen readers, and the same may be said of Enid Blyton, Proust, or William Shakespeare. They, like the most humble letter writer, wrote for a sharply defined audience, and so communication was all the easier than it is when a journalist writes a story to be read variously by devotees of Hemingway, Austen, Blyton, Proust, Shakespeare, or Stanley Morison for that matter. Take a step further along that route and consider the differences in communicating with the

16. There are three elements to most news stories, a headline, the text, and some form of illustration. But which element does the reader see first? The design of a newspaper page is intended to guide readers but in this page many people will look at the attractive picture, read the caption, and turn inside as directed, ignoring the compelling text and headline which themselves are in the wrong sequence.

17 and 18. The first issue of *The Independent* and, 141 issues on, the front page of ... on the ... national ... 1987 UK ... hen the ... fine Dutch ... tly ... the basic ... half-point ... and with ... ury of ... and

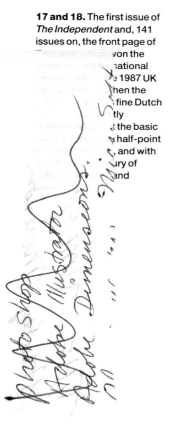

readers of *Woman's Own, Vogue, Harper's Bazaar, Financial Times, Sporting Life,* and that of writing for a local newspaper – whose readers represent that whole spectrum and more besides.

All of us who can read and write are journalists when we write letters. Letters to loved ones are the easiest letters to write, for we know the audience and know instinctively what to say to get across our message. It is not so easy to write to the bank manager about an overdraft, to a possible employer about a job, to pen a complaint to a lawyer or, worse still, to answer one. The better the journalist knows and understands those prospective readers, the people who are likely to read a newspaper if it does its job properly, the easier the process of communication becomes. Newspaper design, we suggest, begins with the commas.

There is much more, of course. Comprehension is all the more effectively gained, and all the more speedily too, when the reader can read in groups of words – in phrases. Read the following four-word sentence one word at a time, pausing between each

word, and see how separate images are put together to form the complete picture which is comprehension:

The
black
dog
growled

How much quicker is the reader's comprehension when the words are all on one line, taken in all at once in the briefest of glances:

The black dog growled

That ease in comprehension, however, also has much to do with the choice of typeface. Imagine that same sentence in some 'olde worlde' typeface:

𝔗𝔥𝔢 𝔟𝔩𝔞𝔠𝔨 𝔡𝔬𝔤 𝔤𝔯𝔬𝔴𝔩𝔢𝔡

or in some elegant Victorian script favoured by the bearers of illegible visiting cards:

The black dog growled

There is indeed a lot to this business of communicating through print.

19 and 20. There are superb text treatments in the five-column grid used by *Die Zeit*.

21, 22 and 23. Three fronts and backs from one of the world's slickest and noisiest tabloids, New York's picture newspaper, the *Daily News*. It doesn't waste words.

22

SPORTS ★ ★ ★ ★ FINAL

DAILY NEWS
Sports

Thursday, July 3, 1986 — Sports starts on Page 74

METS LEAD BY 11½

Sisk's relief stint cuts down Cards
Jim Naughton, Page 75

GUIDRY HURT
Cuts hand, loses 7th in row
Barry Meisel, Page 74

BLUE JAYS HAND BOSOX' CLEMENS FIRST LOSS

14 AND 1

BOSTON — There were no excuses and no complaints . . . but some obvious disappointment from Roger Clemens. "Sure, I'm a little disappointed, but things just didn't work out," the Boston righthander said last night after the Toronto Blue Jays ended his 14-game winning streak with a 4-2 victory over the Red Sox. "I felt strong, felt

See **CLEMENS** Page 93

Roger Clemens tips cap to crowd's cheers as he walks off mound after being lifted in eighth inning.

Lendl tops Mayotte in 5 sets
Harvey Araton, Page 76

SPORTS ★ ★ ★ FINAL

DAILY ◉ NEWS
NEW YORK'S PICTURE NEWSPAPER®
Thursday, July 3, 1986

THE CITY GOES 4TH

LIBERTY WEEKEND
FULL DRAMA OF BIG DASH STARTS ON PAGE 3 & IN CENTERFOLD

23

4 STAR ★ ★ ★ FINAL

DAILY NEWS
Sports

Thursday, November 13, 1986 — Sports starts on Page 64

GIANTS: VIKES NO PUSHOVERS

Gastineau vows to come to the rescue
Needell, Verigan — Pages 66-67

OUR MAN SAYS HUBIE, SCOTTY DESPERATE

KNICKS IN PANIC
Henderson deal proves it — Harvey Araton, Page 64

RANGERS WORK OVERTIME
Overtime has been unkind to the Rangers this season. Not last night. Buffalo's John Tucker (above) moves in to score on Ranger goalie Doug Soetaert, but Walt Poddubny's two goals, including the game winner at 2:01 in OT, lifted New York, 2-1.
Brown, P. 69

Surprise! Clemens wins Cy
Lang, Page 65

ROGER CLEMENS: It was no contest

MacLEAN SCORES 2
Devils clip Red Wings
Poris, Page 69

SHE RAPED ME, PREPPIE SLAY SUSPECT SAYS
Page 3

DAILY ◉ NEWS
NEW YORK'S PICTURE NEWSPAPER®
Thursday, November 13, 1986

WARD & PBA CLASH ON TRANSFERS

SLOWDOWN SHOWDOWN
'This is war,' says Caruso; calls protest march
Stories on pages 4 & 5

FROM BACKS-TO-THE-WALL TO THE ROSE GARDEN

WELL, HAIL, FELLOW METS President Reagan sizes up his own team jacket, presented by Mets boss Fred Wilpon, at White House yesterday. Behind (l. to r.): Bob Ojeda, Rick Aguilera, Lee Mazzilli, Dwight Gooden and Jesse Orosco. **Page 2; other pictures in centerfold**

21

24, 25 and 26. In 1988 *The Guardian* underwent a major redesign, taking on a somewhat Latin look, magazinish in character, in sharp contrast to the traditional dress of the UK's more serious-minded broadsheets. The conventional titlepiece (Figure 24) was abandoned in favour of a controversial typographical flourish which combined the paper's two main display typefaces, the Helvetica of the news pages and Garamond of the features pages, topped by a promotional display of people in the news. BREAKFAST WITH A STRANGER was a headline in *Newspaper Report* summing up the paper's new appearance and it was an apt comment. Perhaps predictably, the departure from traditional titlepiece design drew much criticism from media-watchers as did also the change from serif to sans in news headlines and the extra whiting of headlines generally, Figure 25 shows a typical example. There was considerable praise for the return of column rules and the use of Monotype's Nimrod typeface in text although this was tempered by a mixed reception for feature-page use of unjustified text over a narrow ten-em measure.

TYPOGRAPHY
THE MATHS AND MECHANICS

THE production journalist of today and tomorrow needs to know much more about typography than any previous editorial generation. The simple reason is that in the new world of electronic editing there is so much more to do and so much more that can be done. This is not to denigrate the sub-editors and copy-editors of yesterday who, disciplined by brass rules and metal type, produced newspapers that in many respects were superior to many of those we see today. Today's newspapers, freed from the constraints of hot-metal setting, are to some extent too free, spoiled for choice by a bewildering range of typefaces and no limit to the ways they can be presented. How many journalists, we wonder, can claim to be competent and confident when faced with a mixture of good, bad and indifferent typefaces and the need to choose two that are compatible and yet so different, one for statistical matter requiring high legibility and the other for lengthy text where the requirement is for readability?

How many newspapers have written into their job specifications and contracts the need for an editor or production department editor to make decisions about the purchase of suitable typefaces for editorial needs? Too few, we know. Yet who is there that does this job for our newspapers? Advice abounds, much of it expensive and much of it dangerous if it is not based on good, sound, journalistic understanding and practice allied to local circumstances. The typefaces that best suit one printing press and the kind of newsprint it uses will more often than not be less good, and sometimes be downright awful, on another press even where the newsprint is the same. In that jumble of names brought about by wholly inadequate copyright laws, one typeface may appear to have several different names; and sometimes even the right name may prove an unreliable guide, for different suppliers may supply differing quality.

The typographer who is aware enough to be cautious is clearly of great value in a newspaper, but the things we are discussing are by themselves as nothing without journalistic understanding. Let us assume that journalistic understanding and now graft on to it the necessary knowledge and skills relating to typography, beginning with the point and the pica as used for typographical measurement in most English-speaking countries and called variously the 'American point system' or 'Anglo-American point system'.

The first edition of *Newspaper Design* made only passing reference to the point system's history and practical basis as being of no immediate concern to the newspaper man. Today, however, a little of the system's interesting history will not come amiss, for it serves to emphasise the importance of a method of measurement that is precise and unique in that it bears no relationship to the Imperial inch or to the metric centimetre. Some newspapers employ page plans calibrated in inches or centimetres, sometimes in both, but this has more to do with the sale and positioning of advertisements than with editorial matters. Advertisements are sold in the measurement system the customer understands and are then composed or designed in typefaces measured in points to occupy sufficient space, also measured in points, so that when printing takes place, no matter how much shrinkage (if any) there may be, the advertiser will not get fewer inches or centimetres of space than he has paid for.

In the early days of printing with typefaces there were relatively few alphabets, and they did not conform to any system in measurement or even name. Names, where applied, were quite likely to be based on the use made of a typeface. As so much printing was done by or for the monasteries, many of those still surviving had religious significance. Not all historians agree, but there is a popular belief that the priest's Breviary, or daily office, was often printed in a quite small typeface, undoubtedly called *Brevier* but then bastardised to 'Breveer' by the English (who are notoriously bad at the pronunciation of foreign words and phrases). In the Missal, the book of the Mass, the

27

The first thing to remember about a filmsetter is that it is a camera and that its function is to present language in all its beauty, variety and intricacy. Its products are more versatile than those of casting machines, and they open up to the typographer a whole new vista of design, liberating him from the limitations of a solid three-dimensional metal form. By the photographic process it is possible to cover a wide range of type sizes from one matrix-case; areas of copy can be quite freely reversed from black to white; lines can be placed at an angle or on a curve; rules and borders can be stripped in at the make-up stage; type can be made to run across halftones without great expense; tints and solid panels

The first thing to remember about a filmsetter is that it is a camera and that its function is to present language in all its beauty, variety and intricacy. Its products are more versatile than those of casting machines, and they open up to the typographer a whole new vista of design, liberating him from the limitations of a solid three-dimensional metal form. By the photographic process it is possible to cover a wide range of type sizes from one matrix-case; areas of copy can be quite freely reversed from black to white; lines can be placed at an angle or on a curve; rules and borders can be stripped in at

The first thing to remember about a filmsetter is that it is a camera and that its function is to present language in all its beauty, variety and intricacy. Its products are more versatile than those of casting machines, and they open up to *The first thing to remember about a filmsetter is that it is a camera and that its function is to present language in all its beauty, variety and intricacy. Its*

The first thing to remember about a filmsetter is that it is a camera and that its function is to present language in all its beauty, variety and intricacy. Its products are more versatile than those of casting machines, and they *The first thing to remember about a filmsetter is that it*

The first thing to remember about a filmsetter is that it is a camera and that its function is to present language in all its beauty, variety and intricacy. Its products are more versatile than those of casting machines, and they open up to the typographer a whole new vista of design, liberating him from the limitations of a solid three-dimensional metal form. By the photographic process it is possible to cover a wide range of type sizes from one matrix-case;

The first thing to remember about a filmsetter is that it is a camera and that its function is to present language in all its beauty, variety and intricacy. Its products are more versatile than those of casting machines, *The first thing to remember about a filmsetter is that it is a camera and that its function is to present language in all its beauty, variety and* THE FIRST THING TO REMEMBER ABOUT A FILMSETTER IS The first thing to remember about a filmsetter is that it is a camera and that its function is to present language *The first thing to remember about a filmsetter is that it is a camera and that its function is to present language*

27 and 28. It is easy to choose typefaces by reputation and make the mistake of not considering the way we will use them. Here are 14 different versions of Univers, all from the same type supplier, and all set at 14pt, ranging from Univers Extra Light Extra Condensed to Univers Extra Bold Expanded. The first may be unrivalled for maps and other graphics and the last ideal for wide-measure intros but choosing typefaces without function in mind can be the deadliest of typographical sins.

28

The first thing to remember about a filmsetter is that it is a camera and that its function is to present language in all its beauty, variety and intricacy. Its products are more versatile than those of casting machines, and they

The first thing to remember about a filmsetter is that it is a camera and that its function is to present language in all its beauty, variety and intricacy. Its products are more versatile than those of
The first thing to remember about a filmsetter is that it is a camera and that its function is to present language in all its beauty,

The first thing to remember about a filmsetter is that it is a camera and that its function is to present language in all its beauty, variety and
The first thing to remember about a filmsetter is that it is a camera and that its function is to

The first thing to remember about a filmsetter is that it is a camera and that its function is to present language in all its beauty, variety and intricacy. Its products are more versatile than those of casting machines, and they

The first thing to remember about a filmsetter is that it is a camera and that its function is to present language in all its beauty, variety and intricacy. Its products are more versatile than
The first thing to remember about a filmsetter

The first thing to remember about a filmsetter is that it is a camera and that its function is to present language in all its beauty, variety and intricacy. Its products are more versatile than those of

The first thing to remember about a filmsetter is that it is a camera and that its function is to present language in all its beauty, variety and intricacy. Its products are more versatile than those of

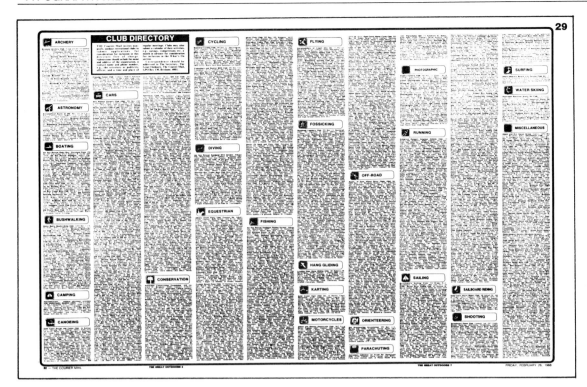

29

29. Solid with detail, a sporting directory from *The Courier-Mail,* Brisbane, in 5pt but presented skilfully with generous gutters between columns and effective section heads in alphabetical order.

Canon would be printed in a large typeface, called 'Canon'. The trouble was that one printer's Breveer, and his Canon too, were not necessarily the same size as the typefaces used by another printer for the same books. As the number of typefaces grew so too did the confusion.

Eventually, after long years of argument and indecision, and several abortive attempts to introduce uniformity of measure, the present point system was adopted in America in 1886, the standard unit evolving from the pica of MacKellar, Smiths & Jordan, whose types had the widest sale and use. The word 'pica' also came from the church, deriving its name from the type used for the Ordinal, the clergy's book of instructions for services, one of the most widely printed of books which made the typeface one of the most common. The Ordinal was black-and-white like a magpie, or 'pica' in Latin, devoid of the rubrics or coloured illuminations so prevalent in church books. The pica type was roughly one sixth of an inch in body depth, which was too large a standard for comfortable fractions in designating the size of other typefaces, so the unit was divided into 12 points, each measuring 0.013837 of an inch. (Something

similar had happened in much earlier times to the sovereign's foot, which was divided into 12 inches as the basis of the Imperial measuring system.)

With 12 points to a pica (taken at 0.166044 of an inch) there are roughly 72 points to an inch – we say 'roughly' because 72 points add up to 0.996264 of an inch. While that may mean six and a half yards or so over a mile, the difference is meaningless in, say, a broadsheet page that may be marked in 22 inches or 56 centimetres but to a typographer is 132 picas. The fact that 72 points made an inch – never mind the approximation – is magical information to anyone who still understands and uses inches. It means that there are eight lines of 9pt to an inch and, of course, nine lines of 8pt. Just as we learned our 'times tables' in junior school, we might begin a study of type measurement by learning our 'types table'. An inch will also give us six lines of 12pt, twelve of 6pt, seven of 10pt, ten of 7pt, five of 14pt, fourteen of 5pt, and so on. We can also say that three lines of a 36pt headline will take up an inch and a half (although we later suggest that it ought to take a little more to accommodate some white space).

The journalist should learn his types table by rote,

even those who are unfamiliar with the inch (for we were not talking of an inch; you will recall from our earlier comments that it is a 72pt unit we are dealing with). A well-known teacher of sub-editing insists that his students learn their tables so that when he asks how many lines of 4.75pt will go into ten centimetres they will chorus 'Sixty' without thinking or interrogating a computer. The same teacher is fond of an architectural analogy, saying that if you want to build a house you need a bricklayer, but that not all bricklayers can build houses, for it takes many skills in addition to that vital one of knowing how to lay bricks. It takes a typographical bricklayer to build a page.

We are neither Luddite nor pedantic in urging the young journalist to master the point system, for it is likely to be with us a lot longer than the efforts to encourage change to a new point based on the millimetre. Indeed it may gain in importance now that computers are giving us typesizes measured in fractions of a point. How strange it must seem to the editor of yesterday, used to headline sizes leaping upwards in 6pt and 12pt steps, from 24pt, 30pt, 36pt, 42pt, 48pt to 60pt, 72pt, 84pt, etc., to find it commonplace for headlines to be set in increments of a half point or for classified advertising to be typeset in 4.2pt to make for a comfortable six lines of revenue per column-centimetre. The point system has many advantages, not least of which is that we can always adapt what we know to convert our precise calculations to an approximation in whatever language others may use, inches, centimetres, word counts, line counts or anything else.

While type size is expressed in points, the measure to which type is set, or the type area of a page, is designated by that standard unit the pica, or 12pt em, since the *em* is the square of any given point size. Measures are usually given as being so many picas or so many ems, pica ems being implied. When we say that a particular newspaper has an 11-em column, we are referring to the pica em as being the standard unit for measuring area or space. But it must be noted that em or en (being half a em) will be used in a different sense when referring to indenting copy: here the word 'em' means the square of the point size we are dealing with and an en will be half of that. To avoid confusion, printers called the em and en 'mutton' and 'nut', and the instruction 'nut each side' is a standard instruction in hot-metal setting, the first and last en of each line being left blank in order to inject white space between vertical column rules and the text inside

them. Photocomposition all but put an end to the practice of such indenting, for those two keystrokes per line could be saved by setting text across a shorter measure and 'floating' it in the space available. There are, however, forms of indenting that remain and can be useful to a page designer – for instance, the reverse indent or hanging indent style, very often called '0&1', meaning no indent on the first line of each paragraph but all other lines indented one em. This can be adapted to allow for the kind of setting commonly seen in television timetables where the times of programmes stand out to the left of the programme description. This gutter might be achieved by setting the copy 0&3 or 0&4, any permutation being possible.

But let us return to the measurement of area in newspaper pages. This is where the copy-editor of today has the greatest need for understanding, since the width of a newspaper page is probably its most important dimension so far as design is concerned. Given a width in round terms, perhaps 80 ems, we might say that such a sheet will accommodate eight 10-em columns or, much less happily, ten 8-em columns. There would be no need to allow for space between the columns: we could merely set our text across 9 ems to float in those 10-em columns, effectively providing half a pica space at either end (or what the printer of old called a 'nonprul' or even 'nomple', bastardised from Nonpareil, the old English name for 6pt).

But rarely do we get page widths in round terms, and in this age of spatial awareness who needs column widths anyway? Advertisement managers do, and presumably so do their customers, but there is little need for advertising measures and editorial measures to coincide. They need to co-exist rather than to conform.

Take what might be considered a middle of the road broadsheet with a page width of 92.25 pica ems. Most American broadsheets and a lot of English broadsheets are much narrower than they used to be, around 79 or 80 picas being fairly standard, but around the world there are still some very wide broadsheets of 96 ems or more. At this moment we are not concerned with the ideal width because, for the most part, the page designer has little control over that factor. Our page for this particular exercise is 92.25 pica ems.

The requirements of advertising may be for a page with ten columns. Our page would make ten 9-em columns with 2.25 ems left over, equal to 27 points which we might use to put 3pt divisions between those columns. The same page would clearly give us nine 10-em columns with 2.25 ems left over, or eight 11-em columns with 4.25 ems remaining, and it would be a simple matter to work out any other permutation – a simple division of the page width by the number of columns required and what is left over being distributed between columns just for the moment. We say 'just for the moment' because what we have decided is a basic grid and not a set of measures to be used for headlines, text, and pictures: clearly those divisions of a few points between columns are far too narrow for ease of reading. The setting measures will go *within* this column grid.

The spacing between columns of type is vital and yet the principle is much misunderstood, one of the many such things lost in the move out of hot metal into cold type. The grid of the hot-metal page was formed by those brass rules of old, usually 3pt in base width, printing a 1pt line with 1pt of space at each side. Later soft-metal rules varied in base width, but those that were a neat fraction of the pica, 3pt, 6pt, 9pt and sometimes 12pt, were the most popular (although we recall that the much-mourned *News Chronicle*, which ceased in 1961, had a 4pt column rule and the *Dublin Independent* at one time had an 8pt rule).

Perhaps 90 per cent of newspapers adopted the 6pt rule, but with only two and a half points of space each side of a 1pt line the text inside the columns was cramped; hence the almost universal practice of setting the copy 'half-and-half' or 'nut each side'. With 8pt setting this means 4pts of space at each side of a 6pt rule, thus providing 14pts of space between columns, 1pt of which printed as the line. And that line was a functional device, not only to separate the columns but to help keep the reader in the right place without tiring the eye. If this makes sense then it makes a nonsense of the practice of so many newspapers in throwing away the column rule as a remnant of the past without thought of replacing its function with another device – which in this case could only be the injection of more space. If ease of reading could be achieved only by 14pts of space between columns, and that amount including an actual line, we cannot hope for the same eye comfort with a mere 12pt gutter (and often considerably less) and no line either. A growing number of newspapers, we are pleased to say, seem to have re-invented the rule. It appears increasingly in feature pages where the longer read has always required and usually demanded a high degree of

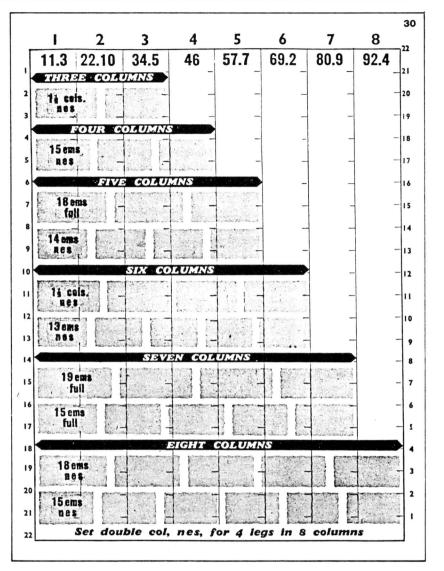

readability. Significantly, the redesign of *The Guardian* included the return of column rules for both news and feature pages.

Returning to our example of that awkward but still very common 92.25-em page, the basic grid may be of eight, nine, or, perhaps much more likely these days, ten columns, which would make for good advertising business but not-so-good editorial quality. The page designer will endeavour to counter the narrow advertising columns with broad measures in the editorial part of the page, but a straightforward conversion is

30. A chart for broad measures taken from the *News Chronicle* style chart in the 1930s.

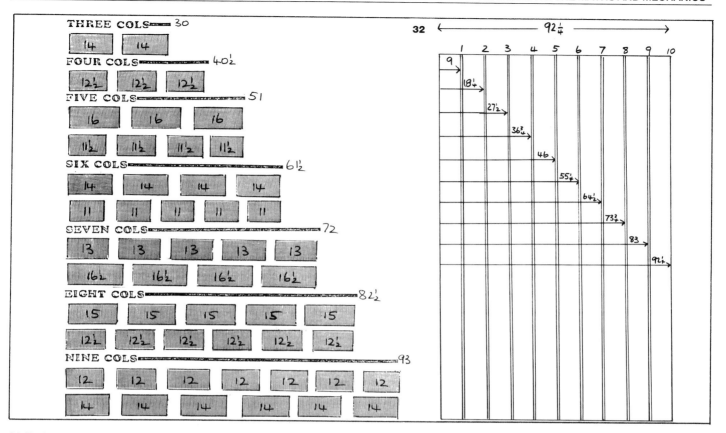

31. Typical chart for broad measures today.

32. The first step in making a chart for a ten-column page of 92.25 ems is to determine the basic grid.

not always easy, especially on a page with advertisements of mixed sizes. The need is for a chart that shows all the possible permutations of advertisement widths, lists the physical dimensions of the editorial space remaining and offers suggested measures for use in those areas. Examples are given in Figure 30 which dates back to the *News Chronicle* of half a century ago, and Figure 31 which is fairly typical of those in use today. Figures 32 to 40 show how the chart may be made up for the 92.25-em page (or any other page width for that matter). Figure 32 shows the ten-column grid with the editorial permutations left by any mix of advertisements. Figure 33 shows the same positions each reduced by 9pts to allow what we might call 'scalpel space', about three points at each side of a headline to be fitted into the space available. Figure 34 shows some of the possible permutations of text measures that might be accommodated.

In every case we begin by allowing what we may consider to be the ideal amount of space between legs of type, 18pts or one-and-a-half pica ems, multiplied

by the number of gutters, and subtract this total from what would be the headline width. The number of ems left is then divided by the number of legs required to give a measure that can be rounded up or down to the nearest half em, which would effectively increase or reduce the space between the legs of type by a maximum of 3pts either way. With a computer or calculator to help, that is by no means as complicated a problem as it must have been to the pencil-and-paper copy-editors of the *News Chronicle* who were doing it in hot metal half a century ago without so much as a pocket calculator to help.

Production journalists grown used to calculators and computers may occasionally think that such sophisticated tools do all the work, thus rendering it a waste of time to have gone through all that painful business of learning about casting off. There is a similar argument about shorthand for reporters that questions its value now that tape recorders are widely available. But in the same way that the reporter with shorthand is better equipped for all occasions, so too

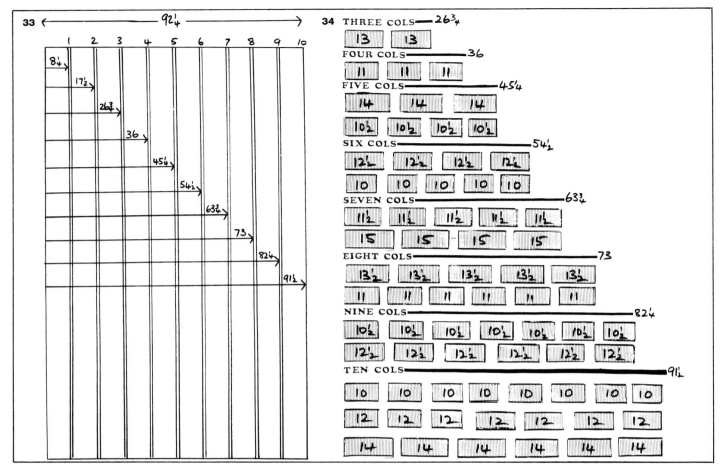

is the copy-editor who can do his own sums and not be retricted to those things that someone else has programmed the machine to do. An even better analogy might be that, just as a child who has mastered the 'times tables' can all the more easily tackle the creative tasks of mathematics, using a calculator and understanding its use, so will the journalist who has learned en theory be all the more creative.

By casting off we mean the ability to do three things:

1. calculate the amount of space required for a given amount of copy;
2. calculate the amount of copy required for a given amount of space;
3. given copy that cannot be cut or altered, and space that is similarly inflexible, choose the type face, size and setting to ensure a comfortable fit.

En theory is a basic formula that converts the measure into ens or characters, calculates how many there will be in an inch of type, turns the answer into words per inch and allows for paragraphing and word breaks. It takes many forms, but all will be similar to that which follows:

$$\frac{\text{Measure} \times 12 \times 2}{\text{Point size}} = \text{ens per line}$$

$$\frac{\text{Measure} \times 12 \times 2}{\text{Point size}} \times \frac{72}{\text{Body size}} = \text{ens per inch}$$

$$\frac{\text{Measure} \times 12 \times 2}{\text{Point size}} \times \frac{72}{\text{Body size}} \times \frac{1}{6}$$
$$= \text{words per inch (in theory)}$$

33. The measures in the basic grid are each reduced by 9pts of 'scalpel space'.

34. The finished chart.

We say 'in theory' because the formula so far assumes that all lines are full and there are no paragraphs or even hyphenations. We allow ten per cent for such things, and the formula becomes:

$$\frac{\text{Measure} \times 12 \times 2}{\text{Point size}} \times \frac{72}{\text{Body size}} \times \frac{1}{6} \times \frac{9}{10}$$
$$= \text{words per inch (in practice)}$$

Inserting real figures in the above example, for example 8/9pt type to a measure of 10 ems, gives 30 ens per line, 240 ens per inch, 40 words per inch (in theory) and 36 words per inch (in practice). This is basic theory, the main value of which lies in acquiring that understanding of type measurement we wish to encourage. Its weakness in practical value is in asuming that all type faces are average: its answers, therefore, are only approximate. It is not a far cry, though, from understanding en theory to using a set of type manfuacturer's tables listing how many characters there will be per pica em for every type face and size in their library.

Even more valuable in the copy-editor's armoury is the mental ability to calculate how many words will be needed to provide exactly three lines of caption for the late picture being schemed into the front page, or how many lines of 14pt something or other will the front page 'intro' make. En theory can be adapted quite easily: if we take that first piece of the formula, ens per line, and divide by 6 (being the average number of characters per word, including space between that word and the next) we obtain the number of words per line:

$$\frac{\text{Measure} \times 12 \times 2}{\text{Point size}} \times \frac{1}{6} = \text{words per line}$$

By reducing the constants in this formula we can shorten the procedure to:

$$\frac{\text{Measure} \times 4}{\text{Point size}} = \text{words per line}$$

Which points the way towards simplifying en theory itself. There are only three variable elements in the formula: the measure, the point size and body depth. By multiplying and dividing out all the remaining elements we arrive at a factor of 259. Therefore:

$$\frac{\text{Measure} \times 259}{\text{Point size} \times \text{Body size}} = \text{words per inch}$$

Those who prefer metric measures may take the figure 259, representing an inch, and divide by 2.54, being centimetres per inch, and alter the formula to:

$$\frac{\text{Measure} \times 102}{\text{Point size} \times \text{Body size}} = \text{words per centimetre}$$

There are many variations possible, from calculating units for a headline to copy for a five-pointed star. Again, though, it must be emphasised that at best these are quick guides, more rule of thumb than exact, and the principal value is in teaching that all-important understanding of type measurement.

Just a few years ago it was commonplace among sub-editors and copy-editors the world over to mark their copy for setting in crude but effective codes such as '10×1' against the first paragraph, '8×1' against the second, '7×1' against the third, and no code at all after that. The typesetter knew the style and set the 'intro' in 10pt, the following paragraph in 8pt, and the rest of the story in 7pt, all across one column. There had been no need to indicate the type face by name because house rules dictated which one was to be used for text. House rules were usually very strict, and any departure from style would have to be clearly marked; even then a messenger was likely to be dispatched to the editorial department to query the intention.

Today the journalist may sit at a keyboard and type computer codes – *C1 or >10F or some other strange but short alphanumeric sequence might be the cryptic code to trigger off a longer code instructing the typesetting equipment to set what follows in perhaps the most complicated format. Imagine, say, the lengthy typesetting formula for a horse-racing programme with tabulations for past form, current form, horse's name, owner, trainer, jockey, weight and draw, using perhaps two typefaces and in bold, roman and italic, and all to fit across 20 ems. A code that says *R1 might be enough (* to signal a typesetting instruction, R for racing, and 1 for the preferred style), while other minor cards might be coded *R2, *R3 and so on, each of these calling up typesetting codes as long as your arm! A vast acreage of copy may need no codes at all. If the bulk of a newspaper's setting is in 9pt Times New Roman condensed to 85 per cent across 11 ems with a half point between lines, why bother to tell the computer anything? In the absence of instructions a default system takes over.

So what's new? Not a lot, you may think. Computers have given us much more firepower, enabling us to do much more than ever before and a whole lot quicker, but they have not yet taken over. Someone must still decide just what is to be done. The computer's job is to do it.

The role of a sub-editor or copy-editor (call that person what you will) has not changed significantly. Only the *way* the job is done has changed, and that is the least significant thing about it. The journalist must do what has always been done, adapting the journalism to the techniques available. The person who thinks that job is one of learning codes and applying them is thinking of what we used to call a 'parmarker', an individual who does not read the copy but merely processes it for the computer. No, the sub-editor we are thinking about is the journalist Henry Wickham Steed, Editor of *The Times* from 1919 to 1922, was thinking about when he wrote:

> Among the members of a newspaper staff I am inclined to give first place to the sub-editors as a body. Without their devotion and goodwill an editor may be impotent. They can make or mar his paper. They are the infantry who win newspaper battles. Their names rarely reach the public except in brief obituary notices, but in more ways than one they can justly say of themselves that without their labours 'the Press' could not exist. When a sub-editorial staff are really interested in the policy of their paper or are keen to make the paper 'tell' in other respects, they can do more for it than an editor and all his assistants put together.

To conclude this chapter, a few more words will assist understanding. Collective terms are, first, the *fount* or (increasingly) 'font', both words being pronounced the same way (font) and meaning the collection of characters of one size and one design, covering the alphabet, figures and the usual punctuation marks; second is the *series*, or number of founts of different sizes of an identical design (e.g., the Times Roman Series); third is the *family*, or group of series derived from a basic design, whose name they bear with the addition of a qualifying term indicating variation by weight, width, or special treatment, (e.g., the Gill Sans family, which includes Light, Bold, Extra Bold, Condensed, Bold Condensed, Shadow, Shadowline and Cameo).

The term *type face* is used for the actual design of the letter; it is more often used as one word, typeface, and often abbreviated to 'face'. Letter design is the most complex theme in the entire range of the graphic arts, as a glance at the monumental Jaspert, Berry & Johnson *Encyclopaedia of Type Faces* will show. The journalist of yesteryear hardly needed to do more than wet his feet at the shore of this vast ocean, but today, in the computer age, there is a greater need to know so that the editorial voice may prevail in choosing

typefaces and deciding how best to use them in the journalistic context.

The appearance in print of a given type is considerably conditioned by its *weight* (defined as 'degree of blackness') and *width*, or the combination of these two, which determine what is often called its 'colour'. A medley of terms is currently used under both heads; sometimes the same term has different meanings, and sometimes different terms have the same meaning in the case of different types. Repeated efforts to bring about uniform terms have not enjoyed much success. When one encounters the vast difference between, say, the very wide letters of a Century face called 'Extended' and the somewhat narrow letters of another Century called 'Expanded' it becomes obvious that individual names have to be memorised as needed. Specially to be noted is the loose use of 'Bold' and 'Heavy' (and the prefixing of 'Extra-' in either case), the use of 'Black' instead of 'Extra-Bold' or 'Extra-Heavy', the alternation of 'Wide Expanded', 'Extended', and the occasional substitution of 'Compressed' for 'Condensed'. Most confusing of all are the terms not relating to weight; thus the fat letter commonly called Ultra Bodoni is also known as Bodoni Black, Poster Bodoni, and Bodoni Modern, although this latter name is also applied to one of the lightest Bodoni faces available.

A normal fount includes both CAPITALS and lower-case letters; the SMALL CAPS of the book world are rare in newspaper work. Some founts are of capitals only and are known as *titling founts* in which the face of the type usually, although not always, occupies the whole or nearly the whole of the depth of the body; a 60pt letter in a titling fount may therefore appear to be considerably bigger than another 60pt of the same family in a non-titling fount.

The normal *roman* fount is named after the straight-up-and-down style of Roman lettering as distinct from the italic companion which is usually available, but there is an increasing tendency to use the word 'Roman' to mean 'of medium weight' as distinct from 'Bold' – despite the obvious problems associated with typefaces referred to as being 'Roman Bold'. It should be noted that the true *italic* is differentiated from its roman mate by details in letter structure as well as by its slope; a so-called italic that is simply the roman pushed out of the vertical is correctly called a *Sloped Roman*.

Another important element is the *x-height* of a type, which is the actual height of the printing surface of the lower-case letters such as x, m, n, c, o, and so on. The greater the x-height, the shorter will be the extending portions of b, d, f, h, k, etc., (the *ascenders*) and of g, p, q, y, j (the *descenders*), and so the larger the type will appear. In text this has an important relation to legibility and in headlines and other forms of newspaper display it is especially significant, for a 36pt 'big on the body' face such as Caslon may look as large as a 42pt character in a 'small-on-the-body' face such as Bodoni, a fact that a page designer needs constantly to bear in mind.

The other most important anatomical features of a typeface are the *serifs*, or lack of them in *sans serif* typefaces, and mainstroke or stem, and the stress or shading; these factors largely determine the features of a typeface. Serifs are the small terminal strokes at the top or foot of the mainstroke of a letter. Serifs may be bracketed (that is, rounded-in to the mainstroke), or unbracketed, oblique or horizontal, fine or slab, and there can be subsidiary variations, for instance when a bracketed slab serif is given a sharper note by chamfering its ends. The *mainstroke* is the thick or, in using a pen, the down-stroke of a letter, contrasting with the thin up-stroke. *Stress* is the direction of the shading, or thickest part of the curved strokes in letters like 'o', 'e', 'd', 'b' and so on. It may be diagonal, oblique, or vertical. A further term to note is the *counter*, being the enclosed portion of letters like 'p', 'o', 'e', 'a', which may be of enormous importance in choosing text faces for high-speed printing in less than ideal circumstances.

35 and 36. Legibility is the chief criterion when it comes to presenting matter for reference, as in these pages listing Parliamentary nominations and election results.

35

36

THE PAGE
ITS SHAPE AND FORM

DESIGN in all things can be a very personal matter; beauty, they say, is in the eye of the beholder, and you can be sure that some of the things that send us into raptures will dispatch others in a different direction altogether. There can be no unanimity about what makes the perfect page; there will always be those who know they can improve it. And anyway, as we have already said, design is not a thing that can be judged on its own as so many judges of newspaper design have discovered – it is part of the journalism itself – and, as such, the most important criterion is that of appropriateness.

Interestingly, the panel of judges in the 1986 UK Newspaper Design Awards wrestled with this problem, for their brief was to judge the design rather than the journalism. That might seem to be the very antithesis of what newspaper design awards should be all about, but it makes sense in that a panel of judges, faced with the newspapers they do not know, cannot attempt to judge the journalism itself, since that is to do with its appropriateness for the market. The UK judges in 1986 pointed out their dilemma in the official report. They said:

The consumers ought to be the best of all judges for after all a newspaper is a consumer product just like any other and if it isn't what the customer wants he won't read it. The trouble with that popular view, of course, is that newspaper consumers are a varied lot and while we all know what we like, or would like, it's not so easy to choose for other people's likes and dislikes.

We found that out ourselves right at the start when in the first argument of the day a certain newspaper was described by one of our number as a 'a bit po-faced and ponderous' while someone else thought it 'reflective, serious, and appealing'. The ensuing discussion enabled us to decide on our interpretation of the judges' rules that direct them to the design rather than to the journalism. These things are hard to separate but we agreed that the main tasks were to consider layout, including visual balance, use of pictures, the arrangement of columns, choice and use of typefaces and sizes, the design of headlines, consistency on style throughout the paper and, in general, ease of reading. We could not, however, divorce ourselves from the important thought that what really counts in the end is how well a newspaper caters for the people who are likely to read it if it does the job properly. That's a deep thought we will leave with the editors who are in effect the product managers!

That judging panel, by the way, was made up of an editor, a production director and a typography professor. While recognising their problem and approving of the way they tackled it, one can only reaffirm that appropriateness comes above all else in the criteria for assessing what makes good newspaper design.

While opinion counts for a lot it does not count for everything. Certainly that old excuse that 'well, it's all a matter of opinion' will not wash because all must agree that some opinions do not count at all. Opinions matter only when we are faced with two or more acceptable alternatives and there is disagreement over which is better or best. If one or more of the alternatives is unacceptable because, perhaps, it offends against what Morison called the ocular laws, it will remain unacceptable, and no amount of opinion will make the slightest difference.

One editor may favour italic capitals for headlines on news pages and argue eloquently that the italic imparts a flavour of urgency, which helps tell the news. Another may detest the device, arguing (especially in the case of the artificial sloped romans) that type on the slant cannot be as easy to read as the true roman. Each is entitled to his opinion and preference, perhaps even prejudice, because there is nothing inherently wrong with either argument. However, no one could argue a case for the use of large slabs of text in wide lines of a small italic sans serif face; no amount of opinion would make that acceptable.

We once heard the story of a designer who schemed a long feature across the top of a broadsheet page, headed with wide, wide lines of a small and not-very-readable face, and then expressed surprise and dis-

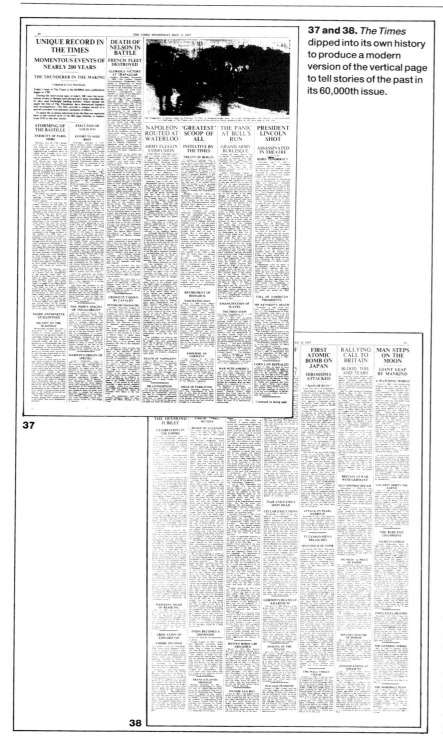

37 and 38. *The Times* dipped into its own history to produce a modern version of the vertical page to tell stories of the past in its 60,000th issue.

appointment when his editor condemned it. 'To me it looks absolutely beautiful,' he claimed. Beauty very rarely comes into it. Journalism is a functional process of communication by means of the printed word; and while matters of presentation are an important and integral part of that function, they do not have an over-riding importance.

Generations of sub-editors and copy-editors have been called 'butchers' by their writers because they mistakenly put the pattern before the content and needlessly cut stories to fit the page plan. A designer who looks for a 500-word story to fit a predetermined layout and chooses by length rather than news value or, even worse, takes a much better but longer story and hacks it into shape, ought to be designing wallpaper not newspapers. The pattern is all important in wallpaper; it is not meant to be read. Here is the gap between graphic design and journalism that must somehow be closed if newspapers are to do their jobs properly. Let no reader think that presentation is unimportant, but let us talk about it in terms of *projection* rather than of packaging. The aim of a newspaper must be to project its stories and pictures for what they are worth, not to parcel them up into pretty packages.

There are various schools of thought relating to page design, much discussed by such gurus as Edmund C. Arnold and Harold Evans, and valuable their examination is for what we can discover about the way people read. However, it is advisable to regard what follows as theory, useful in exposition but not so useful that the designer might wish to ape such pages. The repertoire of a good designer is rather like that of a good writer – open to a thousand and one influences, but taking a little from here and there, adding the touch of personality that helps fashion what comes out as a distinctive, even unique, style.

The first and clearly oldest formula for making up a page is the *vertical* grid. A page is divided into columns and these are filled with single-column stories. In the nineteenth century the news was told as it happened, in chronological order: it made good sense to begin at the beginning, at the top left of the page, and fill the columns one after another, story after story, until there was no more space.

A more sophisticated style, often called the 'tombstone style', ran headlines side by side, the original single-column tops, rather in the manner of Figure 37. The space left underneath these stories could be filled with minor matter, the 'down-page stories' if you like. More modern still, the style shown in Figure 38 would

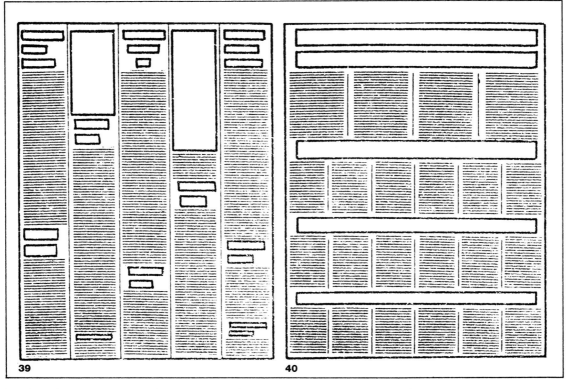

39. Vertical make-up, an old style with modern values.

40. Horizontal make-up, providing easy reads for long stories.

break up the page in a neat and attractive way, but still without injecting much of a scale of priorities to the elements other than drawing attention to those at the top of the page. That in itself may be taken as a warning that too many newspapers too often strive for a page lead because the layout demands a page lead, rather than the story demanding one. Another virtue in this sort of design is that there is little chance of the reader losing his way. Headlines are immediately above the story (a virtue in itself to be commended to those who see little connection between the points where a headline ends and the story begins), and the text runs in an entirely logical fashion down the page without the eye hazards associated with changes in direction.

Reading small type from the top of a column to the bottom may be logical but can be very tiring, and there is even more eye-strain associated with lifting the eye from the bottom of one column to the top of the next. *Horizontal* make-up, Figure 40, where the text runs in a series of short legs across the page, is easier on the eye and in many respects is rather like the style of a book, where the reader gets a rest at the bottom of

each page. Indeed the depth of the octavo page may be taken as a good guide to the maximum depth of the legs of text in horizontal layout. Certainly the distance between the bottom of one flight of text and the top of the next ought to be short enough to enable the reader to see, out of the corner of his eye as it were, where to go next.

Another good rule is to endeavour to turn from one leg to the next in mid-sentence and certainly never at the end of a paragraph lest the readers feel that they have reached the end of the story. In hot-metal days this was never the problem that it is now because compositors, highly-trained craftsmen who had an incredibly long (seven years) apprenticeship, were so disciplined as to move two lines forward or backwards rather than turn on a full stop. Moving two lines, of course, prevented that other dread occurrence, the lonely widow line, sometimes called 'jack' line, in which less than a full line of type would sit at the top of a column. Such discipline disappeared with the advent of the scalpel in photocomposition when it was obviously so much easier to cut between spaced paragraphs than in mid-paragraph and also a lot more

41. Diagonal make-up, a guide to the way readers look at a page.

42. Quadrant make-up, best suited to the brash tabloid.

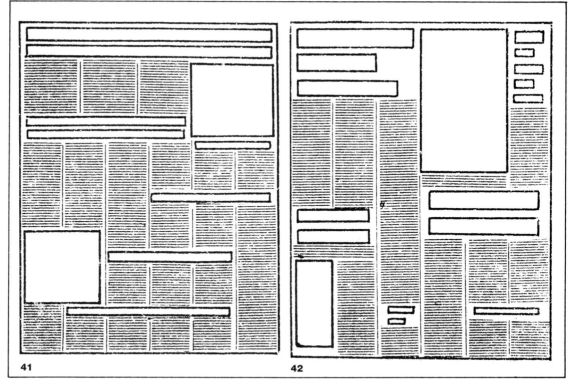

41

42

difficult to move individual lines. Many sub-editors failed to spot the change, probably because such things had been taken for granted.

Wide measures are recommended for the lengthy story, up to around 50 characters per line for the really 'solid read' of a couple of thousand words or more. Legs of even length are also advised so that there is more rhythm as the reader moves from one flight of text to the next. Crossheads and other such devices are usually unnecessary except in the longest articles, where even horizontal layout requires deep legs of type.

Diagonal make-up was one of those subjects that first brought the co-authors of this book together, for it was Allen Hutt who explained to the youthful Bob James just why old hands would run a finger across a broadsheet page from any corner to the opposite corner and expect that line to touch or pass through all the important elements of the page. When pressed, those old hands would mutter the inadequate explanation that somehow this diagonal arrangement would 'give the page movement' which was apparently some mystical quality never explained other than

with the warning that, young man, you ought never to let a column rule run from the top of the page to the bottom: breaking it at some point with a multi-column element would ensure the achievement of that mysterious 'movement'. The Hutt explanation was much easier to understand. It concerns the way in which people look at pages, particularly the big broadsheet pages. Something will take the eye, a good headline perhaps, possibly a picture, maybe something the reader was looking for in the first place, like the crossword. Readers will see different things first. Naturally, much may depend on the direction that they are coming from, the top of the facing page or (quite logically) from the bottom, and there is no accounting for the people who like to read from back page to front.

Whatever the reader sees first is immaterial; the important thing is that *after* seeing that element the reader will be inclined to look *around* the page in a clockwise direction, and that will be helped by the diagonal arrangement and its movement.

There is more. Another school of thought suggests that the reader will look at a broadsheet page in much the same manner as looking at an approaching person. Whatever it is you see first (and it could be anything from the carbuncle on his nose to the dead rat she is swinging) it is highly unlikely that it will be that person's scalp. Why then do we as a matter of course put the main headline at the very top of the page? Those layout people who favour the main headline at a level about a quarter of the way down the page may take comfort from the fact that that is probably about the level of a smile on the face of that approaching person. Most layout people, we are sure, would agree that it does not really matter all that much where you put the lead provided that it is obvious that it *is* the lead.

If diagonal make-up best suits the broadsheets, then *quadrant* make-up is more likely to be encountered in the tabloids, especially those that are tabloid by nature rather than by size – by which we give the word that new meaning of 'loud', 'noisy', 'sensational', or just 'lively', which is probably the fairer judgment. The idea is that on this kind of a page, of the biff-bang-wallop-and-the-page-is-full style, the reader does not need to be guided. Everything can be seen at one glance and you are unlikely to lose your place when you stop to read something. The other name for this style, in truly tabloid vernacular, is 'the four-ringed circus', meaning that you can see all the acts at the same time. The word quadrant means little. The style of this page is to divide the area into two, three, four, perhaps five positions, and to scheme something strong in each. When pages are compared, the one that is truly quartered will probably win fewest votes because of its square shape (see Figure 63).

There is perfect symmetry, we feel, in a crossword puzzle. One solid square one in and two down at the top left requires the same treatment at top right and bottom left and bottom right as well. The same sort of crossword balance is required in the *symmetrical* page, as shown in what was perhaps the world's most famous exponent of symmetrical make-up, *The New York Times* of a bygone age. The idea demonstrated in our diagram is that if you draw a line down the middle of the page the left and right sides of that line provide a mirror image. If that story in column one is worth, say, 500 words then the matching story in column eight has to be 500 words long, worth it or not.

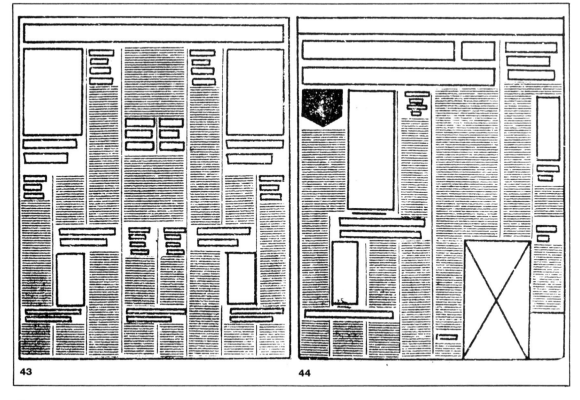

43

44

43. Symmetrical make-up, which may be modified to achieve ordered arrangement.

44. Asymmetrical make-up, a style that reflects varied elements.

45. Modular make-up, most popular and most misunderstood of the styles.

46. *The Financial Post* of Canada with a modular front page which combines elegance and discipline with liberal use of colour. All five pictures are in colour and the hand-lettered script title and digest columns include spot colour. Headlines are in Century Old Style Bold with Century Old Style Roman text, slightly condensed, across 13 ems.

45

46

If that two-column story at bottom left has an associated picture then the matching story in bottom right has to have a same-size picture, so go and find one . . . It does not do much for the journalism.

On the other hand (and we would always urge you to think laterally) there may be good value in the sort of layout suggested in the bottom half of our diagram. Would it not suit the sports page composite of a dozen-and-one match reports in which individual readers are interested in just one or two at most?

The higgledy-piggledy nature of such pages – and the same goes for non-sport composites such as the collection of items in a news backgrounder, or from a newsworthy convention, conference, or council meeting – demands some thought as to an ordered, disciplined arrangement to help the readers find what they are looking for. Symmetry should not be cast aside as an outmoded fad.

Figure 44 is intended to recapture the look of a Fleet Street broadsheet of the 1950s and 1960s, a distinctive genre that seemed to be exported to all corners of the globe, with variations of course. We encounter it

still in those quiet backwaters of journalism where too little has changed in a long time. *Asymmetry* describes quite aptly the uneven balance that can exist between the different kinds of story we might see on a front page – some happy, some sad, some important and some frivolous – and with pictures that may be entirely unrelated. It is a good, mixed diet, suits the popular broadsheet, and is achieved by matching shapes horizontal with shapes vertical, matching a big headline here with a big picture there.

In many respects it is the ideal newspaper make-up, allowing the page planner to react to the news, to juggle with an assortment of items in shapes that might seem equally assorted but which in fact match each item's requirement. Matters of virtue in such pages include the style of a vertical page with the stories, where possible, running down the page in a single flight. Those two at bottom left flight from leg to leg, but in each case the change of direction is slight, the legs short, and there could be nowhere else to go. Remarkably, too, neither of those elements has a multi-column intro, which enables us to make the point that multi-column setting, as in a two-column or three-column intro to a story, is usually overdone.

There are two basic reasons for multi-column setting. One is the clearly apparent need for an important story to have a commanding first paragraph and it may be difficult, to say the least, to set a long intro in 14pt single-column. Such reasoning may be applied to the front-page lead, perhaps the back-page lead, and maybe to other stories inside – but not to three or four stories on every page. The other explanation is that of providing a shoulder position, one side or the other, as the story runs down the page. If a three-column headline is to be held up by a three-column text treatment underneath then it is better that the text be in two or three legs of constant measure than to use a three-column intro and struggle to find some device, like a byline or sub-heading, to hold the angle between the intro and the single-column legs that run beneath it.

Modular, the most popular yet most misunderstood of our formulae, sometimes called 'block' make-up, is often regarded as being dull and stodgy. Yet forms of it can be seen in the most exciting of metropolitan tabloids. Modular make-up stems from the premise that the page is a rectangle and can be broken into a series of smaller rectangles, each containing one element of the page (Figure 45). Related elements may be drawn together to form a further rectangle, and there are adaptations of the formula to allow elements that are not rectangular to be put together, jigsaw fashion, to form a rectangle.

The common feature of all forms of modular make-up is the rectangle or series of rectangles remaining after each step in the design of a page. This fits perfectly the philosophy that a page should be designed as a whole, each stage of its building being so controlled as to produce shapes or positions for the next stage. In this way page planners do not solve the problems of their own making, putting a story or picture into a page and then working out what to do next, but rather do they proceed in such a way as to remove problems altogether. Each step creates a position for the next element; it is the difference between planning a page and merely filling one.

We may liken a newspaper page to a jigsaw. If the pieces of our jigsaw are all even rectangles, often so flexible that they may be used just about anywhere, the puzzle will be a lot easier to put together than those interlocking jigsaws wherre each piece is unique and requires a special place in the intricate pattern. Returning to the analogy of the bricklayer who builds

47. Symmetry in a features page from *The Observer*. It is a fine text treatment of the News Plantin typeface.

48. Over-condensed type, especially in sans serif faces, can be almost painful to read.

49. Daily Swift, a fascinating demonstration of Gerard Unger's new typeface, Swift, in the forms most suited to newspaper text and headlines. Swift is strong in outline with open counters and sturdy serifs to stand up well in economical sizes on cheap, grey and rough newsprint. The typeface has the readability and legibility to make it eminently suitable for such things as dictionaries, catalogues and price-lists and is also elegant enough to dress magazines, supplements, and paperbacks.

houses, that task is eased by the uniformity in size and shape of the basic ingredient – it is a lot quicker to build a wall with bricks than with assorted rocks.

At this point those critics of 'dull and stodgy' modular make-up are likely to point out that brick walls are boring. The answer is that they do not have to be; our bricks, or jigsaw pieces, or modules, can be any size we require. Euclid taught us that the square is a dull shape, static and inanimate, and we will see in our study of pictures that the farther we divorce their shape from square the more dynamic they become. Most pictures reaching the page planner will be slightly off-square, of 10:8 proportion or similar, either vertical or horizontal, and when the proportion changes through cropping to increase the vertical or horizontal stress the result will be a better picture (provided that the cropping has been done properly). Apply that same thinking to the text. We have infinitely greater flexibility, being able to fashion headline and story to any sort of shape – deep

verticals, shallow horizontals – and also vary the measures within the chosen shapes to benefit from the longer lines to be associated with the longer reads. Look again at the pages shown in the set of quadrant pages; they are all modular pages too, and it is quite likely that their popular appeal will be decided by the dynamics of the shapes employed. It is significant that the least successful page is that of four almost identical squares.

A system of truly modular make-up must concern the whole page and not just the editorial part of it. The advertisements will themselves be arranged so as to leave a clear rectangle for the editorial matter that follows. In many newspaper offices this means upgrading the job of the advertisement paper planner, for it is no longer a question of plonking advertisements where there seems to be space, with little thought as to the consequence of building pyramids by putting single-column advertisements on top of two column advertisements, above a three-column with a four-column below that, and so on.

Sometimes, in even more chaotic fashion, the pile of advertisements grows like a stalagmite upwards from the floor of the page, usually in the middle of a two-page spread. The result is a disorganised jumble. Generations of newspaper people have told themselves that this is what advertisers want – to have their advertisements somehow touching editorial matter. If this is the case with some advertisers then they must have been conditioned by newspaper people promising them a space next to editorial matter.

What advertisers really want is to be part of an attractive page, a page with a lot of 'reader traffic', by which we mean the numbers of people who stop at a particular page and spend some time reading it. Still, that is a matter perhaps best dealt with elsewhere; for the moment our mission is to suggest that a good system of page design concerns the whole page and the advertising content is part of that page.

An artist, faced with a blank canvas (which will be a rectangle too), will draw us a picture with ease; but give him a canvas the shape of the editorial part of a pyramid page and he will have considerably more difficulty composing a picture to take up all those illogical angles. Make life a little more difficult for the artist and fill in the rest of the page first while denying him the opportunity to see whether you have used line-work, halftones, display faces or text, and you have created the problem that so many editorial planners have to deal with each and every day.

Not only is this situation difficult to defend, it is

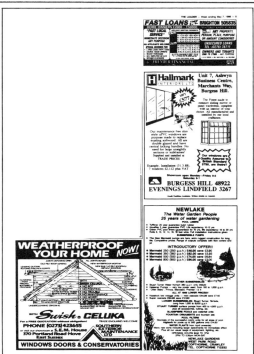

difficult to understand why anyone would wish it to continue. To plan advertisements in modules, stacking them in rectangles if you like, is a rewarding and quite skilful job in itself, and to leave the rest of the page as a clean rectangle will immediately improve the productivity of everyone else concerned with that page. The page planners, artists that they are, will scheme many clean canvases in the time it takes in the vain struggle to get the best out of a pyramid page.

Could it be that the problem lies in the way advertisements are sold almost instinctively in depths of 5, 10, 15, 20 centimetres, etc? Put those sort of shapes up the sides of a 39-centimetre page and there will always be gaps of 4cm or 9cm at the top. We are loth to suggest that the answer is to go out and sell 4cm instead of 5cm, 9cm instead of 10cm, or to fill those remaining shapes with house blurbs of our own.

In the 'green field' operation of a new newspaper it has proved possible to establish ground rules to remove this sort of problem. Typical might be the advertisement page planner's brief not to run advertisements up the side of a page beyond the halfway mark unless it be to go to the very top. The human problem is obviously one connected with a change of

brief; there is no problem with a new brief altogether. A temporary compromise may be to say that, while it is our aim not to go beyond the halfway mark without reaching the top of the column, there will be situations concerned with existing advertising practices, but even here the advertisements will not encroach within 10cm or so of the top of the page. Another compromise, much more controversial, is to allow the editorial planner to move advertisements to another page if they are causing layout problems.

We know of offices where all these things have worked quite successfully. That last one, painful though it was at the start, proved probably the most successful of all when the advertising page planners stopped the scheming of advertisements in those positions where they were likely to be moved. The rewards for removing this whole problem are great. The job of the advertisement planner becomes more creative, the editorial planner becomes more productive and less frustrated, and the newspaper looks all the better, pleasing the advertiser and therefore the accountant.

In considering the suitability of typefaces for text setting, we must first define what we mean by the

56

58

57

59

56, 57, 58 and 59. The importance of a new look was reflected in this preview edition (Figure 56) of the *Winnipeg Free Press* at a time the paper was locked in a fight-to-the-death with a newly redesigned rival. The new design was to replace what was described as a fat, drab, ugly, and inconsistent appearance and it helped do the trick, for the rival paper folded (Figure 57). The distinctive titlepiece is an adaptation of Franklin Gothic while all headings are in Century Schoolbook with Imperial text set to a basic measure of 12.2 ems. Figures 58 and 59 show how the design has evolved in recent years in both the weekday and Sunday editions. Headlines have become much smaller.

60 and 61. Horizontal versus vertical in the same-size page. Choice of picture often dictates the style, as here, although the *Evening News* scores on this occasion with the more dynamic page.

60

London: Wednesday
December 20, 1978
Price: Ten pence

STANDARD

CITY PRICES

Four killed in Brighton line crash

DISASTE
SWEET H

FOUR people died when two trains crashed on the London - Brighton line last night. Seven people were seriously injured, and the accident toll could be as high as 40.

The crash occured in a 40ft cutting at Sweet Hill Bridge, 3 miles from Brighton.

The 9.40 Victoria to Littlehampton train ploughed into the rear of a 9.50 Victoria to Brighton train, halted at signals because of a report of a woman on the rail line near Brighton station.

One coach was hurled 30 feet into the air and crashed on to another carriage. Thr

IRA gunman fires on police—Back Page

BRITAIN'S BIGGEST EVENING SALE
01 353 6000

Evening News

LONDON WEDNESDAY DECEMBER 20 1978   8p

NIGHT SPECIAL
CLOSING PRICES

TRAIN DEATH LEAP AT SWEET HILL

THIS is the grim scene at Sweet Hill Bridge outside Brighton today.

A Victoria to Littlehampton train ploughed into the back of a stationary Victoria to Brighton service, killing at least four people.

Two rear carriages leapt into the air. One ended on its side on the up-line, the other landed on top of the Littlehampton train's front coach and smashed into the bridge.

Four bodies have been found in the horrifying wreckage. A fifth is believed to be still hidden under the mangled debris.

Rescuers continually call for silence in case some passengers are still alive in there.

One of the seven passengers

Story and pictures Pages 2-3

injured was still in hospital, seriously ill and in a coma.

Southern Region said the Littlehampton train, which was travelling at up to 50 miles per hour, should have stopped at a danger signal half a mile up the track.

Mr Bill Mackmurdie the region's central division manager said: "We don't know yet whether the signal was working. In normal circumstances no train should come close up to the back of another."

Sir Peter Parker, chairman of British Rail, visited the scene and said he was dismayed by the crash and promised a full inquiry.

Picture by KEN TOWNER.

61

62. *The Globe and Mail,* Canada, a fine example of modular make-up, avoiding the boring blocks of so many pages put together like rows of bricks. The small and informative headlines add to the busy look.

63. A form of quadrant make-up in *Today.* The squares are dull, static shapes and lack excitement.

64, 65, 66 and 67. *The Daily Telegraph* sticks to its traditional eight-column format but the measure is no more than ten ems in these days of narrowing broadsheets. A one-subject feature page (Figure 65) provides opportunity for a more comfortable read at seven columns to the page, improved further by the use of column rules. The leader page (Figure 66) employs even wider measures with a 20-em leader and five 12-em columns.

From the same stable, *The Sunday Telegraph* (Figure 67) often employs a format of six 13½-em columns for lengthy features.

68. It is important that layout sub-editors should consider eye-flow as one of the most important elements of page make-up. The main headline is apt to take the reader away from the start of the story and it can be difficult to find the way back when the text wanders haphazardly, as in this page, all the way from column two to column ten.

69. Freedom from the column grid permits this sort of design, a superb front page, in full colour, to celebrate a rare occasion.

70. A good headline interfering badly with a good picture and both of these elements interrupting the flow of text.

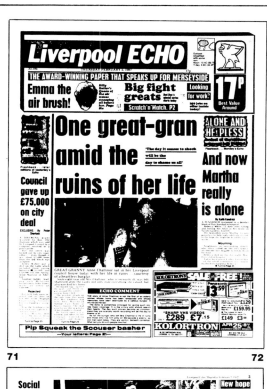

71, 72 and 73. The *Liverpool Echo* combines the razzmatazz of a metropolitan tabloid with the high story-count associated with successful parish-pump newspapers. The typical reader cannot fail to find something of interest in these action-packed pages. Figure 73 shows the sub-editor's page plan for Page Three.

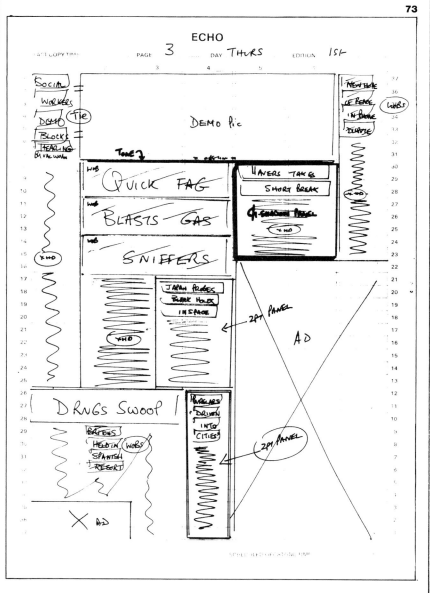

74

75

74, 75, 76 and 77. A splendid text treatment for a lengthy survey in *The Financial Times*, but it is difficult to work out whether the sub-headings in columns two and four are eyebreaks or crossheads or separate headings. The heavy crossbar above each of them may be a barrier to continued reading, especially after the paragraph break and with a flush left start to the next sentence.

Effective eyebreaks do not interrupt the reader nor should they present a puzzle to the reader who has to jump back and forth as in Figure 75 where it becomes difficult to move from the bottom of the second leg of type to the top of the third. Compare these eye-hazards to the smooth and logical sequence of text in the other two articles on the page.

Figures 76 and 77 show two pages from the same edition of *The Age*, Melbourne, both superb treatments of the readable Bedford text face but one suffering from a series of eye-flow problems caused by a quote pulled out of the story for display purposes.

78. A very English look for the Malay-language *Berita Harian*, Kuala Lumpur.

79

79, 80 and 81. The shape of pages to come . . . Three run-of-the-mill pages from *The Boston Globe* showing no trace of a column grid; a page is a page, measured in pica ems, and that's where design begins.

81

The Boston Globe

SUNDAY, JULY 19, 1987

FOCUS

Editorials 86

THE IRAN-CONTRA HEARINGS

America finally gets an earful

The colonel was the star, but the admiral provided the crucial testimony

By David Nyhan

He can't remember whether it was in London or Frankfurt, but Oliver North is sure that his conversation with Manucher Ghorbanifar took place in a bathroom.

When a foreign arms trader offers you a million-dollar bribe in the john, it's the kind of thing you tend to remember.

The Iranian middleman in the initial arms-for-hostages deal supposedly made the Marine officer an offer he only half-refused. Why not use profits from the arms sales to help the contras? And why don't you take a million for your trouble?

Lt. Col. North forgets if he alerted his superiors about the bribe offer he spurned. But he told his boss, Rear Adm. John Poindexter, about the "neat idea" he got from Ghorbanifar. Poindexter didn't want to tell President Reagan about it, "so that I could insulate him and provide some future deniability for the president if it ever leaked out."

This is the tale America was asked to believe last week, that a mysterious Iranian could propose a fantastic link between two super-secret American policies, and the key details were kept from the president by his most trusted advisers.

A question of misplaced trust

Reagan had two simple goals: He wanted the hostages back, and he wanted the contras funded, period. In Poindexter's words, "The president is not a man for great detail." It was as if a modern Henry II raged before his officers, "Will no one rid me of this troublesome Congress?" And this pair of obscure military adventurers took it upon themselves to do his bidding.

No one worried that the CIA regarded Ghorbanifar as a liar, cheat and an agent for the Israelis. Ghorbanifar himself told a "Nightline" audience from England on Thursday night that North is lying. The HEARINGS, Page 82

David Nyhan is a columnist and an associate editor of the Globe.

THE MUSE OF THE WEEK IN REVIEW

The cream of serials

When the Northern lights glowed in the hearings, they showed
A public less willing to dwell on
An act that's illicit than gaily dismissed
With "Ollie is a jolly good felon."

Olliegiance was pledged as North lectured and hedged
While he stuck to his guilt-free motif,
Despite counsel's desire to pluck from their liar
A tune giving hell to the chief.

Sincere and endearing, clean-living, God-fearing,
Ollie shone as a media star –
But his luster was gummed up when Hamilton summed up:
North had gone much too Ghorbanifar.

Who'd have dreamed North began on his Contr-Iran plan
At a word from an Eastern civilian,
A bathroom aside, plus an offer (denied)
Of baksheesh to the tune of a million?

A much less direct stir was made by Poindexter
Who came on as dully reliable,
Causing Ron's heart to lift with the fabulous gift
Of making his "finding" "deniable."

Then the hearings suspended
As Congress attended
A fete for our great Constitution,
Before getting back to take one further crack
At exploring its near-dissolution.

– Felicia Lamport

David Cowles Illustration

CAMPAIGN '88

Dukakis courts centrist image

His decisions draw criticism at home but may be helping him on the road

By Joan Vennochi

By Massachusetts standards, Michael Dukakis has always been something of a political hybrid. In his first term, he outraged traditional liberals by drastically cutting the state's welfare budget, and antagonized business interests with strict regulatory policies. In his second term, he has worked harder to please competing interest groups. Helped by a growing state surplus, he has increased spending for social programs, and he has provided more economic incentives to keep the business community happy.

But maintaining that balancing act has proved difficult, and Dukakis has been facing some strong criticism lately, with the fire coming mainly from liberal supporters.

They have blasted his policy that makes it virtually impossible for gays to become foster parents and his recent proposal to allow insurance companies to test for AIDS. His insurance commissioner, revered by pro-consumer groups, resigned two weeks ago in protest of the testing plan. Even the American Civil Liberties Union has expressed doubts about Dukakis, who has proudly called himself a "card-carrying member" of the group.

Is it conscious image-building?

If Dukakis were just another chief executive, worried about losing a portion of his political base, the last few weeks might seem like a bad dream. But for Dukakis the presidential candidate, they could turn out to be a blessing. While the governor's troubles may wound him at home, they are not hurting him on the campaign trail.

"I think his recent behavior fits the image he is trying to portray to a national audience – that he is a pro-business, pro-growth Democrat," said Steven Pizer, research director for Mass. Fair Share, one of the groups that counts itself as growingly disillusioned with Dukakis, the presidential candidate.

If Dukakis has a political soft spot as a national candidate, it is his continuing need to fight off any attempt to paint him as a repackaged version of a Ted Kennedy liberal. The Massachusetts "economic miracle" helps him. So does the tax rebate he announced several weeks ago, without ever mentioning that he opposed the referendum petition that resulted in the refund. But suspicions about him still linger in the South and West, key areas he must win if he is to be the party's nominee.

Though Dukakis is still firmly positioned as a liberal on litmus-test social issues such as abortion and the death penalty, Illinois Sen. Paul Simon clearly commands the left of the political spectrum among the declared presidential candidates. Dukakis' recent policy decisions have moved him closer to the center on the national stage and helped him tone down his image as an Eastern liberal.

US Rep. Richard Gephardt (D-Mo.), coming from the other side of the political spectrum, also seems to be heading toward the same centrist haven. In what some see as an effort to modify his conservative image, presidential candidate DUKAKIS, Page 84

Joan Vennochi covers the Dukakis campaign for the Globe.

One of South Korea's "Darth Vaders."

Matsumoto/Sygma

LETTER FROM SEOUL

DEMONSTRATION MODELS

By Colin Nickerson

SEOUL – The hottest-selling items in Seoul's open-air markets these days are swim goggles.

It's not that South Koreans have suddenly discovered a passion for the free stroke: rather, they have learned that underwater eyewear offers some protection against the sting of the city's No. 1 air pollutant of late – tear gas.

And so, market stalls that until recently offered only the humdrum staple – boiled pigs' heads, dried squid, full-size replicas of armless Greek goddesses, chirruping song birds, wind-up frogmen splashing circles in plastic tubs and so on – are now doing a brisk business in goggles, surgical masks and surplus gas masks.

"Oh, I sell many, many goggles to many peoples," boasted a vendor in sprawling Namdaemun Market. "Maybe for Olympics, but I don't think so."

For the last two months, antigovernment demonstrations have been a near daily occurrence in Seoul. And when the protests turn violent, which is often, the Chun-too Kyung-chal – the special riot police – break them up with tear gas, the only weapon at LETTER, Page 84

Colin Nickerson is a Globe foreign correspondent.

Gov. Dukakis meets the media at Logan after a campaign trip.

Globe staff photo/Keith Jenkins

82

83

terms readability and legibility, for in typographical usage the words are not synonymous. *Readability* is a quality concerned with the ease and comfort with which we read text, with the eye moving across the page in a series of rapid jerks and taking in a number of characters at each pause. *Legibility* is concerned with the speed with which the eye picks out an individual character or word or short compact group of words as in a narrow headline, or a very big headline, when the eye is fixed and focused. Readability, then, is the test of the suitability of a typeface for lengthy text, while legibility is the test of typefaces to be used for headlines, crossheads, sub-headings of all kinds, and also that kind of text matter where the reader's need is to pick out individual words, or groups of words, as in lists of results, race-cards, television programme guides, classified advertisements, etc.

Some typefaces are rated highly for readability but not legibility, and some typefaces have high legibility but rate less well in terms of readability. Some score highly on both counts. A useful rule of thumb, although not entirely reliable, is that old-style typefaces and slab-serif typefaces are apt to be both readable and legible, while moderns tend more towards readability and sans-serif faces towards legibility.

However, there is much more to consider. Type-size does not determine readability, and indeed may militate against it in the context of narrow-column measures. There is an important relationship (touched on elsewhere) of type-size to measure in order to achieve a suitable number of characters per line so that we may read in phrases.

What is to be regarded as suitable will vary according to the kind of content and the mood of the reader. The reader of fine literature in a well-printed book may be best served by ten, eleven, or twelve words per line in order to best savour flowing phrases, while the reader of one-, two- and three-paragraph news briefs will find little difficulty in dealing with much narrower measures. Generally speaking, though, we may say that in newspapers there is a lot that is in between the two extremes, and the reader of text of any substance is unlikely to be comfortable with less than five or six words per line. In terms of characters this might cause us to lay down a minimum of around 30 letters and spaces per line for sustained newspaper reading; the longer the piece the wider the lines ought to be. Spacing between columns will be crucial, as may spacing between lines of typefaces that

82. Dynamic shapes in this front page of the German-language edition of *Pravda.*

83. Juxtaposition is one of the biggest problems of the popular newspaper, using an assortment of shapes to create excitement. Readers are used to pictures with related headlines above them and the visual link here is compounded by picture-cropping which joins the two elements typographically.

are so big on the body that they may seem cramped when set solid.

Other factors are *reproduction:* the type must print clearly even on poor quality newsprint, and this means that it has to have a clean and open cut; *colour:* the drawing of the letter should be strong enough to avoid greyness, even with thin inks and high-speed printing, while sustaining sufficient contrast between thick and thin strokes to break monotony; *proportion:* the height/width relationship should be oblong, not square, and the body of the type (or x-height) must not seriously encroach on the ascenders, those upper distinguishing strokes which perform an essential optical function.

In the 1920s, the first two of these factors were telling heavily against the modern romans, which in many variations had been the normal newspaper text face since John Bell introduced the first (French-inspired) 'modern' at the end of the eighteenth century. The light-faced moderns, with their weak serifs and tendency to create ink-traps in complex lower-case letters, could not withstand the demands of punishing printing speeds. The introduction of Ionic, strongly-coloured, open and large-bodied, re-volutionised newspaper text setting and initiated a whole series of similar specially-designed text types which became known as the Legibility Group. Ionic caused a sensation and is said to have been adopted by 3,000 newspapers inside eighteen months. However, it was by no means perfect in readability terms, for its abnormal x-height and set-width meant that it was too strong to be served 'neat'. It needed 'diluting' with inter-linear white space; that is, instead of being set solid, it had to be set on a body at least one point larger. In terms of line count, and in characters per line, the typeface was greedy for space. A modified successor, Excelsior, was fractionally lighter in weight and less extreme in proportions; then this variation was made first a little heavier (Opticon) and then even lighter (Paragon). The typeface Ideal was similar to Excelsior and was then modified into Regal; and finally there came Corona, described as a composite of this entire Legibility Group.

Stanley Morison's Times Roman (at first called Times New Roman), evolved in the period from 1930 to 1932, combining legibility, readability, good colour and space economy, the qualities which to this day have made it the most popular serif face in the roman alphabet. In the early 1950s two more popular faces were launched: Jubilee (standing somewhere between Times and Excelsior) and the quite independent

Imperial (regarded as a descendant of the Ionic-Excelsior group). Towards the end of the 1960s came Walter Tracy's Telegraph Modern and, later, Matthew Carter's Olympian, which was to win enormous popularity in North America; and also Walter Tracy's Times Europa, which for a period replaced Times Roman in *The Times* of London.

Choosing typefaces from among those named was perhaps a simple task before the advent of computerised typesetting, when the tried and trusted faces had to be digitised and were not immediately suited to what in its early stages was an exceptionally clumsy process. Versions of Times Roman proliferated, under all sorts of names, and a great many were substandard; the same must be said of many of the other existing faces, which were digitised, often hurriedly, to meet popular demand. Choosing typefaces for new electronic systems became something of a nightmare. The problems have since eased and will become easier still with the enormous improvements in methods of digitisation and other methods of producing images by means of computers. Some fine new typefaces have been designed for computerised setting, and technological advances coupled with marketing pressures have increased compatibility between typeface suppliers.

One of the most popular introductions of recent years has been that of Monotype Nimrod, the work of a young designer, Robin Nicholas, which has been likened to a great many of the most successful newspaper text faces of the past, including Plantin, Times, and Ionic. In one sense this must be considered flattering, yet in truth Nimrod must be described as a new face, designed for computers and capable of withstanding the degradation so often inescapable under the demands of modern newspaper production.

Figure 87 shows Nimrod in various sizes with differences in inter-linear spacing. Clearly it is a typeface that, in its most readable forms, benefits from being set on a slightly larger body. There are, however, versions of Nimrod designed specifically for display, for text and also for classified advertising, with different set-widths to suit the obviously differing needs of newspapers, which charge by the line or by the word. The very fact that there are so many forms of this new typeface – and we have not even mentioned its excellent italic or the companion bold – must be sufficient indication of the difficulties associated with the choice of just one typeface. The fact that there is a growing number of new typefaces and variations pinpoints the need for an increased understanding of form and content.

84

Galfra 5pt.

AAA's TICKETS. Phantom, Les Mis., all sport & pop. 01 999 8888/7777. Fax 666 5555.

ALL TICKETS Phantom, Les Mis; S Winwood, M Jackson Springsteen, Cliff Richard, Cricket Prince & all Theatres Credit cards Accepted Tel: 01 010 0101 or 01 232 3232.

ALL TICKETS theatre, pop concerts and sporting events 01 456 7890

BABY GRAND PIANO Modern style, figured walnut case with stool. £1,450. After 6p.m. 01 987 6543.

BANK HOLIDAY week, 27 Aug. Lakeland cottage. Sleeps 8. 0665 455445

BOOK CLUBS Research being undertaken on your experiences. Write to—Box Number 2400 Daily Clarion, E14.

BRITISH TIPPED Kittens for sale. Show/Pet quality. CH fired. Tel. 021 544 9669 or 021 724 6997.

Nimrod Classified Ads. Extended 5pt.

AAA's TICKETS. Phantom, Les Mis., all sport & pop. 01 999 8888/7777. Fax 666 5555.

ALL TICKETS Phantom, Les Mis; S Winwood, M Jackson Springsteen, Cliff Richard, Cricket Prince & all Theatres Credit cards Accepted Tel: 01 010 0101 or 01 232 3232.

ALL TICKETS theatre, pop concerts and sporting events 01 456 7890

BABY GRAND PIANO Modern style, figured walnut case with stool. £1,450. After 6p.m. 01 987 6543.

BANK HOLIDAY week, 27 Aug. Lakeland cottage. Sleeps 8. 0665 455445

BOOK CLUBS Research being undertaken on your experiences. Write to—Box Number 2400 Daily Clarion, E14.

BRITISH TIPPED Kittens for sale. Show/Pet quality. CH fired. Tel. 021 544 9669 or 021 724 6997.

Nimrod Classified Ads. 5pt.

AAA's TICKETS. Phantom, Les Mis., all sport & pop. 01 999 8888/7777. Fax 666 5555.

ALL TICKETS Phantom, Les Mis; S Winwood, M Jackson Springsteen, Cliff Richard, Cricket Prince & all Theatres Credit cards Accepted Tel: 01 010 0101 or 01 232 3232.

ALL TICKETS theatre, pop concerts and sporting events 01 456 7890

BABY GRAND PIANO Modern style, figured walnut case with stool. £1,450. After 6p.m. 01 987 6543.

BANK HOLIDAY week, 27 Aug. Lakeland cottage. Sleeps 8. 0665 455445

BOOK CLUBS Research being undertaken on your experiences. Write to—Box Number 2400 Daily Clarion, E14.

BRITISH TIPPED Kittens for sale. Show/Pet quality. CH fired. Tel. 021 544 9669 or 021 724 6997.

Times Small Ads. 5pt.

AAA's TICKETS. Phantom, Les Mis., all sport & pop. 01 999 8888/7777. Fax 666 5555.

ALL TICKETS Phantom, Les Mis; S Winwood, M Jackson Springsteen, Cliff Richard, Cricket Prince & all Theatres Credit cards Accepted Tel: 01 010 0101 or 01 232 3232.

ALL TICKETS theatre, pop concerts and sporting events 01 456 7890

20th Century Classified 5pt.

AAA's TICKETS. Phantom, Les Mis., all sport & pop. 01 999 8888/7777. Fax 666 5555.

ALL TICKETS Phantom, Les Mis; S Winwood, M Jackson Springsteen, Cliff Richard, Cricket Prince & all Theatres Credit cards Accepted Tel: 01 010 0101 or 01 232 3232.

ALL TICKETS theatre, pop concerts and sporting events 01 456 7890

BABY GRAND PIANO Modern style, figured walnut case with stool. £1,450. After 6p.m. 01 987 6543.

85

Abadi medium roman 8 on 8a over 12 ems width

A well-designed paper explains itself at a glance. The typographical treatment distinguishes different kinds of news stories, and separates features. Further, it maintains interest throughout. There

Abadi medium italic 8 on 8a over 12 ems width

A well-designed paper explains itself at a glance. The typographical treatment distinguishes different kinds of news stories, and separates features. Further, it maintains interest throughout. There should be a

Abadi bold roman 8 on 8a over 12 ems width

A well-designed paper explains itself at a glance. The typographical treatment distinguishes different kinds of news stories, and separates features. Further, it maintains interest throughout. There

Calisto roman 8 on 8a over 12 ems width

A well-designed paper explains itself at a glance. The typographical treatment distinguishes different kinds of news stories, and separates features. Further, it maintains interest throughout. There

Calisto italic 8 on 8a over 12 ems width

A well-designed paper explains itself at a glance. The typographical treatment distinguishes different kinds of news stories, and separates features. Further, it maintains interest throughout.

Calisto Bold roman 8 on 8a over 12 ems width

A well-designed paper explains itself at a glance. The typographical treatment distinguishes different kinds of news stories, and separates features. Further, it maintains interest throughout.

Times New Roman 8 on 8a over 12 ems width

A well-designed paper explains itself at a glance. The typographical treatment distinguishes different kinds of news stories, and separates features. Further, it maintains interest throughout.

Times Postscript roman 8 on 8a over 12 ems width

A well-designed paper explains itself at a glance. The typographical treatment distinguishes different kinds of news stories, and separates features. Further, it maintains interest throughout.

Excelsior roman 8 on 8a over 12 ems width

A well-designed paper explains itself at a glance. The typographical treatment distinguishes different kinds of news stories, and separates features. Further, it maintains interest throughout.

84. Galfra is a remarkable new typeface designed for use in Italian telephone directories but destined, surely, to gain an even wider audience in newspaper columns such as classified advertising and stocks and shares prices, where there is equal need for high legibility in small sizes and sharp, precise figures. In this illustration we can see Galfra in two weights, medium and semi-bold, at 5pt. Monotype offer two versions of Nimrod for classified advertisements: one recommended for advertisements sold by the word and the other for lineage. Figure 84 shows Nimrod Class Ads and Class Ads Extended, alongside two other excellent faces, Times Small Ads and 20th Century Classified.

85. Abadi, an excellent new sans face designed by Ong Chong Wah, made its newspaper debut in 1989. Here it is seen headlined in the first issue of the free newspaper *Keighley Target*. Calisto is a new text face, which appears in newspapers for the first time in 1989. Sturdier than Times, more uniform too, this typeface design by Ron Carpenter of Monotype may enjoy a big success. Times Roman and Times PostScript are also shown here, together with an excellent new version of Excelsior.

86. A new version of Times New Roman, produced for PostScript typesetting, shown here at 144pt.

87. The new Nimrod 8141 typeface from Monotype, seen here in various sizes and measures. The letters *a*, *b*, and *c* in the typesetting descriptions represent an extra quarter-point, half-point, or three-quarter-point on the body.

86

S012
abijp

87

8141 7 on 7a over 8b ems width

A well-designed paper explains itself at a glance. The typographical treatment distinguishes different kinds of news stories, and separates features. Further, it maintains interest throughout.

8141 7 on 7a over 9 ems width

A well-designed paper explains itself at a glance. The typographical treatment distinguishes different kinds of news stories, and separates features. Further, it maintains interest throughout.

8141 7 on 7a over 10 ems width

A well-designed paper explains itself at a glance. The typographical treatment distinguishes different kinds of news stories, and separates features. Further, it maintains interest throughout.

8141 7 on 7a over 12 ems width

A well-designed paper explains itself at a glance. The typographical treatment distinguishes different kinds of news stories, and separates features. Further, it maintains interest throughout.

8141 7 on 7b over 8b ems width

A well-designed paper explains itself at a glance. The typographical treatment distinguishes different kinds of news stories, and separates features. Further, it maintains interest throughout.

8141 7 on 7b over 9 ems width

A well-designed paper explains itself at a glance. The typographical treatment distinguishes different kinds of news stories, and separates features. Further, it maintains interest throughout.

8141 7 on 7b over 10 ems width

A well-designed paper explains itself at a glance. The typographical treatment distinguishes different kinds of news stories, and separates features. Further, it maintains interest throughout.

8141 7 on 7b over 12 ems width

A well-designed paper explains itself at a glance. The typographical treatment distinguishes different kinds of news stories, and separates features. Further, it maintains interest throughout.

8141 8 on 8a over 12 ems width

A well-designed paper explains itself at a glance. The typographical treatment distinguishes different kinds of news stories, and separates features. Further, it maintains interest throughout.

8141 7b on 8 pt over 12 ems width

A well-designed paper explains itself at a glance. The typographical treatment distinguishes different kinds of news stories, and separates features. Further, it maintains interest throughout.

8141 9 on 9b over 12 ems width

A well-designed paper explains itself at a glance. The typographical treatment distinguishes different kinds of news stories, and separates features. Further, it maintains interest throughout.

HEADLINES
AND OTHER FORMS OF DISPLAY

THE typography of the newspaper headline is sharply conditioned by its function and its technical circumstances. We may describe its function as being at once that of a *signal* and of a *summary*, attracting attention and helping readers to make a selection of those items they wish to read; this it has to do within a fixed and inflexible measure to which its set width, or unit count, and consequent reasonable ease of writing, have to be related. Even with the use of very wide headlines the determining fact of measure, from the standpoint of headline typography, remains the width of the single-column or narrowest headline, for it is useless to choose a basic headline type too wide for easy and lucid use in a single column, no matter how conveniently it may display in three-column or four-column heads.

But if the importance of this mechanical factor of measure is recognised it has to be conceded that the effective determination of headline types fit to perform this dual function depends upon a whole series of complex secondary considerations. Reasonable regard may be had for tradition, though this does not mean blindly following the styles of long ago. Fashions in typography change as fashions in all things change, and we are apt to see what is currently fashionable as being an improvement on what went before. Present-day headline types are of strong 'colour' – the day of the light, spindle-shanked headline swimming almost indistinguishably in the grey ocean of the text is long since done. It was, though, once fashionable.

Colour, or degree of blackness, is of some primary concern in our choice of headline types. Allied to this are *crispness* and to some degree *contrast*, two qualities that require a word of explanation. Crispness implies a clear-cut, sharp design of letter; one that tends to angularity or harshness rather than being elegant or even handsome, so that it could never be classed as being delicate, florid or soft in its outline or serif structure. Contrast is a quality concerned with thin up-strokes and thick down-strokes, which is regarded by many as essential in the most satisfactory types for news headlines, more so in the UK than in America, where there is a strong liking for the even-stroked Egyptian letters of types such as Rockwell, Memphis, Stymie and Karnak. Contrast is perhaps of less importance in the fashions of today than it was when this book was first published more than quarter of a century ago. It is significant that the contrast of thick and thin strokes was never a requirement in anybody's mind when considering the virtues of sans serif types, which more often than not are of monoline nature. However, in the case of sans serif types there is contrast of a different kind, resulting from sharp cut and strong colour accentuated by the absence of serifs.

Knowing what you want is an all-important part of the task of choosing types for a newspaper. Some typefaces are elegant and upmarket, others are down-to-earth and downright downmarket too. A typeface designed for selling soap powder, screaming from the supermarket shelves, will be quite at home shouting from a tabloid news page. Tempo Heavy is such a typeface which is why it has suited newspapers such as *The Sun* in Fleet Street; to see the same typographical treatments in *The Sun* in Fiji, or *The Sun* in Brisbane, both in the nature of look-alikes, would seem to be ill-fitting unless those two newspapers happened to be selling the same goods. (It is interesting to note that *The Sun* in Brisbane changed its lookalike cornerpiece title for a horizontal version when in 1988 it turned from morning to afternoon publication.) Not all Tempo faces have the same stark quality; Tempo Black has it, but not Tempo Bold, which is too clean, too neat, while another member of the family, Tempo Medium, and especially its italic, is a great typeface for selling greetings cards.

One editor we know, searching for a powerful sans serif face for a new newspaper, actually did find it in a supermarket, on a packet of frozen chips. That was

88, 89, 90 and 91.
Typefaces old and new that are among those likely to be popular headline choices through the 1990s. All the samples are in the same point size.

58

88

Calisto Bold 24pt.

NEWSPAPER DESIGN TODAY

Newspaper Design Today

Monotype Clearface bold 24pt.

NEWSPAPER DESIGN TODAY

Newspaper Design Today

Bodoni bold 24pt.

NEWSPAPER DESIGN TODAY

Newspaper Design Today

Bodoni bold condensed 24pt.

NEWSPAPER DESIGN TODAY

Newspaper Design Today

Helvetica medium condensed 24pt.

NEWSPAPER DESIGN TODAY

Newspaper Design Today

Helvetica extra compressed 24pt.

NEWSPAPER DESIGN TODAY

Newspaper Design Today

89

Helvetica Inserat 24pt.

NEWSPAPER DESIGN TODAY

Newspaper Design Today

Franklin Gothic extra condensed roman 24pt.

NEWSPAPER DESIGN TODAY

Newspaper Design Today

Franklin Gothic extra condensed italic 24pt.

NEWSPAPER DESIGN TODAY

Newspaper Design Today

Optima 24pt.

NEWSPAPER DESIGN TODAY

Newspaper Design Today

Abadi bold condensed 24pt.

NEWSPAPER DESIGN TODAY

Newspaper Design Today

Abadi extra bold condensed 24pt.

NEWSPAPER DESIGN TODAY

Newspaper Design Today

Century Schoolbook 24pt.

NEWSPAPER DESIGN TODAY
Newspaper Design Today

Century Schoolbook bold 24pt.

NEWSPAPER DESIGN TODAY
Newspaper Design Today

Rockwell bold condensed 24pt.

NEWSPAPER DESIGN TODAY
Newspaper Design Today

Plantin bold condensed 24pt.

NEWSPAPER DESIGN TODAY
Newspaper Design Today

News Plantin bold 24pt.

NEWSPAPER DESIGN TODAY
Newspaper Design Today

Placard bold condensed 24pt.

NEWSPAPER DESIGN TODAY
Newspaper Design Today

91

Nimrod Headline 24pt.

NEWSPAPER DESIGN TODAY
Newspaper Design Today

Nimrod Headline bold 24pt.

NEWSPAPER DESIGN TODAY
Newspaper Design Today

Times New Roman 24pt.

NEWSPAPER DESIGN TODAY
Newspaper Design Today

Times New Roman italic 24pt.

NEWSPAPER DESIGN TODAY
Newspaper Design Today

Times semi bold 24pt.

NEWSPAPER DESIGN TODAY
Newspaper Design Today

Times bold 24pt.

NEWSPAPER DESIGN TODAY
Newspaper Design Today

92. A new version of Times New Roman from Monotype showing the superb clarity of letter structure that has made Stanley Morison's typeface the most popular serif in the world.

ABCDEF GHIJKL MNOPQ RSTUV WXYZ&

how the typeface Anzeigen Grotesque was first introduced to newspapers in Britain, to be copied, quickly and often badly, by a good many newspapers. This is a common problem, especially among small newspapers that ape the practices of bigger and different papers, believing no doubt that they are following a good example. The typographical razzmatazz of a metropolitan tabloid is unlikely to suit the country weekly, which has a different kind of content and a different style of writing.

Sans serif faces such as Univers, eminently suitable for brochures, company reports and the like, have an air of upmarket elegance to impart, although not all who use them recognise or exploit that quality. Univers is perhaps not as 'newsy' as Helvetica, with which it is often wrongly classified; Helvetica of one sort of another – its features can be recognised in at least a dozen and one typefaces under different names – is not as brash as, say, Franklin Gothic. Futura sits somewhere in the middle.

But these are all well-known typefaces, seen in newspapers the world over and often said to be the best because they are the most commonly encountered. Too many newspapers are over-influenced by this sort of list and perpetuate the fashion by choosing from what is already popular. Others, keen for innovation but shy of adventure, will wait until something new comes along, something that looks good enough to mimic without too much thought about the suitability of its translation from one kind of paper to another.

When a much talked about American paper, *The Ledger* in Lakeland, won a series of circulation awards after a series of far-reaching changes, much of the talk centred on its redesign and the fact that all of its headlines were in small sizes of Avant Garde; there was little doubt that this would spawn a fashion. Avant Garde is a fine face, but a change of typeface by itself is unlikely to alter the fortunes of a newspaper even when used as well as Avant Garde is in *The Ledger*. The same typeface was used well in the short-lived UK news magazine *Now!* but it could not sell a product for which there was insufficient demand.

The sans serif types cover a field of great variety and indeed complexity, which affords rich study for the scholars; but newspaper people have not the time for scholastic classification and will look for a face that can offer varying weights and widths. A Bold, a Bold Condensed, and a slightly lighter Extra Condensed are the main basic ingredients for the brash tabloid,

but so limited a range may be too heavy and 'bludgeoning' for unrelieved broadsheet display.

It is remarkable that the great Gill family of sans serif faces, equipped as it is with all the necessary variants, has not been regarded as being suitable for newspapers. One day, perhaps, this superior style, demanding as it does the delicacy of first-rate composition, may come into increased favour.

Clearly a similar range of popular names can be found among the seriffed ranks, although those we are likely to find in newspapers have perhaps more versatility than many of their sans cousins. Times Bold, for instance, communicates an air of sure authority in the neatly shaped headlines of *The Financial Times* while it fair squeals with excitement in the big sizes of some noisy tabloids. Century, the biggest family of newspaper serifs, has the same versatility as have some of the heavy Caslons. It is significant that in the trend towards more colour in

93. Headlines do not have to be big to command attention. *The Ledger,* from Lakeland, produces a lively front page with quite small headlines in Avant Garde.

94 and 95. *The New York Times* combines excellence and tradition in its tightly-ruled columns but its wordy headlines are not easy to read, especially in the all-caps style.

96

our types there has been a move towards heavier serifs, brought about in some measure no doubt by the degradation that occurs in the rough processes of newspaper printing: the blunter the serif at the outset the more likelihood there is of something appearing to be a serif in the finished product. This can account for the rise of the Rockwells and other slab serifs, which also have the versatility of being all things to all papers if we choose the right versions for the right places, from the small and light to the big and black.

While some types rise in popularity and new types are designed with the computer in mind, some must wane in popularity. The first edition of this book referred at length to the Edwardian Cheltenham family of faces (Figure 96) whose longevity and ubiquity were described as proverbial. Cheltenham, an even-toned letter without sharp serifs, essentially contravenes the requirements of crispness and contrast as outlined here yet it continued through generations, and continues still in a number of newspapers, on the important qualifying grounds of tradition and association. As we continue to say, a newspaper must look like a newspaper and should not break radically with tradition so as to make itself provocatively unfashionable; so we cannot argue against such grounds. Yet times change, and over the years Cheltenham acquired a marked air of a provincialism that no longer suited newspapers striving to reflect the lifestyle and tastes of present-day readers. The great

96. Once one of the most popular typefaces in country newspapers, Cheltenham is enjoying a revival. Figure 96 shows a good treatment of it in the *Malton Gazette & Herald*, although the sans titlepiece seems to be out of place in such a setting.

97 and 98. Two front pages from separate editions. There are more than 20 typographical differences but the most significant are those between the two lead headlines. Neither really succeeds because of the unnecessary underscore.

value of Cheltenham in its heyday was concerned as much as anything with the enormous range of variations in weight and width. Few typefaces could offer its range of styles from condensed to extended in different weights – although today, thanks to the computer, this in itself would seem extremely limited. We can see in Figures 27 and 28 some fourteen examples of Univers, all in one size, from one supplier, and there seems little reason why the selection should not be wider, given the need.

Need is a crucial factor. New typefaces are designed to meet needs rather than create them. A newspaper man might look at that remarkable range of 14pt Univers samples and wonder what on earth they must look like in 6pt and why anyone would possibly want such an extraordinary type as 6pt Univers Extra Light and Extra Condensed; and yet, on thinking about the needs of a map-maker in pinpointing communities from tiny villages to cities, rivers and mountains and every other kind of geographical feature and boundary to be found in a map, such a typeface must be very useful indeed. It is a short step from such understanding to the thought that there is a need today for such suitable typefaces in newspaper graphics, and they might not be readily available from among those in traditional use.

History will record Bodoni as one of the greatest of newspaper typefaces. The family of types bearing the name of the illustrious Parmesan printer and type-cutter of the late eighteenth and early nineteenth centuries is not a reproduction of any one of his faces but, as has often been pointed out, a synthesis of the main features of all of them. So it emphasises the characteristics of the so-called 'mechanically perfect' letter, the great divide between Old Face and Modern. Extreme sharpness and straightness of cut, absence of curvature, the greatest possible contrast between up-strokes and down-strokes, straight hairline serifs – these are the characteristics that give Bodoni its special, acute and arresting quality. The modern face we call Bodoni was devised in America, the standard weight first being cut in 1911 by Morris Benton, chief designer of the American Type Founders Company. It was shortly afterwards made available by Linotype and then in other versions including a Bold and Bold Italic, which set the seal on its use for news headlines.

If Bodoni has a disadvantage (some would view what we are about to say as a virtue) it is that, like other moderns, it will not mix happily with other display faces. A Bodoni page is at its best when the display is wholly Bodoni without contrast of any kind. Unlike most of the other newspaper types mentioned in this book, Bodoni is exceptionally small in body, retaining the long descenders of its prototype, and this has to be kept in mind – a Bodoni of, say, 42pt will appear smaller than the 36pt point of many other faces. There is some advantage to be gained here, of course, for Bodoni can be set solid in situations where the bigger-faced types require inter-linear spacing if they are not to look cramped and crushed. The biggest virtue of Bodoni for editorial display lies in the Bold italic, which is truly outstanding among italics (and sloped romans as most ought to be called). The Bodoni italic is both colourful and crisp, and its cursive effect contrasts well not only with its own roman but with almost any other, including rounded serifs and sans faces.

Associated with Bodoni, at least in trade parlance, are ranges of extra heavy and extra condensed letters which have nothing to do with the great typographer but share the thick-thin contrast and hairline serifs. These 'ultra' styles are versions of the English Regency 'fat face' later called Elephant by the typefounders and are useful as auxiliaries for crossheads, straplines, logos and other elements of display associated with headlines, but not for main news headlines, for which they seem totally unsuitable despite their sometimes quite successful appearance in feature treatments.

Where Bodoni has lost some of its traditional popularity as a news headline face is in its unsuitability for the over-sized headlines that sprang into vogue during the boom years of the early 1970s, when the demands of advertising necessitated increased paging with acres of unexpected space not easy to fill. Headlines more than doubled in size in some newspapers, a device that does not suit the heavily contrasted strokes of Bodoni and other moderns, for in appearance the thin strokes become thinner while the thick strokes grow to a point where the distortion loses all of that Bodoni elegance. It is also unsuited to headings in capitals, and in many newspapers the inevitable consequence was to bring in another face, often Century, to carry first the front page lead and then spreading inside to other page leads, gradually squeezing out the Bodoni look. That look is still to be found in many American papers, while the most notable example of it in the UK is to be found in *The Daily Telegraph*, where it stands as a hallmark of typographical quality. If fashions do indeed turn full circle, we shall one day see the return of many Bodoni newspapers.

The ever-extending Century family shares the widest popularity for headline purposes. This is another type of American origin which began life in 1894, cut by Linn Boyd Benton in collaboration with that famous printer Theodore L. De Vinne for his production of the *Century Magazine*. De Vinne wanted a bolder, more readable typeface than its thin-faced predecessor and of slightly condensed style to suit the magazine's column widths. The result was a face of fairly even tone, falling short of the complete monotone of Cheltenham and well-suited in pre-Ionic days for newspaper text. The original roman subsequently proliferated into a near-Cheltenham medley of variations in weight and width, the Bold and Bold Italic of which became the most useful and most used variants for newspaper headlining.

No one can contend that Century Bold is a handsome letter: it possesses neither the richness of Caslon Old Face Heavy, nor the distinction of Times Bold, but it has one important practical affinity with the last-named, a relatively condensed lower case, which is not the least of its virtues in the modern narrow measure. The essential proportions of Century Bold, that is to say, are the 'upright oblong' of the Moderns; it is big on its body; its unassuming but sturdy appearance admirably fits it for newspaper purpose. Also it has a fully satisfactory italic sorting most faithfully and acceptably with its roman which is again an important practical point. From its early days, Century was popular for school textbooks, and the variants called Century Schoolbook and Century Schoolbook Bold have been exploited effectively by

99

100

99 and 100. Dramatic shapes in a front page from *The Vancouver Sun*, headlined in two weights of Clarendon over Corona text. Helvetica adds to the legibility of text on tints. The titlepiece is an artist's rendering of an Old English blackletter, the thin strokes fattened and serifs strengthened to stand out on a yellow background. Figure 100 shows the same powerful Clarendon style in an inside news page.

newspapers of all kinds over the last twenty or thirty years. Other versions of similar name, such as Century Textbook, have helped in what has been a major typographical innovation in newspapers.

No doubt the next such triumph will be the exploitation of the new generation of types designed for computers, which can generate any size imaginable in any weight and width. One of the most successful of these may well be the Nimrod face discussed in another chapter.

This is not a book about typeface selection, a subject that these days might not be dealt with fully within the pages of a single volume. Rather, we wish to point towards the need for careful selection, going far beyond whim and fancy and taking into account not only what would be ideal and what is unsuitable

101

but allowing for that undeniable element that is concerned with what is available for the typesetting system we are to use.

Even allowing for the difficulties of availability, we can say from the outset that every paper has or should have a personality or character as determined by its policy and its readership. The type dress of its headlines should express that character and should fit the purpose of the particular paper. Thus a 'class' journal might choose from the Bodoni or Times range, or even Caledonia Bold, which is a face yet to achieve the popularity it deserves. A so-called 'popular' journal could get a colourful and strong result from a bold and varied handling of Caslon, or could find the answer to all of the problems in Century with a 'kicker' in Bold or Medium Condensed Sans serif.

102

101 and 102. *The Alabama Journal* imparts an air of quality, dressed throughout in Optima headlines. Figure 102 shows a light Optima, roman and italic, on the Opinion page.

There are various typographical styles of heading in use around the world, and much depends on where you are as to the arguments for and against each of them. The most common form of agreement we are likely to find is that an all-capitals style has virtually died out, although lines of caps for individual page leads, followed by lower case for the rest of the page is universally acceptable.

There is likely to be near agreement that the once common style of upper-case and lower-case heads where the first letter of each word is capitalised is now outmoded; the style to be preferred is one where every word is in lower case apart, naturally, from the first word and any proper names.

There are four methods of securing headline variation no matter what the basic style. These are:

1. By size: this primary variation, while obviously applying in general to any scheme of graded headlines is rarely employed as an exclusive method.

2. By weight: this is a further stage employing the differentiation between Bold and Light, Bold and Condensed, etc, in one type family. As in variation by size only, variation by weight implies uniformity of style but it achieves the aim of varied colour on the page; a page of headlines in Century Schoolbook and Schoolbook Bold is a good example.

3. By style: in its simplest form this uses the caps and lower case of one typeface, either all roman or, more unusually, all italic. With two alphabets, the caps and the lower case, it thus increases the possible variety in appearance of headlines but retains a uniformity of structure and colour which may make for monotony in a page as a whole unless whiting is generous. This monotony can be overcome, even within the confines of the same series, by using both the roman and the italic; this use of four alphabets (roman and italic caps, roman and italic lower case) in a suitable range of sizes provides the backbone for sound headline display in a modern style.

4. By contrast: this method of securing variation, by the use of contrasting types, can easily go wrong. Certain types will not mix – Bodoni for one – and some will mix happily with one face but not with another. If we group our typefaces as far as is possible into Old Style, Moderns, Sans serif, and Slab serif (Egyptians) we can establish some simple ground rules:

(a) Moderns are best left to themselves.

(b) Old Style will contrast well with the neutral sans serif as in the traditional 'kicker' treatment where one headline is out of tune with the rest of the page and so catches the reader's eye. The reverse style, an old style 'kicker' in a page of sans headings, will also work, although slightly less successfully. (It should be pointed out that the term 'kicker' is used differently in some countries, including America, where it describes a kind of strapline, usually underscored.)

(c) Sans serif faces and slab serifs will usually make a happy mix, especially where the two are monoline and the only real difference between the two letters is the presence or absence of serifs.

(d) Old Style and slab serif faces are not a safe mix for the styles of serif may clash severely. They may, however, be mixed as a last resort without too much damage to style.

The size range for headlines has varied over the years. A quarter of a century ago very few newspapers used headlines bigger than 60pt or 72pt, and even this was apt to be regarded as outrageous by some of the elder statesmen of newspapers reared on an upper limit of 30pt or maybe 36pt for 'class' make-up. Today there are no real limits, save those of technical considerations and the fact that big headlines consume a lot of space – and, of course, the need to keep something in reserve for the biggest story of all time.

In the days of hot metal there were constraints in the limited number of sizes available, the usual run being 12, 14, 18, 24, 30, 36, 42, 48, 60pt and increasing after that, when possible and permitted, in 12pt leaps. Current technology enables us to have just about any size we wish and in quarter of a point increments if necessary; but the absence of constraint brings with it a need for discipline if we are to achieve the desired effects of changes in headline size.

These aims are usually in the cause of guiding the readers around the page from first lead to second, third and so on, offering the menu in such a way that readers are unlikely to miss anything. It is this scale that goes wrong when readers express surprise on hearing stories they must have missed when they read the paper. Shading down in 12pt steps may seem logical and easy to achieve but one also has to take into account the spread of a headline, which will affect its apparent size. A 60pt line s-t-r-e-t-c-h-e-d- across six columns is in many respects weaker than 60pt across three columns. A 'kicker' in the wrong place or the wrong size, a bloated white-on-black or other misplaced reverses can all ruin the scale.

The well-organised papers will have ground rules on the typefaces to be used and where and at what weight and widths, where they should be roman or italic, caps or lower case, with rules for reverses,

103. Wordy headlines in the *Toronto Star* but Times Roman in these sizes enable the headline-writers to tell a story as well as fulfil a design function. The paper goes to great lengths to get the best out of its Corona text, set in 9.6pt on a 9.8pt body with a slightly tighter 9.2pt set width across 12.4 pica ems.

104. Helvetica comes in all sorts of weights and widths. There is tremendous variety in these front-page headlines but they are all Helvetica.

underscores, straplines, picture lines, captions, borders, boxes, panels, standfirsts, standing lines, logos, intros, and quite a few other things too, but these will be golden rules designed for understanding rather than to be followed slavishly.

The guideline that works does not say that page leads will be one line of 84pt something-or-other across 'x' number of columns but might say that page leads will be in such-and-such a typeface with the sort of weight achieved by one line of 84pt. This leaves the way open for creativity to produce the best headline while achieving the desired 'weight'. Flexible guidelines will allow for a four-line deck of 36pt to be changed, after due consultation, to a five-line deck of 30pt to allow, say, the use of a vital word that would not fit in the bigger type size. Inflexible guidelines will put the pattern first and foremost – which is little better, journalistically, than having no guidelines at all.

Although mention is made of an 84pt headline this is not to be suggested as the norm for any particular kind of paper. We subscribe to the view that whatever the starting point, be it 60pt or 120pt, other headlines should be in scale with it. The higher the starting point, of course, the more space is consumed right down the line, especially with the broadsheet page where scale, as a guide to the reader, is more important.

While we advocate flexibility this is not to be confused with the sort of freedom that allows whim and fancy to dictate the design of individual pages. There will be some very firm ground rules laying down design policy on such things as pictures, captions and above all the style for shorts; shorts are meant to be short and we commend a rule that says they will be graded according to whether they make one paragraph, two paragraphs or three, and the headline sizes for each will be stipulated.

Once a suitable type dress has been selected and the basic ground rules determined it becomes a tolerably simple task to demonstrate the aims of page design by drawing up sample headings for specimen sheets to be inserted in the editorial style-book. We recommend a style-book – a series of loose sheets in a ring-binder is good enough – to emphasise the guidelines and enable all concerned to see them in action. In these days, when typefaces are apt to be referred to in alphanumeric codes, the good style-book will be a useful reminder of their names and may also contain brief descriptions to increase the understanding of those who use them.

71

105 to 110.

Modern newspaper typography owes much to the late Arthur Christiansen who became editor of the *Daily Express* in 1933 and revolutionised the paper in both content and design. His new journalism, described by a critic (Francis Williams, *Dangerous Estate,* 1957) as 'sophisticated escapism and the bright romantic treatment of news' was to achieve far and away the largest circulation that any broadsheet morning newspaper had ever known.

It was his choice of type and handling of it that made an important mark in the history of newspaper design; it determined what became the characteristic headline typography of the English newspaper, both national and local, a style which was to influence popular newspapers in many parts of the world.

He chose the Century family of typefaces which had gained currency among a number of American typefaces since the arrival of the Ludlow type-setting machine in the late 1920s had permitted the slug-casting of headlines of all sizes from hand-set matrices. Century Bold (roman and italic) and Century Bold Extended were Christiansen's principal choices, with Bodoni Italic providing the secondary contrast.

Figure 105 shows a typical *Daily Express* front page (1930) before the Christiansen revolution. Figure 106 shows the Christiansen treatment, sensational in its day, of the Munich front page of 29 September 1938. After the war the typographical revolution continued, as seen in Figure 107 (1946) with the development of the centrally placed single-column sans-serif 'kicker'. The old blackletter title had been dropped in a space-saving exercise in 1942 in favour of the famous Morison title which the designer himself described as 'a super-fatted and extended Perpetua'. Morison,

who had 'romanised' *The Times* title ten years earlier, had dealt the first two serious blows to the blackletter tradition.

Two decades on, Figure 108 shows the *Daily Express* (1966) after the modification of the traditional 'streamer' to allow powerful headlines to run down the page rather than across it.

Two decades more, Figure 109, and the *Daily Express* (1986) in tabloid format with a brutally heavy Rockwell titlepiece and banner headline making an unhappy contrast with what remains of Christiansen's style for Century. Two years later, something of the old style is back (Figure 110) showing a new Clarendon titlepiece and Century in command.

The extent to which Christiansen was inspired by America is debatable and not of very great importance. His revolutionised *Express* was in any event entirely English, bearing no resemblance to any American model; and John E. Allen's 'streamlining' campaign in the United States did not win a decisive victory until 1937 – after the *Express* transformation – when the *Los Angeles Times,* restyled on Allen's lines, received the coveted Ayer design award and started a general fashion. By this time inspiration was rather travelling the other way. The Hearst papers, for example, were under orders to study and follow *Express* typography while American journalism textbooks held up pages of the *Express* and the other 'populars' from Fleet Street as models for their students.

Sample headings are the best way to guide headline writers as to the kind of shapes to aim for. The shape of a headline will never be as important as its content, but that is not to say that it is unimportant. The rule should be first to get the content right and then to consider the shape so that we may endeavour to improve a poor shape without undue interference with what it says. There are several variations in shape to consider:

1. Flush left, with the lines ending unevenly at the right, but not too uneven, an obvious temptation with this style, padding out a weak headline to make an extra line. Flush left headlines have the considerable advantage of ease of writing. It is a mistake to set the lines full out to the left where column rules are in use; a slight indent of 6pt or so will remove the cramped look. One variation on the theme is to centre the longest line of the headline and range all the other lines left with it.

2. Centred, the most usual style for multi-line display, almost as easy to write as the flush left headline (for most headlines in that style could also be centred) and with the advantage that it distributes its surrounding white space more evenly. Some newspapers insist on all the lines being snug or fairly tight, but this is an unnecessary constraint and can give the page a cramped look. Good shapes for a typical three-liner are:

(a) Long-short-long, in which the first line should almost approach the full measure, the second being perhaps two units shorter each end, and the third reaching almost to the length of the first, perhaps half a unit to a unit shorter at each end; a fault to avoid is making the third line the longest.

(b) Short-long-short is less satisfactory than (a) and looks best when the two short lines are about the same length and one-and-a-half to two units shorter than an almost full measure centre line. This style is best limited to the occasional single-column top and is apt to look better in caps than lower case.

(c) Long-shorter-shortest, i.e., an inverted pyramid, is a self-explanatory style. It requires some skill in writing; the first line should be full or very nearly so with the succeeding lines shortening by up to two and three units respectively.

Where centred headlines are to have four lines the pattern should be extended to add an extra short or long line to match the sequence and this can be continued in even deeper headlines. Naturally there are limits to the inverted pyramid style which is at its best in the three-liner.

For down-page two-line headings the top line ought always to be the longer and almost full with the second line being centred. Two-liners ranging left, or with a short first line, should be avoided.

3. Stepped headlines are perfectly shaped when the first and last lines respectively are full out left and full out right and the middle line (if a three-liner) is centred. The step is a classical American style and calls for great precision in writing so that each line gauges exactly the same measure. There is little worse in headline shape than a step where the lines are uneven or too short; a fair average for stepping is to aim to write each line about two units short of its measure.

The use of *straplines* or 'kickers' over headings is highly fashionable and often used more for cosmetic reasons than the need for a subordinate heading, as in providing a kind of buffer between a newspaper's titlepiece and the splash heading. Clearly it is a modern form of the somewhat out-of-favour second deck; as far as the content is concerned it ought to carry the secondary or subordinate thought, with the

109

110

main news in the main headline. Typographically, a strapline ought to be slightly less than half the point size of the main heading and of shorter measure; it may be underscored and with a slight change of signal, italic to roman, caps to lower case, light to bold, etc, but these are matters to be dictated by house style.

The strapline or 'kicker' may also be set left, preferably when the main line is no more than two or three columns and there is a need for something in the nature of a scene-setter or signpost to say something about the content – that it is about Australian soccer, a City scandal or a trade union conference.

Although multi-deck headlines are no longer the height of fashion there may be the occasional need for two decks. The best style is for the second deck to be not one but two sizes below the main heading and to use a companion italic to follow a roman first deck; in general a roman second deck looks ungainly after a main italic even when they are of the same family.

The *tag-line* often used to carry some weak attribution (e.g., '—Court told', '—Chairman's reply', etc) should be unobtrusive but not neglected. Set full out right, perhaps three sizes below the heading they follow, (perhaps 14pt for a 30pt heading, 18pt for 36pt), it is also sound practice to reverse the style of their main heading; e.g., an italic cap tag to a roman lower case, and so on.

Care should be taken when adding rules or borders to headings by way of underscores and boxes. These are devices to be used sparingly when the reason is journalistic, as in adding emphasis, rather than in ornamentation. When headlines are dropped a size in order to accommodate words vital to the story the addition of an underscore will raise the headline weight back to the original intention; an underscored single column heading between two multi-column headings will provide useful contrast; such are good reasons for the addition of rulework.

Having said that, there are certain typographic conventions to consider and the first is that a plain rule is always to be preferred over the 'fancy' border or wavy line. It should approximate in weight to the weight of the face. Look at the mainstroke of the headline face in the chosen size and if it approximates to 2pt to 3pt then stipulate a 2pt or 3pt underscore. Nothing looks more unbalanced than a light rule under a heavy headline, while too heavy a line dilutes the words; the heavier the headline the less likely it is that an underscore should be necessary. The device should be avoided for caps headlines.

Cutting underscores to allow for descenders is unnecessary with modern newspaper types, few of which have descenders of any great depth, and it looks fussy and untidy too when two or three descenders come together as in words like 'happy' and 'leggy' or when they are separated by only one or two other letters as in 'pay' or, even worse, 'paying'. We are reminded of the wise old editor who told his sub-editors that if they wished to use underscores they must write headlines without descenders and thus removed the problem without instituting a total ban! Typefaces that do have long descenders, like the elegant Bodoni, are better off without underscores.

The fashion for hooded, curtained or boxed headings of varying kinds comes and goes. When in season, as it were, these are likely to be most effective when the rulework is lighter than the headline type being used. A boxed heading should never be cut off from the story that follows, the bottom rule being 'broken' or the last line of the heading being cut in.

Reversed headings of varying kinds abound in present-day newspapers, although a growing number of newspapers eschew them. There are so many reverses in advertisements that it makes sense to abandon the device or at least to limit its use, and if this reduces the amount of ink that comes off on the hands of readers – a matter deserving of much more attention than it gets – this must be all to the good. Where reverses are used, however, great care must be taken with them, particularly on news pages where headings in white-on-black, white-on-tint, black-on-tint and both white and black on patterned stipples can so easily interfere with scale and also detract from the news itself.

One popular and eminently successful use for the reverse, and one we could not argue against, is as a theme for overlines to picture stories, helping to establish a consistent overall type livery for a paper. The typefaces to be used for reverses will depend on the rest of the livery, but the best will be some arrangement of sans serif or a face with a chunky serif that will cut a clean and legible image into the background colour be it black or tint. Typefaces with fine or medium serifs, including Bodoni, Times and all the Century family, are best avoided.

Two final style points deserve attention, since they have a direct relation to headline appearance.

Quotes: quotation marks in headings should always be single. Double quotes waste space and are irritating. Quotation marks should also be ignored in the centring of lines, and with flush-left headings they should hang in the white outside the true left edge

111, 112 and 113.
Excellent use of space in *The Providence Journal*, especially in the neat and distinctive titlepiece designed and executed by Peter Palazzo about 11 years ago. It is the only design aspect of that time left in the paper which has evolved slowly into the firm but flexible format as seen in these two front pages. Headlines are in Times Bold with sub-decks in Times New Roman and the text is an admirable treatment of Autologic Bedford (which equates with the older and better known Imperial) 10.4pt on a 10pt body, tightly set to achieve a 'European fit' over the basic 12-pica measure. Note the excellent whiting between the columns.
Figures 111 and 112 show different permutations within the framework.
Figure 113 demonstrates the same sort of style, freely spaced, in a features page from the stablemate *Journal-Bulletin*.

where the opening letters of each line stand one above the other.

Full points in initials: it is common to omit these in acceptable abbreviations, but it is helpful to have a thin space between the letters, particulary in caps headings, where the effect is anyhow not very agreeable; to avoid certain obvious confusions, 'U.S.' and 'US' for instance, the points have sometimes to be retained.

Some headline writers will use a sophisticated headline fitting program as might be found in the best electronic editing systems, where the computer measures each letter and thus casts off headlines perfectly, but it is as well for all headline writers to be familiar with a good unit counting system that allows for the varying widths of characters, etc., making up the headline alphabet. A 'good' system is one that works every time and we commend that put forward in *The Compleat Sub-editor*, the program we have mentioned elsewhere as being used to train many sub-

75

114

115

114. The ultimate in type-size for a tabloid front page? The heaviest Helvetica yet on the front page of the *Daily Mirror*.

115. *The Christian Science Monitor* with a surprisingly weak Garamond title above the strong display of Times Roman and Times Bold and Century Book text. Near perfect.

116, 117, 118 and 119. The transformation of the highly successful *Yorkshire Evening Press* from hot metal to cold composition, letterpress printing to offset lithography with full colour daily, offers an interesting case study in design changes. The changes were gradual, the first stage being to adopt modular make-up within the original typographical framework, and the next being to change the typefaces on introducing photocomposition. The paper then converted to direct input in readiness for the final step, moving to a new plant and offices in a £7 million operation. Figure 116 shows the original *Yorkshire Evening Press* with Goudy title piece and a mix of headline typefaces including Century Bold, Ionic Bold and sans. Figure 117 shows make-up changes and a simplification of typefaces with the paper still under its old flag. The typographical transformation is complete in Figure 119 with a new titlepiece in Clearface Bold (with extra large initials), headlines and text in Century Textbook and Textbook Bold with Helios for contrast. Figure 118 shows an interesting use of Stymie for both text and headline treatment in advertising features to distinguish them from editorial counterparts.

editors in the UK. It requires a type-chart that gives a sample of all typefaces in each size available; the best sample will be a plain alphabet, or as much as can be accommodated on the page, printed on a pica grid with a counting scale across top and bottom.

Type samples made up in words are not very useful editorially and are usually hand-me-downs from an advertisement department where there is some subliminal intention in inviting prospective advertisers to choose their lettering from a chart that carries an advertising slogan or message. Occasionally editorial departments will print their own, often including the famous line 'The quick brown fox jumped over the lazy dog' containing every letter of the alphabet, and we know of one newspaper in Dublin that has a chart bearing the question 'What goes in the next at Leopardstown?'. Such charts are likely to throw out the count, for the word-spaces will inevitably vary, often wildly, in order to accommodate the line, whereas the counting system allows a half unit as the average.

The important thing to remember about calculating a headline count is that it is a count of units not of letters and spaces. When a headline is set in lower case but, with an initial cap for the first word and other proper nouns, the lower-case letters are generally counted as one unit each, except for the 'm' and 'w' which are counted as one and a half units each, and 'i', 'l', 't', 'f', and 'j', which are counted as half units. The

upper case letters are counted as one and a half units each with only three exceptions: 'M' and 'W' are counted as two units each, and 'I' is counted as one unit. In some styles of type the letter 'J' may also be counted as one unit, but it is best to avoid making allowances for varying letters since they are necessary to the averaging out principle. Figures, which are about the same size as capital letters, are counted as one and a half units each, except for the figure '1' which is counted as one unit. Most punctuation marks are considered to be a half unit each. Spaces are set down as half units, which are considered to be sufficient; some systems recommend counting spaces as a unit each but this is too much and tempts headline writers to risk 'tight' heads. The system as described is one that works.

When a headline is set entirely in capital letters there is a different and simpler system in which all letters except 'M', 'W' and 'I' are counted as one unit each. 'M' and 'W' are counted as a unit and a half each and 'I' as half a unit. Punctuation marks and spaces are counted as half a unit each.

The system is used on the type sample to gauge how many units can be accommodated in a given measure and then the headline is counted as it is written. A great advantage to be gained from the system is that the count immediately shows the headline shape, which could never be gauged by a count of letters and spaces.

116

118

119

117

THE NEWS PAGES

NEWS is the staple diet of a newspaper. It is the element that makes the reader reach out to see what is in the paper – and this first conscious decision is all important. A good newspaper is one that makes people seek it out because they feel they need it; it is not like a coffee-table magazine, to be picked up in an idle moment. It is far easier to get the cover price (say 20p or 50c) out of readers than it is to buy twenty or fifty minutes of their time to read what we offer. People who do not *need* newspapers are unlikely to read them. That applies equally to paid for newspapers and those that are free; good newspapers are those that are read.

We have already expressed the view that the make-up of a news page is its own menu; as with any menu, this must be an inviting, appetising guide to all that is available. It is not a list of competing items; the elements of a news page should demand attention but they should not fight with one another for that attention. The main story on a news page will announce itself as the most important on the page because it has the biggest headline. It is, if you like, the 'dish of the day' and you ought to know what it is even if you do not buy it. You can choose instead the second lead, or third lead, and so the menu goes on, saying, in effect, 'do not miss this story, or that', pointing to a picture story here and an amusing tale there, and reminding the reader that there is some good stuff at the bottom, perhaps 'for dessert'. There may appear to be more need to conduct the readers on a tour of a busy page containing lots of stories than a page with but a few items. However, it would be wrong to regard signposts as a device for the broadsheet page alone; there are some very busy tabloids.

News pages should be planned as a whole rather than just filled item by item. The editor who fills a page will invariably start at the top, scheming the lead and then thinking about what to do next; page make-up, as a result, becomes a series of problem-solving situations in which the pictures and stories that fit take precedence over news values. That is where butchery begins – a 500-word story being cut to fit into a 300-word position, a wide picture being cut to fit into a narrow position, and so on. The reverse will also be true: the 300-word story being inflated into a 500-word position and the small picture being blown up into a large one. But planning the page as a whole does not mean shaping the news to fit a pre-determined pattern. Formula make-up is useful in certain circumstances but it is not to be recommended for news pages, apart, perhaps, from the allocation of fixed positions for such items as flights of shorts, news digests and the like. The make-up of a news page ought to reflect the news itself, imparting its sense of excitement, drama and importance.

Newspapers are at their best when reacting to the big event. This is when they pull out all the stops and invariably do something different because the situation demands it, perhaps splashing a picture or devoting the whole page to one story. Clearly, on these occasions the story will dictate the layout; it ought to happen more often, for news is news and ought always to demand its shape and place whether the story has a hundred words or a thousand. Page planners must resist the soft option of cliché design, which moulds everything into familiar and manageable shapes and which may even reject or underplay stories and pictures that will not fit easily into the usual pattern.

Cliché design is not to be confused with that kind of formula make-up in which repetition has enormous value. Readers like to know their way around the television and radio section, and the best guides will be laid out with the clarity, legibility and predictability of a good railway timetable or telephone directory. Design, as with so many elements in a newspaper, is finely balanced between originality and familiarity. It is a question of knowing the readers and serving their interests. Everything that we do in the name of design is for the benefit of the readers – regular readers and newcomers alike. We have already made much of the need to win over the potential reader, but it will be a hollow success if we do so at the expense of the existing readership.

In our introductory chapter we quoted some words of Stanley Morison who in turn was quoting a writer in *The Daily Courant* of 1702 warning of the dangers of dressing pages 'with the air of news when there was none'. Page designers must always be alert to these dangers, particularly in news pages, where the all-important aim is to make the best of the stories and pictures available. It is but a short step from making the best of what we have to that point where we make too much of it and the story becomes distorted. Even the slightest distortion is apt to cost heavily in terms of a newspaper's credibility. Exaggeration – for that is the most frequent offence of this nature – is as futile as those old-fashioned news billboards that proclaimed 'FAMOUS FILM STAR SENSATION' in the hope that people would rush to buy the paper and not mind

unduly at the very ordinary revelations concerning a film actor nobody had heard of.

It is a fortunate 'copy-taster' who has never been short of a front-page lead, for there must inevitably be days when there are acres of space to fill and seemingly little to put into them. When there is no obvious lead and a lesser story is dressed up, one that ordinarily would have gone 'down page' or even inside the paper, there is a knock-on effect throughout the news pages as just about everything is upgraded. It may seem to be commonsense to say that a paper must lead on *something*, but is it commonsense to say that it must be a big story and must have the usual two lines of 96pt Heavyweight Bold? Is it sensible, therefore, to go further and indicate the make-up criteria for page leads inside the paper, for second leads, even for anchor stories? This is where cliché design begins.

How different it is on those few remaining newspapers that carry only advertisements on their front pages. If there is no front-page lead there is never a

120

121

120. A crowded page of nine narrow columns in the *South China Morning Post* (from Hong Kong), the inevitable cramped look being relieved by good whiting and an airy titlepiece.

121. *The Courier-Mail* from Brisbane, one of Australia's fine State papers, gives a feel of quality in its clearly-disciplined pages, eight wide columns to the 90-em page, although a little more space between them would be an improvement.

need to manufacture one, nor a real need for lead stories on other pages. In such newspapers the news tends to take the place it requires, long stories being long and short ones being short, without too much need to evaluate their make-up value in terms of length or to consider whether there are pictures to go with them. The *Darlington & Stockton Times*, a remarkable publication that circulates mainly in the dales of Yorkshire and Durham in the north of England, yet selling relatively few copies in either of the towns mentioned in its title, is a good example of this kind of newspaper. The paper is modern in that it is photocomposed and publishes the occasional colour supplement, but the front page is reserved exclusively for property advertising; the news starts inside, with the major stories as likely as not in 36pt across two columns, or three if it is a particularly long story. It is a country paper for dales families, most of whom have been brought up to read 'the Darlington paper' as it is called, and it reflects the country life-style in all matters from parish-pump politics to sheep and cattle sales, agricultural shows, hunt reports and what is happening in the social whirl of the area at all levels. The paper sells 35,000 copies a week, is an enormous success, and is much loved and respected by its readers. They would probably regard the arrival of front-page news as the beginning of the end, as it has proved for so many newspapers of that ilk; where indeed are they all now?

Clearly, the recipe for success enjoyed by the *Darlington & Stockton Times* – call it a formula if you wish – is not one we would urge others to follow. It is right for its particular readers, reflects their life-style and suits the newspaper's content perfectly. A much livelier, noisier style is more likely to meet the needs of a more mobile metropolitan audience. What we are saying is that the design of a newspaper is dictated by the needs and news values of the readers for whom it is produced and not by some stereotyped idea fashionable among newspaper people as to what makes a good-looking paper.

Let us examine a kind of make-up for news pages that combines the advantages of a regular format with the flexibility necessary for the content to dictate its own shape. It is a style that has evolved quite naturally in different forms in a great many newspapers, as can be seen in any study of newspaper design influences over the last half century.

We begin with an advertisement dummy showing the sizes and shapes of the advertising booked. The good dummy will stack the advertisements neatly,

122

122. An unusual front page and, alas, the last one from the *Telegraph,* Brisbane's oldest newspaper. Every word is in sans serif, an excellent example of legibility.

123, 124 and 125. The *Darlington & Stockton Times* still has an advertisements-only front page (Figure 123) but the paper known as the Dalesman's Bible is as modern as most when it comes to layout. Figures 124 and 125 are facing pages from a commemorative issue of 16 pages, each of them like this with a six-column editorial format above a ten-column advertisement block and an identical style for headlines and text.

showing some effort and co-operation in endeavouring to produce the known preferred shapes for editorial purposes, and there may be an indication as to which advertisements contain halftones, line illustrations or some other element that might affect editorial display.

Page make-up is a matter concerning both the advertisement and the editorial departments, so teamwork is essential if advertisers and readers alike are to be best served by what the two departments do on their behalf. In an age when marketing skills are as essential for editorial executives as for advertisement executives it is foolish that age-old rivalries and ill-feeling should persist in some newspaper offices. Editorial integrity is not lost or diluted nor is the advertisement department's first bite at the page lost or weakened merely because the page planners of these departments talk to each other. Nevertheless there are still some advertisement dummies that indicate no more than the sizes of the advertisement bookings. It ought to be an easy step forward to add to this information the names of advertisers, which will give some hint as to the likely content; advertisers too have a certain consistency in the style of their advertisements.

In an ideal world, of course, the actual advertisements would be pasted into a life-size dummy,

123

124

125

illustrations and all. It happens in some newspapers and there seems no reason why it should not happen more often even if only for the advertisements booked early.

However, to return to that neat dummy: we see in Figure 126 a broadsheet of nine columns with portions marked off for advertising, which amounts to about a third of the page. The place to begin would seem to be with whatever is the most important element, perhaps a page lead, but the basis of this kind of news page make-up involves creating suitable positions for the elements, and as yet there is no position for a page lead. We begin to create positions as soon as we put any kind of shape into the page: the most manageable and manoeuvrable shape to begin with is probably a picture of some kind. It is a common practice to plan a page around a picture, and it is usually successful in that the main picture on a page will be given the size and shape it deserves. When

that happens the paper will begin to establish a reputation for being 'good with pictures'.

For purposes of demonstration we will choose a fairly deep picture: Figures 127 to 130 show that, if it is to be a three-column picture, wherever it is placed at the top of the page creates positions of varying size at either side and underneath. A two-column or four-column picture would obviously create a different set of positions and, of course, if the picture were to be moved away from the top of the page this would in turn open up the possibility of positions above it. We could indeed abandon the column grid altogether once the advertisements have been fixed and thus allow the picture to make whatever width seems best. If this width is expressed in pica ems the positions created can be treated as being 'so many ems'. Whatever we decide, there are many permutations of shape and position open to us. The one we choose will be that which best suits the next element.

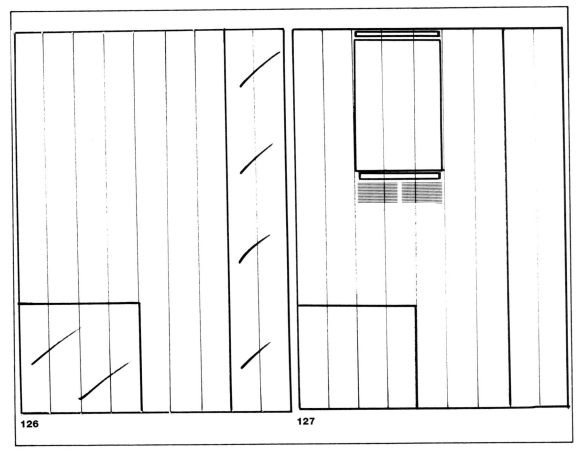

126

127

126. The page grid with advertisement shapes marked.

127. Placing the main picture inevitably creates positions for the other main elements.

Putting our three-column picture shape at the top of columns four, five, and six creates a three-column position for a page lead of perhaps typical length. A bigger lead story would probably have demanded a bigger position. We are at the start of the process that allows the news to make what it makes; two or three major stories will demand two or three major positions, but if there are no major stories for the page we may have to create lots of small- to medium-sized positions.

Figures 127 to 130 show three simple possibilities with a caption story. Were we to follow a modular theme for the page, the first, with the story in two or three even legs, would be preferable. The others, running the caption story in a single leg, create different positions for a further element. Our page will not be truly modular. The shapes will be rectangles, but some will be made up of two rectangles, one being the headline and intro and the other being made up of the rest of the text. Stories will run down the page where possible and multi-column setting will be used to create angles and shoulder positions.

Although we have created the page lead position, it is still flexible. Using, say, a three-line headline of a certain point size could be decreed as correct style for this sort of lead, supported by an intro to match the headline spread with the rest of the story running down one of the three columns, which in turn creates further positions of different sizes. The depth of intro, however, is flexible in that it can range from one paragraph across three columns to two sizeable chunks of column-and-a-half setting. Let us therefore look further ahead to allow the following element to decide what will be in fact most suitable.

Given a second picture caption story to be schemed as a double somewhere under the lead it would be sensible to tackle this as step two. Figure 132 shows how it and its headline can be allowed to take

128 and 129. Changing the position of the main picture, together with variations in the shape of its caption story, offers a wide permutation of make-up possibilities.

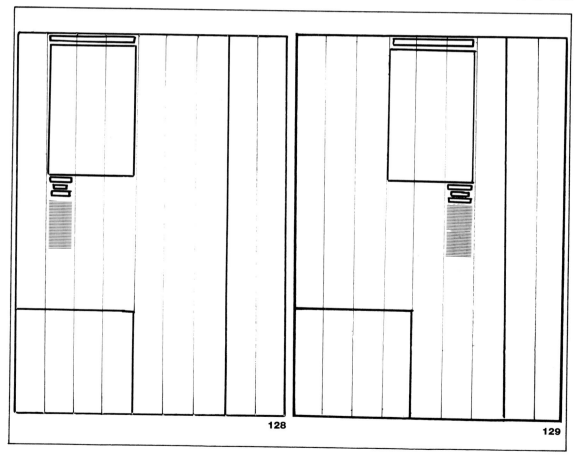

128

129

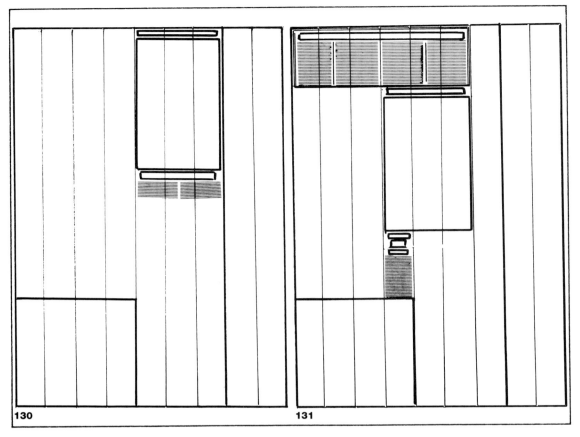

130

131

the space merited, provided that room enough remains for the three-line deck and a reasonable amount of intro depth. Had the page lead been put in first, coupled with an arbitrary decision as to the depth of its multi-column text spread, there would not have been the same flexibility for the picture story, which would have had to fit the remaining space. Figure 133 shows the page at this stage. Note how the lead story also has flexibility, the text running into an open column to be filled up as necessary with a short or shorts. On the other side of the picture, there is a single-column position that can be used for a flight of shorts or a strong single-column top with other stories underneath. Under the picture we place the single-column caption story and where this ends scheme a two-column treatment to hold and break the line of the advertisement; this treatment may have two legs of text or, where space is limited, a two-column intro may hold the angle better.

The bottom of the page needs something in the nature of an anchor. This could be a shallow three-column or two-column treatment, the size and position being determined perhaps by the space to be commanded by the elements placed above it and, we hope, with reference to the advertisements to ensure that there is not a channel of display types running from one side of the page to the other. We introduce a two-column anchor, helpfully breaking the long line running between columns six and seven, and the page is completed by stripping single column stories into the spaces still empty.

Our page does not follow a pattern as such, although Figure 136 shows that it is a neat arrangement of rectangles. We have been making up the most simple kind of jigsaw where all the pieces have straight edges, unlike the interlocking puzzles that do not easily fall apart. It may be likened to playing with a child's building blocks, although here the blocks do not have to be of fixed and similar sizes. This is a pattern that is easy to assemble and easy to take apart

132. Placing the second picture caption story defines the page lead position and determines how much multi-column setting will be required for the story introduction.

133. Positioning the lead story becomes the third step in making up this page.

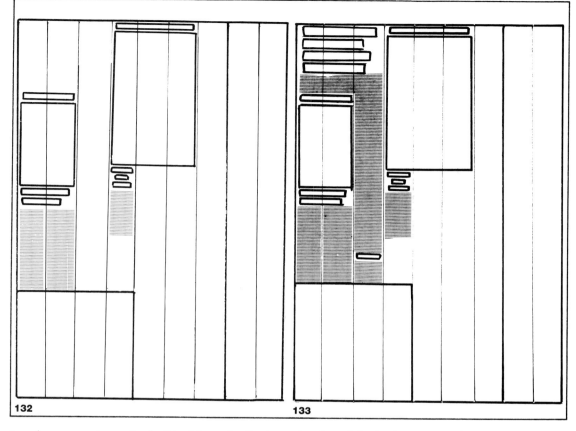

132

133

in order to meet the needs of editionising, of re-jigging rather than the replacement of one odd shape by another that must be of identical shape.

Our page used an average amount of advertising, but this style of page make-up may be fitted to just about any kind of page, resulting in a layout that is more practical than aesthetically pleasing. The aim is to be highly practical in putting together a news page where the news values come first and both speed and ease of change have high priorities. Every decision in the process is influenced by what comes next; every step creates the position for what comes next. There is no limit to the permutations available.

The page we have completed is fairly 'busy' and contains a reasonable number of items. A much higher item count may be considered desirable by many papers, and this would require the placement of many shorts. The same style of make-up would permit this without the page becoming bitty. For instance, a hamper above the page lead would effectively reduce

the size of the lead position. This could be broken down further for a page without any stories of length.

The importance of item count should not be underestimated. At its most simple level we may look at two publications, Newspaper 'A' containing 100 items and Newspaper 'B' containing 200; the reader of Newspaper 'B' has twice the chance of finding something of interest. Going a stage further, we must hope that readers will find something of interest on as many pages as possible for it is this kind of reader traffic that conditions their attitude to the paper and is of high value to advertisers. Let us assume that Newspaper 'A' is a lively tabloid with three big stories on the front page. No matter how 'big' or how 'good' these stories are, some readers will not be interested in any of them and will immediately turn to the inside of the paper. Page two contains the television guide, so readers not interested in television at that moment will turn on to a page dominated by advertisements and but three or four news items. Page four is the readers' letters page and after that comes a full-page advertisement. A lot of readers will by now have reached page six without having read anything at all. It is at about this stage that they begin to think there is nothing in the paper . . .

Newspaper 'B' has three fairly big stories on the front page too, but there is also a flight of shorts, a pocket cartoon, a two-line 'Thought for Today' and perhaps the weather forecast too. Most readers will find something of interest while browsing through a page like this. Page two is all news, as are three, four and five, and every page has a good run of shorts. By the time the readers get to page six they will be convinced of the paper's value – and there's a lot more to come! There will, of course, be advertising on every page but not so much that it weakens the story count. Pages like these may even command a premium on advertisement rates.

Take such a success story a stage further. Perhaps Newspaper 'B' also uses those first five pages for the major edition changes, displaying a strong common core of regional news backed by a high count of parish-pump items in each edition, with perhaps localised advertisements too. There is much more to the design of news pages than the creation of pretty patterns.

Appropriateness is the key word when it comes to dressing the news pages. Everything depends on what kind of a paper we are talking about. The bright and brash metropolitan tabloid may scream the news in extra-large sans serif headings, with dominating pictures, bold intros, short and sharp paragraphs encapsulated in all manner of hampers, boxes, panels and other ornamentation, while the sober broadsheet professing to be a 'quality' newspaper will endeavour to demonstrate seriousness and authority with a restrained, and indeed sometimes solemn, appear-

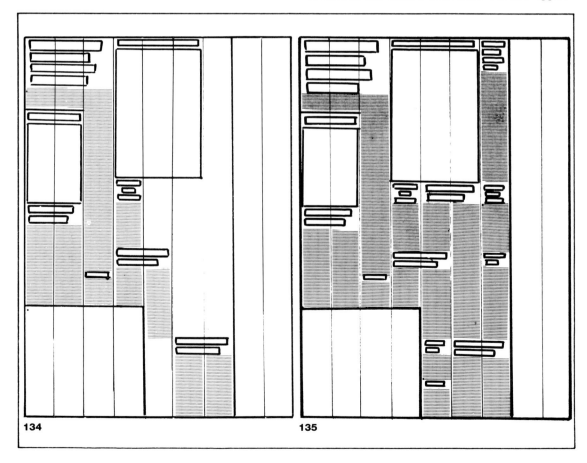

134 and 135. Each further step allows us to create positions of the size best suited for the remaining elements.

134

135

ance. Who can say that one is right and one wrong or even that one is better than the other? If a newspaper's aim is to excite its readers then it must aim for excitement in presentation without, perhaps, becoming too excitable – overkill comes about when every headline seems to end with an exclamation mark or ellipsis and has its own typographical gimmick as well. That is when the reader begins to be aware of the typography.

The same sort of problems affect the serious newspaper too. In aiming for authority, respectability and such qualities, a newspaper can exaggerate its severity to the point where it becomes boring. A newspaper story can be serious without being dull.

But there are rules. Rule number one should be to decide on a type dress and then stick to it, thus achieving the familiarity that is essential. A news page ought to look like a news page.

136. The finished page as a series of shapes. All the pieces of our jigsaw have straight edges.

137 and 138. The style may be adapted in many ways to suit news pages with high story-counts, as in these examples of modular design from the broadsheet *Western Morning News* and tabloid *Manchester Evening News*.

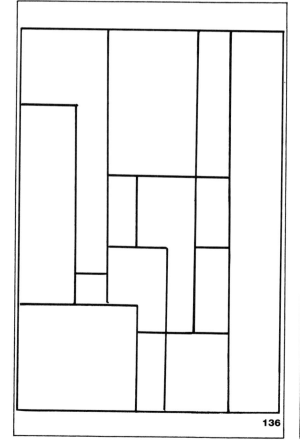

136

137

138

139, 140, 141 and 142. Bold shapes ring the changes in the enormously varied and yet tightly-disciplined front pages of *The Canberra Times.*

140

139

141

The Canberra Times

To serve the National City and through it the Nation

Vol 61. No. 18,721   MONDAY, JANUARY 5, 1987   Price 40 cents

22 Pages plus TV and Radio Guide

Income tax is matter for states: Sinclair

Explosion at school worries police

Death at Casuarina Sands

The Canberra Times

To serve the National City and through it the Nation

Vol 61. No. 18,774   FRIDAY, FEBRUARY 27, 1987   Price 40 cents

20 pages plus 8-page tabloid rugby league liftout

Landscape 'essential but not top priority'

ACT hospitals: doctors offered 21pc increase

Territories cuts staff after $1m 'overshoot'

Talk of preselecting 'stars'

Liberals may challenge in NP seats

Parachute tears tail off plane

Australians are due back tonight

Lebanese must go despite family, war

F27 water-bomber drops in

Morgan Ryan charged

Marcos volunteers

Schools turn open carpark to own account

142

89

143 and 144. The *Auckland Star* (Figure 144), struggles manfully against a grid of ten 8.6 em columns, helped by stacking long stories in short legs across the page with generous whiting. Figure 143 shows the first edition of the companion Sunday morning edition with a front page set almost entirely in wide measure. Headlines in both are a mix of Century Schoolbook and Helvetica, the serif dominating in the weekday issue and the sans commanding the Sunday treatment. Text is in 8pt Olympian with an extra quarter point on the body.

143

144

145, 146 and 147. Varying treatments from New Zealand's *Waikato Times*, reacting to the news. Figure 147 gives a bold banner to the dramatic story of a kidnap, only the third such abduction in the country's history. Figure 145 reflects the 'soft' news day on the eve of St Valentine's Day. Figure 146 is the more typical treatment of a day in the life of a bright and breezy daily broadsheet. While the treatments vary the typography remains constant, Century Schoolbook in display and Crown in text. The titlepiece is a heavy Clarendon.

148

149

148–152. *The Herald,* Melbourne, is one of the most changed newspapers in Australia. Gone at last is the faint and feeble floating titlepiece which could appear in a different place daily (Figures 151 and 152). Gone, too, is the antiquated practice of presenting summary leads to major stories in alternate paragraphs of bold sans and roman serif. The cramped column has been abandoned, along with all the wavy lines and other ornamental borders used for picture stories, the stark clash of different sans-serif headline faces, some too heavy and some too light, and lots of other remnants of a perhaps exciting and romantic age but one quite irrelevant to the modern newspaper reader accustomed and attuned to a different style of presentation. There will be those that mourn the passing of the old *Herald,* just as there are always those reluctant to accept change, but there can be little doubt that *The Herald* of Figures 148, 149 and 150 will win the same loyalty from readers of the 1980s and 1990s. There is still a little room for sentiment in the adaptation of the old Blackletter title-line.

Chicago Tribune
THE WORLD'S GREATEST NEWSPAPER

FRIDAY, JULY 15, 1966

SEARCH FOR MASS SLAYER

Girl Slain, 10 Cops Shot on W

118 SEIZED IN OUTBREAK OF VIOLENCE

Many Others Are Wounded

Victims of Dormitory Attacker

HUNT FOR CLEW OF EIGHT NURSES

Neighbors Tell of Awakening to Tragedy

SLOW PA THRU MO SOBS, T

Asks Probe of Brewers' Gifts

Ethical Questions Raised, Says Rep. Goodell

Hospital Staff Job After Tra

154

Chicago Tribune
Thursday, February 26, 1987
Sports Final

Judge bars Deaver indictment

By George E. Curry

Fresh from his Democratic primary victory the night before, Mayor Harold Washington displays several moods Wednesday morning at a City Hall press conference.

Court OKs race-based job quotas

By Glen Elsasser

2d wave of opponents hits mayor

By R. Bruce Dold and Mitchell Locin

How Washington won

Irish upset De Paul

Football banned at SMU

Ueberroth suspends Hoyt

Canadian rally ties Hawks

Soviets in nuclear test

Dire prediction from Bears

The man of many masks

Warrant issued for bishop

Actor James Coco dies

A Mediterranean winner

Overnight Chicago

School contraceptive clinics face battle

By Daniel Egler

Colonel who supplied contras asks immunity

By Christopher Drew and George de Lama

153

153 and 154. Two faces of the *Chicago Tribune,* more than 20 years apart. Little remains of the 1966 version (Figure 153) apart from a famous title-line now reversed on a blue background. The wide-measured text and serif headlines of the current issue are a big improvement on cramped columns and clashing headline styles but the earlier paper wins on the sheer excitement of news display.

155 and 156. Some of the world's most influential newspapers have the smallest headlines and the most text. Quantity equates with quality as far as these two financial giants are concerned, especially in their digests of world news.

155

156

157, 158 and 159. Two new fronts flank an old page from the *Shields Gazette*. Bigger pictures and bigger headlines give a more attractive look to the shop window but there are fewer items on sale.

158

157

159

THE SPORTS PAGES

160. A mass of detail in the sports section, helped greatly by the generous whiting between columns, but it is still hard on the eye compared with the superb text treatments at the top of the page.

FROM the outset we have argued that design is part of journalism and cannot be separated from it. Nowhere is this better demonstrated than in the *good* sports page where content and presentation will capture and re-create the drama and excitement of struggle, strength, triumph, sorrow, or what the sports reporter would undoubtedly refer to as the whole gamut of human emotion represented in sporting achievement. We emphasise the phrase 'good' sports page because, alas, there are many that do not live up to such a description.

Moreover, we ought to discuss what is meant by the good sports page, for over and above all the criteria concerned with presentation will be the question of getting the content right. This is where a great many sports pages fail, for although they may look appetising or even exciting, they do not adequately reflect the sporting interests of the likely reader. This is a highly controversial question demanding much deeper thought than the 'gut' reactions of the sports journalists involved, who understandably may be a little too close to their own specialist subjects.

Argument is quite likely to rage over what we mean by 'sport' anyway. In this context it must be the opinion of the reader that counts above that of the journalist. If a reader believes jogging to be a sport then he or she and all others who are like-minded will expect it to be treated as a sport. Clearly, the matter of weighing the likely audience for a particular story or subject is as important in the sports pages as it is in the news pages.

Although readership surveys tell us that many more men than women read the sports pages, it is probably true that the figures are very different during, say, Wimbledon fortnight or the Olympic Games. Ought we not to question our 'copy-tasting' if, as we suspect, significant numbers of 'likely' readers do not look at the sports pages at other times because they know that there will be little or nothing there of interest to them?

A certain newspaper once published on its sports pages a series of instructional graphics under the heading 'Teach your child to swim'. Nor surprisingly, perhaps, the feature attracted a great many parents to the sports pages, and later research showed that this had a lasting effect on sports-page readership. Could it be that those parents who did not usually look at the

160

sport pages were pleasantly surprised to find other items there that interested them? Of course, some editors would not have had the courage to put such a strip on the sports pages in the first place. It is quite possible too that in some newspapers the rest of the content would not have held those first-time readers.

The sports department of a newspaper is often said to function as a newspaper in miniature, catering for its own needs so far as writing and production are concerned, including all the attendant functions of news editing, features editing, picture editing, commissioning material, controlling a budget and perhaps even appointing staff to do these things. It will be a poor sports department that does most of these things well but gets the 'copy-tasting' wrong.

Often the sport pages form a section or supplement accompanying the main paper yet clearly distinguishable from it. Everything about sport suggests that somehow it is different from everything else, and yet in this respect it is no different from, say, the business pages, a life-style section, or a motoring supplement, each of which may be said to have equally specialist attention. But there is one very important difference. A great many readers will buy a newspaper largely for its sports content, and some may look at nothing else; others will turn to the sports pages after reading other parts of the paper. Almost all of them will have special interest in a particular item or items, but very few, if any, will be interested in everything. One of the most important elements in sports page make-up is the way in which it is ordered and organised with an efficient system of signposting.

It is important to group linked items so as to indicate clearly that here is a football page, a baseball page, horse-racing section, etc, but this in itself is not enough. The readers of a football page with a dozen or more reports will be particularly interested in one or more but not in all, and it is the designer's job to help them find what they are looking for. Headlines that merely report that Jones did something great or Carter did something awful may fulfil the criteria for news headlines in that they are live, active and image-making – but yet lack the identification that readers need when seeking a particular report. The same is true when the reader is scouring a page of results looking for the one that interests him most.

There will be a need for signposts to main sections and sub-sections and possibly sub-sections within sub-sections. The typefaces must be compatible, graded carefully in size and, above all, legible. Legibility is the secret of success in a sports section containing

161

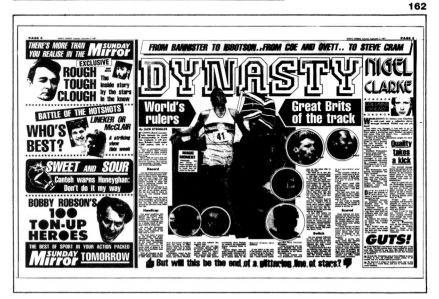

162

163

lots of statistics. Where two or more papers compete for the same readers we may compare their presentation of race-cards and other highly statistical matter; the same detail will be in both, we hope, so we may say that one paper's results are just as good as another's: the difference between them may be a question of legibility. Readers will gravitate to the paper that helps them find what they are looking for and then presents it in an easy-to-read fashion.

Not that legibility is to be achieved at all costs. The designer who decides to set race-cards in 9pt because 'granny cannot pick out the horses' may be thinking well in one respect but will be making a big mistake if the amount of *information* has to be reduced in order to fit the same measure. As we keep repeating, content is paramount and typography is part of that content.

In the good sports page there will be a place for everything of importance to the reader, and everything will be in its place. This calls for a high degree of planning, the first step in which will be to decide how best to reflect the interests of the likely reader. Readership research shows that this is where a number of newspapers fall down. Too little attention is paid to the fact that we live in a rapidly-changing world; and the sporting habits and interests of people today are different from those of twenty, thirty or forty years ago. All of us are likely to have interests different from those of our parents when they were the same age, and their interests were no doubt different from those of a generation earlier. The sports section that does not recognise these changes but caters for readers in much the same way as it did for previous generations must surely come to grief. This may seem to be rather elementary, yet newspapers continue to fail because of it.

It is traditional to give prime emphasis to major spectator sports. No one will suggest otherwise unless the very volume of coverage runs against the interests of significant sections of the likely audience. School sport comes to mind as a subject of enormous value to some newspapers, and yet few do justice to it; the sports pages of local newspapers must cater for the grass roots interests in the same way that news pages do.

Another matter of concern is the imbalance that so often occurs between the competitive and non-competitive aspects of some sports. It is important to record results, scores, league tables, team selections, fixtures and so on, but there are other aspects of sport, concerned with such things as equipment and techniques, that may be of far greater importance to those

164

165

166

164 and 165. Similar pictures on the main sport pages of *The Sun* and *Daily Mirror*. The photograph with least interference works best.

166. Front page of a 20-page sporting section in *The Sun*, Sydney.

who have no direct involvement in competitive elements. This is a difficult matter to define but one worth considerable thought.

For instance, there are millions of anglers, people taking part in a sport that has many forms and crosses all boundaries, young and old, rich and poor, yet so often the coverage of a local newspaper is concerned largely with who caught what, how much it weighed and what the prize was for catching it. Those who describe themselves as keen anglers but who do not take part in fishing competitions may be much more interested in a column concerned with where to fish, when and how, and what sort of bait and tackle to use. They would also be more interested in the report of a match fishing event if an interview with the winner told *how* he fished rather than merely chronicled his success. Substitute other sports for angling and we can see the size of our problem and the enormous scope for improvement it reveals. If much of the matter in our sports columns is contributed copy, often submitted free by the secretaries of local clubs, leagues and associations, it is to be expected that the details will be about those clubs, leagues and associations. With help and guidance the same contributors may well be able to give us what the reader needs in addition to the competitive detail that is mutually beneficial.

There are other things that those responsible for the design of sports pages would do well to consider. If, as we say, the sports section is to be regarded as a newspaper in miniature and some of its readers (albeit a small proportion) do not read anything else, it ought to be as comprehensive as possible. Is it therefore not a good idea to include a 'what's on in sport' guide for television and radio and other sporting versions of such general items, including perhaps a sporting weather forecast, a sporting crossword, cartoon strip, leader column and so on? Once we begin to think laterally, as it were, the faults of certain sports sections that remain as they have always been become all too apparent. The challenge in presenting that *good* sports section becomes both inviting and exciting.

We can say without question that sports journalism at its best is concerned with accuracy and expertise, and these things appear to call for a bold and straightforward typographic form. The sports reader is likely to be a down-to-earth practical sort of person whose diet, so far as the sports pages are concerned, needs to be plain and strong. The indications seem clear enough: they suggest the overall appearance of a sports page should be black rather than comely, with the most appropriate headline style being some version of sans serif. If the headline typography of the main part of the paper is seriffed, here is the opportunity for the sports-page differentiation we have already referred to – perhaps the best means of differentiation available.

While we may appear to support this demarcation, we would not go so far as to say that it is the only way. Indeed, many very successful newspapers – with very successful sports sections – use the same basic heading types for sport as for news; even here though there are probably *some* differences, even if only subtle changes in style: for example, more (or less) emphasis on italic, more underscoring, more ornamentation of all kinds without actually getting to that point where the style of presentation becomes more important than the words.

Even with such excitement ('gimmickry' was the word that first sprang to mind) we would still assert that simplicity is the main point in sports page typography and make-up. No sports page should ever be allowed to succumb to the temptations of type trickery. All that is really needed is for the typography to be a reasonable, flexible, uncomplicated medium for good sports writing; no one will dispute that sport is one newspaper sphere where good writing and objective judgement really matter. This in turn indicates that sports-page text treatments should also be simple. While using variant settings, like roman or bold reverse indent for an entire story, the tendency ought to be to avoid too many text-decorating devices with fussy rules, borders, stars, etc. One must keep close watch on reverses for too many, in too many styles, can be terribly distracting. It is wise to lay down the strictest rules for their use.

Good stories – and that includes the principal by-lined columns – are apt to run to some length. Good measure, good apparent size and good eye-flow are the important elements.

The handling of sports-page pictures does not require any substantial difference in approach from that outlined in our discussion of picture usage generally. There is the obvious point that a good sports picture, even more than a good news picture, needs to be an action picture, and the more startling and dramatic the action the better. Whenever the dynamic quality of such a picture can be enhanced by steps or cut-outs around advertisements in order to scheme greater depth, this should be done, although the more awkward shapes are to be avoided on pages that may be expected to change within a tight schedule for page production.

167 and 168. Two pages of sport in the 1987 award-winning issue of *The Independent,* the judges noting the splendid picture treatments and highly legible statistical sections.

THE FEATURE PAGES

BEFORE considering what we call the feature pages, let us attempt to define what we mean by features and feature pages. In the broadest sense we shall endeavour to cover all those matters which are neither news nor sport; but even this simplification is unsatisfactory, for we must also consider those elements which are called news features and sports features too. The divisions are all the more blurred by the arrival on so many news pages of what we would once have called features, being timeless, undated stories that might quite suitably have appeared three weeks previously, or indeed three weeks hence, but are now dressed and treated as being news of the day. This is a phenomenon brought about by the production problems of the past, which caused the need for more and more 'early' pages with the consequent decline of 'live' news pages. That it has remained is more for the sake of expediency than journalistic value.

In this sense, then, those areas of newspapers that are neither news-of-the-day nor sport-of-the-day are of immense importance and certainly account for the biggest share by far of editorial display. It is quite remarkable, therefore, to note that the features department as such (being the department that works under the aegis and influence of the features editor) is not usually the biggest of the editorial departments. This is because of the sub-division of those non-news and non-sport areas into different sections with an obvious separation of responsibilities; the dangers of each section doing its own thing without regard to a cohesive policy are obvious.

In smaller papers the problems are often more serious, for many of the 'feature' elements are parcelled out to other sections or to individuals as chores; this in turn leads to a lack of overall responsibility or authority to change the way things are done when need arises. For instance, if someone in the newsroom is given the additional task of looking after the crossword every day or every week, ensuring that the grid to be used matches the set of clues, is that same person likely to be concerned with whether or not the grid is the right size, the clues are in a suitable typeface or size, that the crossword is on the right page and in such a position that the clues and grid can be seen together when the paper is folded?

Moreover someone must have responsibility for ensuring that the correct crossword is selected in the first place. So it can be seen that allocating the 'chore' of putting it into the paper is not the end of the matter: someone must have responsibility for worrying about all those elements that are neither news nor sport.

We can divide these elements into two basic categories, which, for want of appropriate names, we shall call the 'topical' and the 'entertaining'. Those which are topical are generally tied to the news in some way, expanding or explaining what lies behind the news, its consequences and so on. Entertainment features cover just about everything else, from that crossword and regular specialist items like the gardening column, religious notes, etc., to the timeless general interest articles. The difference between the two categories is probably a matter of urgency. The topical feature needs to be published immediately if it is to retain its topicality, whereas the regular and timeless features can generally be planned well in advance of publication. It may seem logical, then, that the topical feature, the news feature, is likely to be treated simply, without the use of intricate setting and complicated artwork: such complex treatment may be used, and often overdone, when it comes to the entertainment feature.

Feature articles differ from news stories in one very important respect. Readers peruse them in entirely different ways. The reader flicking through the news pages is looking for things to read immediately and quickly, and does not necessarily intend to read such items from start to finish. All of us read news stories only until our curiosity or interest is satisfied, and that point is different for different people; this is why news stories have that special inverted pyramid construc-

169

Hospitals

Weather

Roads

The Pound

Shares

Bingo

Barrie Hunt

Grass Roots

Ex-Service Notes
Bill Berry

Dates
by Tony Davies

Books
by Tony Davies

Art
by John Hewitt

Music
by Tony Davies

Cinema
by Peter Holdsworth

Steve Kitson

Mike Priestley

North of Watford
Yorkshire Journalist of the Year

169 and 170. Standing heads from the *Telegraph & Argus*, Bradford, all following a theme based on the American Typewriter Bold typeface supported by secondary lines in Helvetica.

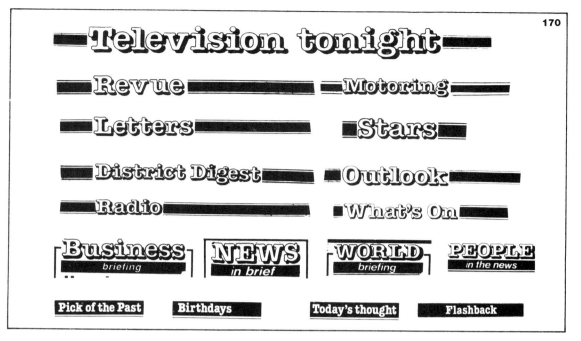

tion, which allows readers to leave at different levels. The usual construction is an introduction based on Kipling's six honest serving men, Who, What, When, Where, How and Why, after which the story goes through them all again, one at a time, amplifying and explaining each point, probably in the order that they were mentioned in the intro. The story then adds the non-narrative detail, comments and background, and gradually trails away with only those deeply interested in the detail staying to the end. We can often cut news stories from the bottom up so that we remove detail in order of ascending importance.

Features are not so easily treated. Readers do not start to read a feature without the intention of reading it all, and in this respect it is like reading a novel. No one picks up a novel intending to read only a bit of it; it is an unsuitable novel, an unsuitable feature, if the reader abandons it half-way through.

The construction of a feature article differs from that of a news story in that it needs, not only a good beginning to attract the reader's attention, but a good middle to hold that attention and a good finish too. The best features are tailor-made, being written to a pre-determined length to fill a given amount of space, or to a length decided by the writer as being best with the necessary space being made available. Very rarely, if ever, can features be cut in the same way as news

stories can be reduced, from the bottom up, for if the writer has done his or her job properly in providing a middle, a connecting theme from introduction to end, there will be linking points and paragraphs not easily separated.

The obvious problems are eased in the case of regular features, for these are generally produced to a formula. The gardening writer, let us say, may write a main piece of 500 words, accompanied by a diary of jobs for the week and a picture caption story; it becomes a simple matter to scheme the same amount of space on the same page each week. The actual make-up of the page may change, perhaps for variety's sake or, more likely, because the advertisement shapes vary, but the main virtue is that of regularity.

It may sometimes be important to stick to the same shapes, as one features editor found when she gave a talk at a meeting of a women's club and came under criticism for the design of a cookery page. At question time an irate member complained that sometimes the recipes in the page were laid out right across the page whereas on other occasions they ran down one or two columns; even more annoyingly they were sometimes split into two pieces, turning from one column to another or jumping over a picture – all of these things made it exceedingly difficult to cut out the recipes for pasting into a school exercise book. The complaint drew loud support from the other women present and the features editor, somewhat embarrassed, said she had learned something about functional design on that occasion. Happily she exploited the experience, starting a cookery column called 'Postcard Recipes', each designed to fit on a postcard, and even went further by producing the postcards and a filing box, suitably emblazoned with the paper's name, as a special offer to readers.

There may be a case for increasing uniformity of treatment by ceasing the practice of writing live headlines for some regular feature items; there is probably more function in a signal that says 'John Smith in the Garden', maybe with a graphic, than in a time-consuming and space-hungry headline. (After all, we do not write headlines for the crossword or the horoscope, and perhaps not for the chess column, contract bridge, the information column and other such items.) Some papers apply the same kind of signposting policy for music, book reviews, do-it-yourself and many other regular features that readers look for. That is just an idea, and there will be good arguments against it, concerned mainly with the need to attract the browsing reader who may not read a column headed simply 'Gardening' but could be interested in its content. What is beyond argument, however, is the value of the signal that says 'here is the

171. Good strong page headings from the *Chicago Tribune.*

172. Simple, elegant, distinctive pagetops from the *Los Angeles Times.*

173. Elegant pagetops in different sizes from *The Age*, Melbourne.

171

172

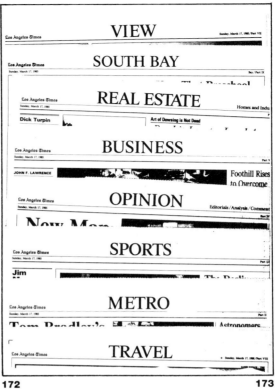

173

174. An artistic centre-spread from *Today* planned for the space available rather than the column grid.

175. An elegant use of Goudy for headlines in this centre-spread from the *Daily Post*, Liverpool. Note how the modular make-up permits the use of varying text measures.

176

176, 177, 178, 179 and 180. There is considerable functional value in keeping regular features in the same place so that readers know where to look for the leader column, their favourite cartoonist, the resident columnist, and so on, but boredom must inevitably set in when there is no change of any kind year in and year out as in the design of this page from *The Sunday Times*.

177

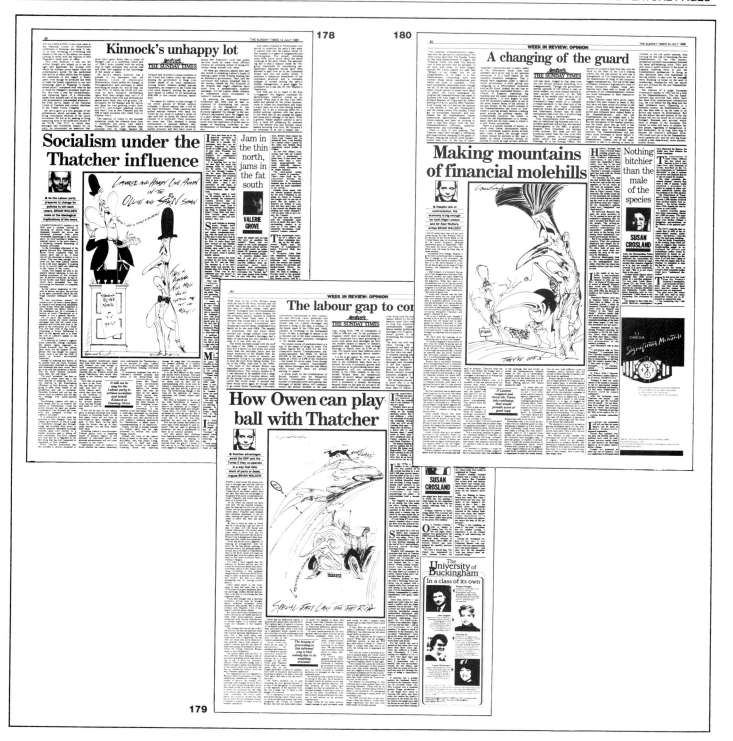

gardening column'; the standing heads or logos that do this job are badly neglected in many newspapers.

A group of editors attending a newspaper design course were given a pair of scissors, a copy of their own newspapers, and asked to cut out everything in the way of a standing head, from the titlepiece to the Stop Press, and paste them on to a single sheet. Not one was at all happy with the results for they made a less than harmonious pattern of different shapes, styles, types and graphics. It is an exercise we would recommend for any editor responsible for design.

The standing head is best regarded as being a kind of street nameplate. Visit any town, looking for an address, and you are unlikely to have any trouble finding the street nameplates; they usually occupy the same sort of position in each street, so the stranger knows where to look. They are invariably in the same typeface throughout the town, the same size and with the same background. They are clearly visible against the plethora of jumbled signs in a busy shopping street and yet do not compete for attention. Could we be laying down the criteria for the signposts we need in a newspaper?

A theme based on the same typeface would seem to be the ideal arrangement for logos. Legibility is the keyword, so a sans serif or slab serif would be ideal, especially if some or all of the logos are to be set in a reverse of some kind. The chosen type ought to be reserved exclusively for the logos, and some kind of graphic could be added. Some well-designed newspapers use the same style of graphic throughout the paper, in news, features and sport, while others have a different style for each section. If the typeface used for a newspaper's titlepiece is suitable then it might also be used for all the logos; we have seen this arrangement in typefaces like Eurostile, Korinna, Souvenir and Antique Olive, all with distinction.

The style may be taken a step further: use the same design for advertising as well as editorial sections.

Turning to that other kind of feature we called 'topical', we may be expected to give and be given much more freedom for the projection of what will often be the finest pieces of writing in the paper. The best of these features will be tailor-made in that they are written to an agreed length, which both writer and presenter decide as being suitable. Ideally, the subject will be discussed in detail before so much as a word is written so that everyone involved has a good idea of what the finished job will be, how much space it will take, how it will be illustrated, and perhaps even how it will be written. Too little of this kind of briefing goes

181

182

181, 182 and 183.
Distinctive feature page from *The Northern Echo* with all headlines in two weights of Albertus, a typeface rarely seen in newspapers and cleverly exploited here. Figure 183 shows the sub-editor's page plan.
Figure 182 shows two fine facing pages from a prize-winning 16-page tabloid supplement about Aids, again headlined throughout in Albertus but with sub-decks in Helios.

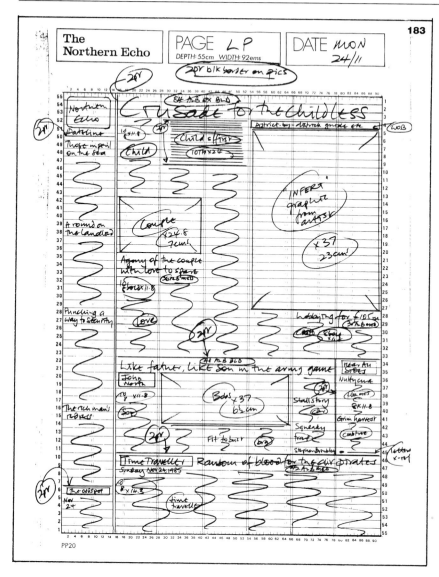

headline, illustration and text. As with all forms of layout, the elements are to fit into the space as in a jigsaw, and in the ideal world, at the briefing stage, the pieces of this particular jigsaw are flexible in that we can make them just about any shape at all. The best shapes will be those that make the most of what we want to say or show. We cannot decide, say, to run a shallow picture across 65 pica ems if the pictures have already been taken and there is not one to suit that shape. It is the same with the headlines and text. We are unlikely to get the best free-flow headline by instructing the headline writer to get it into the straitjacket of a pre-determined unit count and it would be pointless to allow 600 words of text space for a feature tailored to 1,000 words and worth that length.

We are reminded of a fine headline that appeared in the *Liverpool Daily Post* on a backgrounder to some crisis concerned with the finances of the Royal Household. A well-written piece about the difficulties of making ends meet when the Privy Purse is strained was headlined:

THEY'RE GUARDING THE CHANGE AT BUCKINGHAM PALACE

Headlines like that are not written to a prescribed typeface, point size and measure.

The headline has enormous importance in feature pages. We can allow it more freedom than on the news pages, where there is a clearer need for scale and priority in news values. Harold Evans, in *Editing and Design*, Vol V, has this to say about what he calls the free-style headline:

> There are clearly occasions when a news heading to a limited count is not suitable:
> (a) When the ideas in the text are so rich and diffuse that a simple hard news head does not do them justice.
> (b) When the natural headline wording is so attractive (so funny, so apt) that it should be given whatever space it needs.

Whereas there is enormous freedom in allowing the headline to come first and then deciding the type to fit it, there is slightly less flexibility, perhaps, with the illustration. We can discuss with an artist the possibility of pen and ink work and even computerised graphics to fit given shapes, but we have not yet reached the stage where it is possible or advisable to assign a cameraman to a complex job with the instruction to take a two-column picture 14 inches deep with the main subject looking right to suit the layout.

on in our newspaper offices. Sometimes, of course, the writer will be given his head and will write to the length he or she decides is right, the space required then being provided. This may appeal to some writers (usually prima donnas), but very rarely is it the best way to proceed. Nor is it good for the designer to be a prima donna, the writer working in the dark and the resulting piece being massaged into a pre-determined layout.

The prime consideration in feature work is the space available. Into it go three basic elements:

Nevertheless there is always some flexibility in the choice and use of pictures in feature pages. This too will increase with intelligent briefing that involves the cameraman with the presenter and the writer, so that he or she knows the points to be illustrated. Illustration is as much a part of projecting a feature as the other two elements. Just as sometimes it is the headline that sells a feature to a reader, and sometimes the very name of the writer, the illustration will sometimes win the day: it has more chance of doing so with detailed thought, careful planning and expert execution.

Imagine the following true situation. A young reporter is sent out to write a space-filling feature on a day in the life of the local waterworks, a subject most reporters will have tackled at one time or another. This young writer turns in the opening paragraph that any writer would be proud to claim:

> If water were to be delivered in the same way as milk, there would be 480 pints of it outside your front door in the morning – for each member of the family.

What a splendid way that is of presenting the watery and boring statistic that the average daily consumption of water is 60 gallons per head. Imagine the plight of an unfortunate photographer despatched to cover the same job, probably at a different time, and with the same inadequate brief; there is no way that the photographs he or she takes can include anything to project that wonderful intro.

And yet anyone with a creative mind will produce within a minute or two a score of ideas on how we could illustrate the feature in pen and ink or photographic form. If there is a fourth element to the projection of a feature we would add *briefing* to the three already mentioned, headline, illustration and text.

We do not live in an ideal world where everything can be made to measure with matching accessories. Often our features will be bought in, off the peg, but a good contributor knows the sizes that sell best and will also have developed the knack of writing in such a way that complete blocks or situations can be exercised without effort and without interfering with the feature's theme or main argument.

When it comes to the mechanics of feature page design, the greater freedom of display, with its common corollary of greater variety in text setting, demands keen discipline in precision of page-planning. This point must be stressed: it is essential if the freedom we have been describing is not to

184. Strong picture shapes in a fashion page but the text wanders across the page badly and it is doubtful if many readers would reach the last five lines.

degenerate into anarchy. The good feature page may look quite simple as a finished product, but simplicity will have been achieved by meticulous work in page planning. This may well involve the use of full-size make-up sheets instead of the scaled down dummy so often used for the news pages. Not the least important aspect of using full-size sheets is that visualising is much easier. From the start, the picture of the page emerges in exact detail. Headings can be ruled off with an em rule to their exact depth, the required space being allowed for; the text space can be schemed to show all the special items, such as introduction, measure, by-line or other panels, standfirst, eye-breaks or crossheads. Some feature departments like to finish their make-ups with some care, lettering in the headings, shading the illustrations, using colour pencils to indicate spot colour, etc, and even roughing out the text lines so that the make-up sheet resembles an agency's advertisement layout. The real value of

185, 186, 187, 188, 189 and 190.
There is much argument and confusion over the function and use of crossheads and the more substantial typographical features discussed elsewhere in this book which we call 'eye-breaks'. Crossheads are either in fashion or out of it and there is little point in arguing their merits or otherwise apart from emphasising the need for consistency; a newspaper either uses them, in which case they are to be presented in clearly defined fashion, or they are not used at all. Eye-breaks are different; they may be functional or ornamental in providing some kind of relief in a long run of type. Figure 186 shows a slab of type which

has neither crossheads nor eye-breaks and doesn't need either device, for it is a simple read and even the longest legs are little more than half a column. The measure is good, the gutters reasonable, and perhaps the only difficulty is presented by the inordinately long and unnecessarily underscored standfirst. Figure 189 shows a similar run of text but with an eye-break which is more ornamental than functional for the full-measure line top and bottom forces readers to jump over or bounce off to the top of the next column. Figure 188 shows a third treatment with a six-line drop letter that provides an optical rest without interfering with the continuity of the

the extra labour is doubtful. It can certainly be claimed that, like an agency layout, a finished make-up sells itself better to the customer – in this case some editorial executive – but the truth is that to the expert eye an accurately ruled-off full-page sketch should do just as well.

Half a century ago, long before the advent of photocomposition into newspapers, it was a common practice to set feature text slightly narrower than news so that cramped column rules could be removed and replaced with wider channels of white between columns. It made a basic differentiation between the appearance of news and features pages, aiding the readability of the longer feature items by the extra whiting.

The value of this opening up of the page cannot be overestimated, although today the techniques are different. To begin with, it would be rare to set features to a measure narrower than news for in many newspapers (indeed, in the UK we would say most of them) column widths have been squeezed sometimes to ridiculously narrow measures incapable of presenting a decent read of any length. A measure that is barely tolerable in a news page will certainly be inadequate for a features page, where the reader, being in a studying mood, has the greater need to read in phrases. The wider the measure, the wider should be the space between columns of type. We have mentioned this in an earlier chapter (page 28), but it will be as well to deal with the matter again here in the context of the wide measures of the modern feature page. It will be all the easier to understand if the situation is set against that which obtained in the days of the hot-metal newspaper.

Column rules came in all sorts of sizes, but the most common had a base-width of 6pt, and if you held one to the eye as though looking along the barrel of a rifle it would appear to have a central ridge. This printed the line, usually about one point, which allowed for two and a half points of space on each side. In order to increase the space between columns it became fashionable to indent all lines by an en at each end; assuming a 7pt body face, this added three-and-a-half points at each side of the 6pt rule, making a total of 13pt between columns, 1pt of which printed as the rule. With an 8pt body face there would be 14pt between columns. If, as we believe, the column rule is a functional device to help keep the reader's eye in the right place, then to remove it necessitates an increase in whiting, and 15pt (replacing 13pt or 14pt) must be the minimum imaginable. Indeed, as recommended in

another chapter, we would recommend 18pt as being about right for measures wider than the basic column width. Above 24pt, even on the widest measures, is apt to be too much of a dilution.

Remembering that one of the major differences between news and features is the way in which they are read, there are obvious differences in typographical needs. There is rarely a case for the opening paragraph to be set across two or three columns in the bold sans serif made fashionable on so many news pages; the reader has already decided to read the piece throughout, and it is as well to start as we mean to go on, in the same typeface, weight and measure, and even the same point size, although some would doubtless prefer to go up a size for the first paragraph. The value of this straightforward intro style for features is worth some stress since it is the application of an important principle. That is: feature text typography should be unfussy, broken up to ease the eye rather than distract it. All the tricks should go into the headline display and illustration; when the reader has thus been attracted to the feature, he or she should be able to read it more or less as a magazine will be read or almost, perhaps, a book.

This gentle start also accords well with the common device of a standfirst, a summary-cum-blurb disposed in some eye-catching way at the head of the feature, usually heavily indented and set in some suitable display face at a size midway between that of the intro and half that of the headline. Such standfirsts should be one sentence, possibly two short ones, but never giving the look of being a story in their own right. The sight of an overlong and overwide standfirst, set as text but not in a text face, will not act as an appetiser and is likely to be counter-productive.

Broadly speaking, the principles of paragraphing apply more to features than news. The only qualification to be made is that feature paragraphs can with advantage be allowed to run somewhat longer. It is difficult to offer exact prescription since type size, measure, the style of the paper and the character of the particular feature have all to be taken into account, but it seems reasonable to say that for normal feature articles paragraphs may run a third longer than news paragraphs.

Text should rarely be in other than roman although, as with a news page, a short-to-medium piece set in bold throughout may be valuable in giving colour to a rather grey page. This can be very effective when running down the first or end columns. The use of bold paragraphs, already criticised as an outmoded

piece. The column rules also help. The longer the leg of type the more need there is for some kind of break, not necessarily in every column for an eye-break in one column will act as a focal point for the reader in the columns on either side. Figure 187 shows text that cries out for some relief, perhaps eye-breaks in columns one and six or two and seven. The short legs in columns three, four and five do not need breaking up and the rules above and below the byline are functional in directing the reader to the start of the text after reading the headline.

Figure 190 shows a page that would benefit from an eye-break, perhaps in column four. The page in Figure 185 suffers from narrow measure

straggling unevenly around the illustrations but eye-breaks positioned carefully in columns one, five, and eight might ease although not solve the problem.

Problems do not generally exist in 'slabs' of type where the legs of type are of a reasonably good measure, evenly positioned, and well-whited. If a story is worth two, three, or four thousand words then it is perhaps best presented in a slab where the eye-flow runs logically without interruption from start to finish. Nobody ever complained about the absence of crossheads in a book.

and irritating device in news stories, is most undesirable. Where a paragraph or more needs to be picked out for emphasis this will be best achieved by indenting the text by one em. Should there be a series of points to be made, as in a six-point plan or programme, the section concerned may be set in reverse indent with the figures 1 to 6, say, set as drop initials in the gutter left by the indent.

Drop initials, now out of fashion for opening the intros of news stories, are still very useful in feature treatments and offer wide scope for opening up a lengthy piece and unobtrusively decorating the page. Used not only to start the story but also within it, perhaps taking the place of crosshead or eye-break, they can be particularly effective when the typeface chosen is in accord with the main heading and matches the mood of the piece. A feature about the Wild West, for instance, could be headed in 'Wild West' type, i.e., some kind of slab serif (is there any other type for the word 'Saloon'?), and the same face might be used for ornamental drops.

These drops should be designated by the number of lines they are intended to cover, three-line, four-line, five-line drops, etc, and that does not mean simply choosing a 24pt to cover three lines of 8pt. The choice must be by apparent size rather than point size to avoid the problems caused by types that are either big or small on the body. A useful variant, especially welcome in a page that might otherwise seem cramped, is to set the 'drop' initials not as drops at all but as raised or 'cocked-up' initials standing up for three, four, five, or more lines with nothing but space alongside. They introduce a good deal of air into the page. Again, the typeface should be chosen carefully.

One or two matters concerning crossheads and eye-breaks are worth discussing here. These are typographical devices rather than sub-headings in the traditional sense of that description, their function being to rest the eye while keeping the reader in the right place. In the quick read of news stories, the main value is in the space above, below and alongside a short word or two; if the words have value in conveying meaning then that is a bonus.

A reasonable rule of thumb for a crosshead would be to aim to fill half the measure available and to double the point size for spacing, 24pt to accommodate a 12pt crosshead, etc. Where stories are tight the spacing should not be plundered; rather dispense with the crosshead altogether and use the space between paragraphs. So far as type choice is concerned, there are three basic options: 1, of agreement with the main headline, subject to necessary and appropriate variations of size and style; 2, neutrality (e.g., sans serif); and 3, contrast without clash, as in the use of a serif compatible with the text but against a main heading in sans.

In features, where the reader is committed, there is less need for the crosshead – indeed crossheads sprinkled through a long read can be a serious distraction. Remember that we do not have crossheads as such in books, where the reader tends to rest the eyes when turning pages. Where a feature is laid out in short legs stacked across the page there is clearly no need to insert resting points other than the actual turns, but the occasional eye-break is advisable where a lengthy feature must perforce be laid out in a number of deep legs. A break in alternate columns will be enough, and the most satisfactory style will be to set these to less than the full measure so that there is a channel of white at each side to encourage the reader to pass through rather than bounce off to the top of the next column as so often happens when eye-breaks are ruled off top and bottom.

What form the eye-break takes depends on the tone of the feature and the kind of paper publishing it. Whereas the 'popular' paper may use decorative styles, often involving artwork with fancy rules and borders, the more serious journal, whether it regards itself as 'class' or not, would tend to appear overdressed with anything other than a plain and discreet treatment in keeping with the headline.

So it is with other items of display associated with a feature, including by-line, standfirst, boxes, panels and other subsidiary matter. Clearly, the needs of feature pages should be considered carefully where a newspaper follows the fashion to lay down rules for a typographical livery that will run throughout the paper.

Where a newspaper imposes typographical distinctions between news, features and sports pages it may still be possible to have an overall theme for by-lines and logos, but some may wish to distinguish between these matters in the same way. If this is to be the case we would direct attention to one or two matters concerning by-lines, which need to be bold and sufficiently large, perhaps larger than on news pages, although not so large that they become absurd. Given a type sufficiently strong in colour and using caps (normally most suitable for the purpose), a by-line should rarely exceed 18pt unless it be on those columns where the writer's name has an importance that transcends what is written. It is a point of

191. Introducing advertisements as 'natural breaks' in a television guide may seem appropriate but interferes with the design function.

refinement that the 'by' should be kept down, the use of a capital in 'By. . . . .' giving needless emphasis to the preposition. The 'by' may also be set in italic to good effect. When by-lines are panelled or boxed it also improves appearance to cut the 'by' into the top rule, either centred or towards the left, and at the same time the line itself should be reasonably full, letter-spaced if necessary. It is difficult to legislate for the writer with an exceptionally short (or lengthy) name, but one cannot escape from the fact that a short by-line in a box with waste white at each end has a very amateurish air. In panel treatments the top and bottom rules should range a trifle, say 6pt each end, inside the actual type line.

In planning all such elements of subsidiary display material it is necessary to remember that once the overall display has attracted a reader to the feature the text should be capable of being read with the minimum of typographic interruption or distraction. Eye-flow, by which is meant the sequence of text from first word to last, should be as smooth as possible and entirely logical, especially on turns, where a reader should never be in doubt as to where to read next. Eye-flow hazards of this sort are often caused by the use of pictures, by-lines and other typographical elements used to break up slabs of lengthy text; 'slabs' of text may be lightened by such typographical devices, but not at the expense of eye-flow.

A final few words about the choice of headline types in feature pages aiming to be 'different' from news and sports pages. To be 'different' means going all the way and using typefaces that are not being used elsewhere in the paper — the selection of a given type family as a paper's basic news headline style must bar it from features, and the same will be true of the types chosen for sport. In choosing a suitable type it will be of importance to stipulate a good range of variant weight, all the way from light and medium to bold and heavy, for this will give us the main battery for any feature front. This primary approach can either be simple or more complex, according to the resources and needs of the paper, in the following way:

1. One family, one weight: one well-chosen Bold, with its italic, can be manipulated to provide a number of acceptable style variations, beginning with the four alphabets from caps and lower case of roman and italic, plus the use of large initials in roman caps to give a caps and small caps effect. It is also possible to

use initial caps in roman with italic lower case, but this style, once considered the height of fashion, is today rarely seen.

2. Two families: instead of complementing a full range of Bold with a selected range of its Light, it is supplemented with a selected range of an entirely different type, perhaps a shaded and thus somewhat decorative one, but often useful as a contrast. Quite different is the two-family specification that adds to the first full roman-italic range a second full roman-italic range in another face; here the purpose is not to provide contrast on the same page but an entirely different dress for a different kind of page.

3. One family, many weights: display types suitable for feature headlines are usually available in an extraordinary variety of weights, both roman and italic, including Light, Medium, Bold, Heavy, Extra Heavy, perhaps even more, and certainly with further variants in condensed and extra condensed, wide and even extra-wide style. Not all of these variants are happy; the extremes of thinness and fatness need to be treated with caution and are sometimes too distorted for satisfactory use.

Nevertheless, it is quite possible to devise installations of three, four or even five weights in a wide variety of typefaces. Even on the minimum three-weight basis of Light, Medium, and Bold, it is clear that most effective variation and colour contrast can be obtained within one type family; the addition of Condensed and Extended alternatives increase the designer's armoury enormously.

One aspect of typeface choice to be considered is the need or otherwise to distinguish advertisement features from editorial features. This is a sometimes highly controversial matter, for it is not easy to draw lines between the two. In one sense there is little difference between, say, an article about gardening surrounded by the gardening advertisements, and a feature about central heating surrounded by central heating advertisements; and yet in another sense there is a clear distinction, for the gardening article would still be there even if there were no advertisements to accompany it. Where we can draw a line between the feature that is truly editorial and matter where the reader might with some justification exercise a different kind of judgment, then perhaps we could also draw a typographical line between the two; a type family may be reserved exclusively for the advertisement feature, for both display and text.

Let another word of warning be injected here. There is a danger in expanding the typographic

192, 193, 194 and 195. Programme guides for television and radio are like railway timetables with the same sort of function – the need for readers to see what's on now, and later, and tomorrow's details as well. A grid becomes necessary, preferably unchanging, so that the information can be poured into the chosen mould with the minimum of effort for the layout sub-editor and reader alike. Typefaces should be chosen with care, legibility being the need for timings and titles so that they may be picked out by the browser, and readability being the aim for descriptive matter.

The *Daily Post,* Liverpool, has won numerous awards for the design of television and radio programmes like

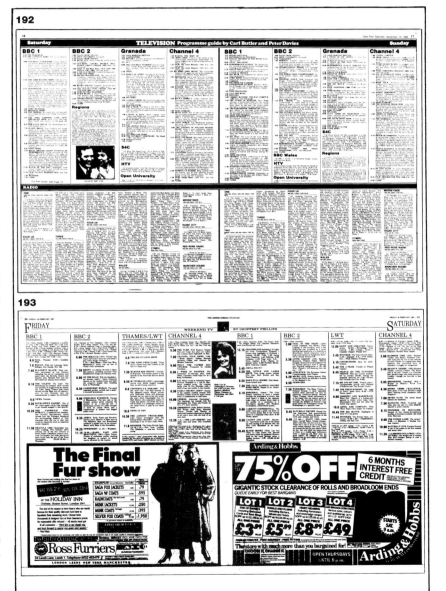

the 1984 version seen in Figure 192. There are similar virtues to be found in Figure 193, London's *Evening Standard;* Figure 194, Bradford's *Telegraph & Argus;* and Figure 195, Sydney's *Daily Mirror.*

repertory of the feature pages too richly – such riches bring embarrassment. A paper that draws on half a dozen different type families for the main lines on as many pages produces an effect of confusion rather than a contrast in effect. Often such procedures arose in the past from the bad old composing-room practices of carrying only a few sizes of each of a large number of faces instead of full ranges (always includ-

ing italic) of one or two carefully chosen faces. Sound feature typography starts there; the types available for feature display should be 'fit – but few', as Sir Francis Meynell once put it. 'Fitness', implying fitness for purpose, can be interpreted in the general sense of the suitability of a typeface for overall feature display, but it can be given another interpretation in the light of what may be called the evocative qualities of different faces. The point has long been familiar to commercial typographers, who would never think of using a heavy Egyptian to suggest feminity or a fancy script to suggest structural strength. Now that technology makes for easy access to a great many typefaces and there is growing use of studio lettering, the fashion for 'mood' typography – floral types for floral stories, vampire type for vampire stories, etc., – can be expected to spread from the colour magazines and supplements to a newspaper's main feature pages. There are obvious dangers.

Turning to the make-up of feature pages we can say that the pattern must be attractive and attention-compelling; yet simplicity is usually best. Complicated, over-elaborate make-up is always to be avoided. The page needs to have a sense of movement, to be dynamic, for the feature page with a layout resembling rows of bricks plonked uniformly on top of one another makes it static and lifeless. More than ever, the designer should wish to be freed wherever possible from the constraints of a single-column grid in order to plan for the space available as a whole. A high degree of visualizing skill is necessary; hence, again, the importance and value of the full-size make-up sheet and precise planning already mentioned.

Make-up procedure on feature pages differs from that on news pages in one obvious respect; it is generally less rushed, less liable to rapid and radical edition changes, and designed to stay through the whole of a run. Nevertheless, certain broad principles of news page make-up apply, including strength below the fold, and the need to guide the reader's eye to all the elements on the page. In pages uncontrolled by column rules, extra emphasis must be placed on logical shape and the need to link related elements, as with the strapline that covers both picture and story, the use of overlays, and so on.

Even more than with news pages, feature pages require generous whiting – in and around the headings and sub-headings, between stories and elsewhere where we might secure the necessary airness. On a feature page above all, where ease of reading is the

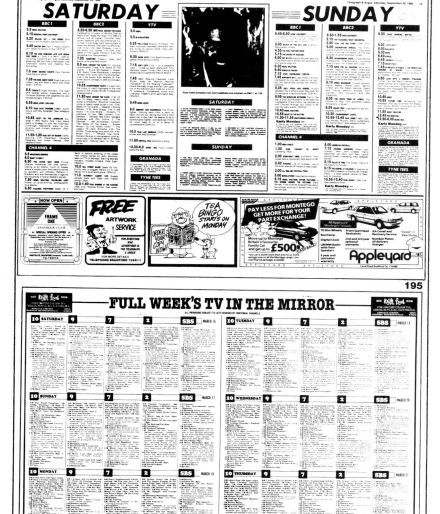

prime need, overcrowding is death and decent white space the breath of life. Ample white is also necessary to accommodate any typographical decoration, a modicum of which undoubtedly helps to enliven a feature page (although, as always, the degree must match the personality of the paper).

It is often said, as though in explanation or excuse for shoddiness, that the small paper lacks the type and other resources needed for smart feature styles. This is not always true and is often patently untrue, for these days the only resources we cannot do without, if we are to produce fitting pages, are those concerned with ability and understanding, which in themselves control that other important resource – the time available to us. The able journalist who can write, edit and design a page to be simple and in keeping with the overall product has little need to envy the resources of the bigger paper down the road. Given the basic creativity we must expect of a journalist, just about all else can be acquired.

196 and 197. The greater the channel choice the greater the need for effective timetabling. It would be difficult to beat the *Chicago Tribune* (Figure 196) for sheer volume while *USA Today* (Figure 197) shows the major networks.

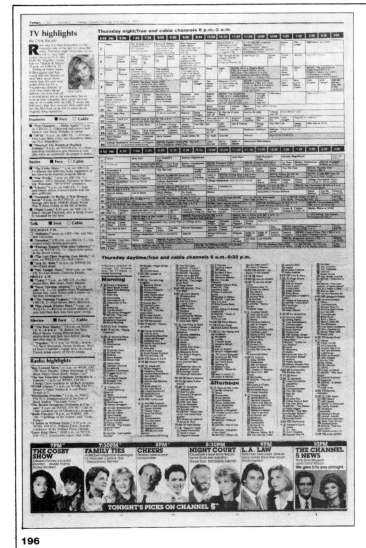

196

197

HANDLING ILLUSTRATIONS

EVERY picture tells a story, the old saying has it. Let us change that very slightly and say there are two kinds of newspaper picture. One is the picture that is the story, and the words associated with it (for there will almost always be some words) are in the way of explanation and amplification. The other kind is the picture that illustrates the story, the words coming first and the picture being subordinate to them. Journalists who grew up as reporters are sometimes inclined to get this wrong because it is perhaps natural to them to put the story first and the picture second. Photographers too can make the reverse mistake, especially when the picture gets less space than they would have wished. Clearly both situations are wrong. The sub-editor or copy-editor is neither a reporter nor a photographer, no matter what his or her background may be, but is the person responsible for projecting the story; he or she must make the most of the raw material available.

To describe the work of writers and photographers as 'raw material' may raise an eyebrow or two and perhaps some hackles as well, but in this instance we are talking of the attitude that an editor must have when handling the work of others. Unless the editor feels that 'this is *my* story to project to *my* readers' he or she is unlikely to get the best out of it, by being subconsciously influenced in processing the work of others. The attitude a reporter must have is different, as is that of the photographer.

We have said before that a sub-editor is not a reporter, and so the approach to a story must be one of assessing its suitability rather than thinking how we would have written it had we been the reporter. It is significant that most copy-editors who were once reporters never have a moment's hesitation in altering a reporter's copy should the angle be wrong or the construction poor. But we suspect there is often much less confidence when it comes to altering the photographer's work – because, well, we aren't really photographers. This is a complex that must be overcome. In the UK in recent years there has been a welcome increase in the number of photographers who have become sub-editors, bringing into that department a much-needed 'feel' for pictures and a confidence in dealing with the work of photographers (but also, no doubt, a lack of confidence in altering a reporter's copy; this complex too must be overcome).

Pictures are enormously important to all but a handful of papers, usually journals like the *Financial Times* of London and similar newspapers around the world for whom the lack of photographs has always seemed to be part of the aura of seriousness. Be that as it may (for who knows if such idiosyncrasy will continue for long), but for most of us illustration is the third basic ingredient, after type and white space, in the make-up of a page. Illustration must naturally include line-work, including the rapidly growing use of information graphics, a rather fashionable phrase taken to describe the bar charts, pie charts, graphs, and all the other things we used to find in our school atlas half a century ago to help us master subjects like economic geography, current affairs and so on. Even the pictureless papers are strong on graphics.

First, though, let us look at the halftone photograph, which makes a vital contribution to the attractiveness of our pages. Just as the typographic pattern of a made-up page must have a journalistic purpose, and not be merely pleasant to look at, so must the picture. It may be decorative, but its function is not decoration. Every picture indeed *should* tell or help tell a story.

Photo-journalism, by which we mean the assessment of news values in pictures, is not within the scope of this chapter but it does bear heavily on the matters we would discuss. Part of that 'feel' for the pictures that we have mentioned is based on the journalistic judgment that will pick out one picture from a dozen, one part of that picture, and plan a whole page around it.

198 and 199. Does it matter that the lady faces out of the page in Figure 199, or that the President looks away from the text?

200. A front-page picture with enormous 'stopping power' when seen on the news-stand. It would be difficult to resist the urge to pick up the paper to see the story-line hidden under the fold.

201. Good pictures *do* need words. The one-word headline in the *Daily Mail* seems to be the picture itself talking.

A complete understanding of the mechanics is essential so that we can crop pictures for their own sake, letting them tell their story in the best possible way, and then size them for enlargement or reduction to go into what may be a fixed grid of columns. We must also be able to size steps in pictures, sometimes for headlines or captions but mainly to stretch pictures around corners to gain extra depth. Finally, we must be confident in cropping pictures to make not only a pre-determined width but a pre-determined depth, as in taking a selection of wedding pictures, all different in size, and scheming them side by side to the same width and depth. All of these things are included in our diagrams, all based on a system of related triangles. Many picture handlers scorn the method, preferring instead the 'magic wheel', sometimes called a proportional calculator, while a growing number use computers, which take away all the hard work. Make no mistake, though: the ability to do one's own sums is no less valuable in the handling of pictures than in all other forms of casting off.

There are a great many things to think about in choosing a picture and deciding how to use it, either to make the best of the picture or to make the best of the page, and there is a subtle but important distinction between those two things. A reader glancing through the pages of a newspaper may see a picture without noticing it. It takes what some call 'stopping power' to halt a reader long enough to take in everything – you will see that stopping power in the *Hendon Times* front page, Figure 200. There could not have been many readers of the paper that day who did not pause to see what the story was all about. Not every picture has this stopping power in such dramatic form, but some can be helped to overcome this.

Glance briefly at Figure 202 overleaf and come back to these words. Without looking again – for readers do not look twice – ask yourself whether it was a happy photograph or an unhappy one, some sort of joyful celebration or an angry demonstration. We would expect a fairly even mix of answers, for although it was an important picture and a good one from a prize-winning portfolio of news pictures, it is not immediately obvious that it shows a Member of Parliament emerging in a throng of well-wishers, having won his way in a constituency party quarrel. It was indeed a happy picture, which is confirmed on close examination: you can see a man giving a thumb's up sign. There would have been no doubt in anybody's mind, though, had there been some prominent words saying in effect, 'Hooray!', 'Thumb's Up', 'Triumph', 'Victory', and so telling the reader what to see. A good picture may be worth a thousand words (probably because it may take the space of a thousand) but there are not many pictures that do not need words at all; some need them more than others.

The power of words can be seen in the collection of pictures of Sebastian Coe winning an Olympic Gold Medal. One version stands out, that in the *Daily Mail* where the one word headline 'ECSTASY' has that quality of speaking to the reader as part of the picture. All the others are in the nature of headlines about the performance.

201

Daily Mail

SATURDAY, AUGUST 2, 1980   12p

8-page TV Mail

Magnificent Coe runs the race of a lifetime to win the Olympic Gold

ECSTASY!

Golden moment as Coe lunges to victory ahead of Straub and Ovett

Picture : Joe Marquette.

THIS is THE moment of Sebastian Coe's lifetime, the split-second of triumph in the Olympic 1,500 metres in Moscow yesterday.

But Coe did more than win the gold medal. He lifted the soul, he ennobled his art, he dignified his country, and he emerged a very great young man.

Watching him run home, invincible, over the

From IAN WOOLDRIDGE in Moscow

last 300 metres in Moscow, was unforgettable. Watching him afterwards made you even prouder, for his conduct in triumph matched his humility in disaster.

Some fool of a non-running poet once called them 'those two imposters,' but when you're down there just living two years of austere living against hundredths of a second, that's a considerable misconception.

Sebastian Coe, 23, and from Sheffield, wasn't here to settle some parochial feud by incinerating Steve Ovett, 24 and from Brighton. For six days Coe had had to live with himself for running so far below his intellect in the 800 metres and losing to Ovett, that his only challenger yesterday was himself.

He accepted that challenge in the Blue Riband of the Games won, permitted himself the luxury of the huge beaming smile of the happiest man in the world on a single lap of honour, and then I swear to God, was the calmest man in a room full of those who came to hear him talk of it.

He said: 'It was nice to climb that mountain. It was an absolute must to win. I felt very much more relaxed than just before the 800, possibly because that was the one I was expected to win. I just felt a different person today.

'It was a very smooth race. That was the key to it. I was able to do what I'm best at—running freely and uncluttered. I started relatively easily and latched on to second or third spot.

Coe went on: 'I was surprised there wasn't more

Turn to Page 2, Col 1

INSIDE: James Wentworth Day 7, Gardening 21, Holiday Mail 22, 23, Prize Crossword 23, City 24, 25, Quick Crossword 24, Junior Letters, Strips and Stars 26, Sport 27-32

202

But to go back several paces to what is probably the first step, that of reading the picture to see what it says. This means literally 'reading' every square em, for until we know what it says *now* we are not going to compare this with what we *want* the picture to say. The picture in Figure 203 demonstrates the dangers there are when someone is given the mechanical chore of sizing up a pile of pictures, perhaps without handling the stories that go with them or even knowing what the pictures are about. The picture might be cropped quite severely at top, bottom and at both sides; in which case what is left will be enlarged so that we may read the words in the bubble appearing to come from the man's mouth, although in truth it is on the exhibition stand behind the group.

Reading the picture prevents mistakes. It also prepares us for the next step of deciding what it is we

203

202. Look at this picture briefly and then turn back to the questions about it on page 123.

203. It pays to 'read' pictures carefully before presenting them. The cartoon balloon that appears to come out of a VIP's mouth is actually on the exhibition stand behind, and with good newspaper reproduction today the reader might just make out the words.

204 and 205. Cameras may not tell lies but the pictures they produce can be altered, perhaps to help a story or even tell a different story altogether as can be seen from the photograph in Figure 204 from the *Daily Express* compared to what happened when *The Star* turned it into two pictures and reversed one of them.

204

205

want the picture to say, enabling us to take out that which is unnecesary, irrelevant or just distracting. It may seem trite to say that the more you take out of a picture the less there is to look at, but put it another way and work on the principle that the more unnecessary detail we can remove from the picture the more the reader's attention is directed to what is left. Picture croppers new to the skills are apt to go overboard with this tight cropping, removing every square centimetre that does not carry vital information. It is as well to remember that many pictures benefit from the atmosphere provided by background detail: an old gardener, for instance, might have interesting weather-beaten features, but to crop tight around his face, removing all trace of the garden where he was photographed, would be to take him out of context, and the result might be a lesser picture of the sort that could have come from a library file.

Occasionally a picture may need touching up to highlight detail lost against the background or to paint out something in the nature of a blemish. This could, in fact, lead to serious distortion, so such operations must be undertaken with care if they are to be allowed at all.

Leslie Sellers, author of that superb manual *The*

Simple Subs Book and other newspaper books, talks of 'repairing the unrepairable' and making a good picture out of a mediocre one using only a pair of scissors, a steady hand and, we must add, a certain amount of ingenuity and licence. He demonstrates how to take a picture apart and put it together again in a much better, more tightly composed form, a technique known in Fleet Street as 'a Hammersmith job' after the London hospital that pioneered transplant surgery. You can see a Hammersmith-type operation in our series of pictures at Figures 204 to 205; decide for yourself where to draw the line, if a line can be drawn at all.

All cropping removes something of the truth, of course, but then so does the actual process of photography, for all we capture is an extract of the full scene as seen though through the viewfinder. The good picture editor is very conscious of this, and while seeking always to make the most of the photograph will not interfere with the reader's understanding of the facts. Readers themselves are aware of this highly selective technique of the still camera; they view it in the same way as the recorded highlights of a televised football game, which may disguise the fact that much of the game was ordinary and uninteresting.

SINATRA: RUMOURS AND A FIRM INVITATION

DAILY MIRROR, Monday, June 19, 1972   PAGE 13

IT IS 370 days since Frank Sinatra went into retirement and obviously it agrees with him. He is pictured here during a game of golf back home in the United States and looks, at 54, as good as ever. Comeback rumours abound, of course, but those talks in London last week about him doing a new musical film seem to have come to nothing. He does have a firm invitation, however, to sing (isn't that the word?) to a Congressional Committee investigating crime.

inside page
Edited by ANTHONY DELANO

206

SINATRA: RUMOUR AND A FIRM INVITATION.

DAILY MIRROR, Monday, June 19, 1972   PAGE 13

IT is 370 days since Frank Sinatra went into retirement and obviously it agrees with him. He is pictured here during a game of golf back home in the United States and looks, at fifty-four, as good as ever. Comeback rumours abound, of course, but those talks in London last week about him doing a new musical film seem to have come to nothing. He does have a firm invitation, however, to sing (isn't that the word?) to a Congressional committee investigating crime.

inside page
Edited by ANTHONY DELANO

207

206, 207. Spot the difference. There are several typographical differences in these cuttings from the London and Manchester editions of the *Daily Mirror,* but the change brought about by tilting the picture is truly remarkable – Frank Sinatra takes on a positively jaunty air.

Editing may change the very personality of those who are pictured. Figures 206 and 207 show cuttings from two editions of the *Daily Mirror,* the work of two different sub-editors, one in London and one in Manchester, working on the same copy to the same instructions. There are several slight differences in the way thay have interpreted their instructions, but the most significant is in the picture treatment. One sub-editor has cropped his subject with a slight tilt and given Frank Sinatra the jaunty air of a motor racing driver. Figures 164 and 165 are also good illustrations of picture tilting, both in space saving and in helping the picture to say what it is we want it to say.

While this is not a textbook that includes practical exercises, some readers might like to put themselves in the position of those who planned the front pages of Britain's coverage of an aircraft disaster at Ringway Airport, Manchester, where 54 people were killed when an aircraft burst into flames as it prepared to take off on a holiday charter flight to Corfu. It happened at breakfast time, and the Press Association, quickly on the scene, had a series of wire pictures on the nation's subs' tables before the early editions went to bed. You can choose from the three pictures (Figures 208, 209 and 210). That was the general order of preference too. In a random survey of 50 newspapers 28 chose versions of Figure 208, 12 chose Figure 209 and 10 took Figure 210, with the remainder using something different. You can see in our three picture strips some of the front pages and the way they used their choice of picture. It is interesting to compare treatments in size, shape, cropping and also the use of other pictures on the page. Generally speaking, the use of two pictures results in the main picture being given perhaps less space than it deserves: the audience is divided, with readers looking from one

208, 209 and 210. Three pictures are available: which would you choose? Would you use more than one? Would you crop any of them and, if so, how?

211. A dramatic shot and a powerful projection in which the picture tells the story and the words are subordinate.

212. Two pictures, neither headlined, are used as illustrations subordinate to the words.

208

209

210

211   212

213

214

215

213, 214 and 215. These were among the most dramatic front pages, with similar pictures cropped tightly.

216, 217, 218 and 219. Four more very different treatments. In Figure 216 the *Yorkshire Evening Post* picture dominates the text but the ambulance dominates the picture, as it does in Figure 219. The *Evening Echo* treatment marries words and pictures superbly while the story is told separately. In Figure 217 the *Evening Post* treatment is fussy and suffers from a disjointed banner headline and misplaced second deck, while the picture effect is diluted by the inset.

picture to the other. There are distinct lessons to be learned by choosing one picture and scheming it big.

Perhaps the picture used least had the most scope for imaginative cropping. Figure 208 is a little off balance, but various versions of this shot produced some of the most dramatic front pages, not least being those of Bradford's *Telegraph & Argus*, London's *Evening Standard*, and The Guardian of the following day, all of which used similar versions of the picture tightly cropped. Our set of front pages, covering half of those surveyed, affords scope for comparison in other spheres, including headlines and text treatments.

We cannot leave the subject of picture editing without dealing with the vexed question of reversing pictures for purely design reasons, usually that of making a central subject look into a page or into the story. Wherever we look there are horror stories of the blunders that occur, like the Australian paper that referred correctly to someone's left leg being amputated when the picture alongside showed convincing evidence that this was incorrect, or the English

220 and 221. The dangers of reversing pictures. Figure 220, like most newspapers that day, shows a fire bomber as being right-handed but Figure 221 shows him left-handed, presumably because he was required to face into the page.

provincial evening paper that had to scrap a much-advertised colour supplement at the last moment when it was discovered that a full-page picture of the Queen showed her with her wedding ring on the wrong hand.

Such mistakes ought to convince journalists that reversing pictures is not good practice, even where design-conscious sub-editors have checked and double-checked that it will make no difference to the way people part their hair, button their coats, shake hands or to a hundred and one other matters that may be affected. We subscribe to the view that to allow it once, even under rigorous supervision, is likely to tempt someone else to use the technique without the same attention to detail. It can be counter-productive, too, as can be seen in the sequences from Figures 220 to 221 where a petrol bomber may be right-handed or left-handed, and from Figures 222 to 223 where reversing a picture meant that a ring had to be painted out. Whatever slight advantage is to be gained has to be weighed against the amount of credibility lost.

Occasionally, of course, it happens by accident. Those of us who pass pages for printing ought always to be alert to the possibility – lest we be remembered as long as the morning newspaper that front-paged an old soldier at the Cenotaph saluting with his left hand and with his medals emblazoned on the wrong side of his chest. He stayed that way all night, through six editions.

Turning to one or two typographical considerations allied to picture treatment, we must nail our colours to the mast and say that no matter what the current fashion or house style may be, a news picture is a story and, as such, ought to have a headline. *Every story* ought to have a headline, even the most humble filler although that word in itself is something we would frown upon, preferring instead to call it a 'short'. Unless news pictures have headlines as well as captions (or 'cut-lines' as they are called in America and some other countries) there is nothing apart from the picture content that says to the reader, 'Hey! You must read this!' Not every good picture has so

222 and 223. Figure 222 shows the tragic Olivia Channon with a ring on her right hand. In order to reverse the picture the *Daily Mirror* (Figure 223) removed the ring.

224. Military-minded readers may spot more than a score of things that are wrong in *Today's* mirror-image front-page picture of Prince Charles.

225. This full-page colour picture, part of a pre-printed wrap-around to mark a Royal occasion, was never published. Just before edition time someone realised that the Queen had her wedding ring on the 'wrong' hand . . . The picture had been reversed in the making and the whole costly production was scrapped.

222

223

224

225

226

227 228

226–233. Powerful combinations of pictures and words catch the drama of tragedy on the front pages of metropolitan tabloids.

229

230

231   232   233

powerful an impact that it speaks for itself. The picture without a heading has a curiously naked appearance on the page.

The most usual style is to place the heading over the picture and the caption underneath it. If the caption is in the nature of a caption-story there may be two headlines, one to the picture, placed above, and the other, something between a second deck and a separate heading to the story, placed between picture and text. The most logical place for a picture caption is under the picture. That is where readers look first. Captions placed above pictures or to one side or another must be so commanding, so obvious, that the reader would look to them first without looking under the picture – and that is a lot to expect. When, again, one considers the way people look at newspapers it is clear that they will see a picture, be stopped by it, and then look at the caption. The caption must be immediate and logical.

When a number of pictures are placed together, as in a composite or picture page, it may seem tidy to group all the captions together as though to make a shape in itself. For the reader this is an abomination. Readers will not look at pictures in a pre-determined order but will be stopped by whatever takes their fancy; certainly they should never be forced to play a kind of hunt-the-caption game, placing the forefinger of one hand on the picture while the other hand traces its way through a series of captions placed some distance away. No amount of typographical assistance in the way of pointers or numbers will replace the simplicity of putting a caption where the reader expects it.

While we are determined on the positioning of headings and captions, there are many possible variations in setting. A two-column picture can have a two-column heading and a caption either two columns or one column wide. A three-column picture may have a three-column heading and a short caption three columns wide; or a long caption of perhaps three legs of single column text, two legs of one-and-a-half columns (or slightly less when we get the spacing right) or one flight of single-column matter. Over more than three columns it is probably unwise to run a caption to full measure, for this will increase the type-size to a point where it becomes unwieldy. Certainly it makes little sense to punish the reader with a wedge of type set caption style in 8pt or 9pt across four, five or six columns.

A basic style for captions is the bold face of the paper's main body face, although this could be considered more fitting for the soberly suited 'serious' newspaper; the more modern, more brash, perhaps more popular newspaper may opt for the contrast of a highly legible bold sans. This latter arrangement is to be preferred where caption stories are set on a tinted or coloured background. One size up from the main body face is advisable. Captions are apt to stand out well when set about an em shorter than the picture measure (an en less in the case of single column pictures) with no paragraph indent on the first line and with the last line centred. In the case of the wider captions it may be important to avoid an ultra-short breakline of only one or two words by judicious rewriting or cutting.

Headings afford considerable typographical variation, but caution is urged. Pictures of exceptional news interest may have news headings in their own right, the typography chosen to accord with the page make-up, but for the less-than-exceptional case, news page pictures should have a fixed style that presents some contrast to the normal headline style. The current vogue in many newspapers is some kind of reverse that clearly marks out the picture story and can break up a horizontal run of news headlines, especially if they are in serif and a suitable sans or slab serif treatment is chosen for the reverses.

Where story and picture stand side by side they may usefully be bound together by some typographical device. The most usual style for page leads will be to run the headline as a multi-column streamer to cover the spread of intro and picture or to run the heading as a dog-leg shape around the picture, as in one line over five columns running into one or two lines over two columns above a two-column intro, with the three-column angle held by a picture. This sort of treatment is at its most effective with the old face or old-style typefaces such as Caslon, Times, etc, which are of irregular shape themselves with diagonal stress in one direction and serifs inclined in the opposite direction. Modern faces, or those typefaces of near-vertical stress, are not suited to the dog-leg treatment.

Main heading and picture may also be bound together under a joint strapline or reverse. Other useful devices include running a headline beside a picture to matching depth, setting it in a reverse of some kind joined to the picture so as to increase the width of a horizontal shape. Headlines may also be overlaid to run into a picture or out of a picture, but this requires care, first to ensure that the edge of the picture runs through a letter and not between letters and also that the picture is light enough to take a black letter or dark enough for lettering lined by white.

So far nothing has been said about complete *picture pages* which are a miscellany of unrelated items. These are no longer very popular. Picture spreads are at their best when there is a theme that joins them together. To scheme a higgledy-piggledy collection of pictures under some banal heading like 'The weekend's events in pictures' will be unproductive if they are all so ordinary that they fail to cause excitement or arouse interest – or, indeed, that they are all so good that it is a waste to put them on the same page where they must compete for attention and divide the audience.

234 and 235. An interesting comparison in picture treatment. In *The Times* the picture tells the story, the words providing amplification and explanation. In *The Daily Telegraph* the words are dominant and the picture is used to illustrate them.

236

237

236 and 237. A dramatic picture makes a good front page and a good full-page advertisement for a car manufacturer.

238. A picture that tells the story; three Queens of England mourning beside the bier of King George VI lying in state in Westminster Abbey. The photographer was an agency man, Ron Case, but there were no bylines for cameraman or reporter in those days.

DAILY EXPRESS

No. 16,113 Price 1½d.   TUESDAY FEBRUARY 12 1952   CONTROLLING SHAREHOLDER LORD BEAVERBROOK   Weather: Cold

The week of tribute...

PICTURE EDITION

TO THE QUEEN ... Our loyal devotion and our complete conviction that she will, with the Blessing of God, uphold the liberties of all her peoples.

TO THE QUEEN MOTHER ... With her aid, the King was able to surmount his trials ... an ordeal he could not have endured without her aid.

TO QUEEN MARY ... May she find comfort in the affection which flows to her from all who have watched and admired her through these long years.

MR. WINSTON CHURCHILL TO THE COMMONS ASSEMBLED IN MOURNING YESTERDAY

THE THREE QUEENS PRAY

AT THE LYING IN STATE

Express Staff Reporter

THREE Queens of England—Queen Elizabeth II, the Queen Mother, and majestic Queen Mary—tried to fight back their tears yesterday as they stood beside the bier of King George VI, lying in state in Westminster Hall.

Queen Elizabeth, mourning a father, stood a little in front at the head of the coffin. On her right, two paces behind, was her mother, mourning a husband. On the other side was Queen Mary, mourning a son.

THE EMOTION

Their heads were bowed. Long veils shrouded their faces. Their emotion was too great for them to join in the singing of "Abide With Me" as a short service drew to its close.

From the assemblage of Lords and Commons and dignitaries of the Realm, there went out a great unspoken wave of sympathy to the three sad queens.

A few steps behind them, finding it hard to bear herself with fortitude, stood Princess Margaret, a frail, pale girl beside the tall, upright Duke of Edinburgh.

There, too, were the Duke and Duchess of Gloucester, the Princess Royal, the Duchess of Kent. The family was gathered.

That was the unforgettable picture in the 20 minutes of heartfelt drama which began when the gun-carriage bearing the royal coffin reached New Palace Yard.

THE SILENCE

It was four o'clock when a great hush fell in the waiting hall. The Gentlemen Ushers in plumed hats, and the Yeomen of the Guard took up positions.

Down one side of the hall ranged the bishops in black and white and the peers in dark dress. On the other side were the Members of Parliament who had walked in procession, Government with Opposition, two by two.

So that Mr. Churchill had walked with Mr. Attlee, Mr. Morrison with Mr. Eden.

It was cold in the hall. The only sound was an occasional cough.

At four minutes past four there was a banging on the great canopied oak doors. Two elderly Yeomen of the Guard swung them open.

THE SALUTE

Outside the guard of honour could be heard moving in rhythmic precision to their salute. As the muffled abbey bells trembled into silence, far-away military commands rang out staccato.

Eyes in the hall were turned towards the great doors. The Heralds came in first, one limping. They moved up each side of the hall with a splash of colour.

Among them was the Minister of Works, Mr. David Eccles, in plain mourning dress. He is Keeper of the Palace of Westminster, a post for which there is no State uniform.

There entered next the Dean of Westminster and Dr. Garbett, the Archbishop of York, taking the place of the Archbishop of Canterbury, who has been ill.

THE CROWN

Then, borne high on the shoulders of eight Guardsmen in long grey coats with white belts, came the coffin of King George VI. The Guardsmen stepped across the thick dull brown carpet.

The clustered lights fell on the coffin of the King draped in the rich colours of the Royal Standard ... on the Imperial Crown resting on the mauve cushion, its jewels glowing with a lustre of sombre beauty ... on that sombre setting ... on the wreath of white and white flowers, the loving tribute of a wife the Queen Mother.

Immediately behind was Queen Elizabeth, looking small and lonely in that huge hall, an effect heightened by her long

➤ PAGE TWO, COL. FIVE

Heavily veiled, the three mourning Queens stand together as the coffin of the King is borne from its gun-carriage to the catafalque in Westminster Hall. ... They joined the procession behind the coffin and as they turned to move the Queen Mother stood back for the Queen to precede her.

239, 240 and 241. Selling power in these excellent front pages from *The Western Mail,* Perth. There is magnetism in a good picture, well presented, the twin qualities of front-page illustration.

The pictures are in colour, as is the splendid titlepiece in Cloister Bold Expanded. Headlines are in Geneva Heavy with text in 9pt Times to varying measures which bear no relation to the newspaper's 8.6 pica em grid.

242 and 243. Picture size has a lot to do with projection, as shown in this comparison between two front pages. Interestingly the positioning of the caption appears to work in *The Star* version although the headline cut-out is rather obtrusive.

242

Daily Mail

TUESDAY, NOVEMBER 11, 1986

The prison officer, arrowed, is paraded on the roof of the jail yesterday by his captors

HOSTAGE OF MURDERER

By JAMES GRYLLS

A PRISON officer was at the mercy of three murderers last night.

They have already threatened to kill their hostage, who has a knife at his throat.

The officer's mother, sobbing and close to collapse, was helped inside Peterhead Prison in Scotland to beg for his freedom.

But the rioting prisoners ignored her pleas.

Hooded

The 25-year-old officer, in the prison service only 18 months, was allowed to send out a letter saying: 'I'm OK.'

One of the men holding him is believed to be Andrew Walker, an Army corporal who shot dead two soldiers and a retired major in a payroll snatch two years ago. His two other captors are believed to be William Ballantyne and James Smith, both serving life for murder.

They seized the officer on Sunday night and used his keys to free 50 more inmates who have been running wild in 'A' Hall.

Police in riot gear were standing by last night as negotiations to end the siege continued. Yesterday hooded inmates, armed with makeshift knives and clubs, appeared on

Turn to Page 2, Col 6

Fashion note as Diana heads for the Gulf

Diana stepping out in pop style

Princess Pop Socks

By ANDREW MORTON
Royal Correspondent

PRINCESS DIANA socked it to the fashion fans yesterday as she and Prince Charles left Britain for a nine-day tour of the Gulf States.

The split in the back of her Prince of Wales check skirt revealed the latest addition to her wardrobe—pop socks.

The royal couple were at RAF Brize Norton, Oxfordshire, to board their plane. But by the time they arrived at Muscat, Oman, to join the royal yacht for the night Diana had changed into the more formal outfit pictured right.

They will tour Oman, Qatar, Bahrain and Saudi Arabia. Prince Charles, a keen artist, is taking 34-year-old landscape painter Martin Yeoman on the tour to help him brush up the royal technique.

Mr Yeoman, from Berkshire, will advise Charles on subjects and style as they sail the Red Sea for four days after the official tour.

Demure Diana in Oman

THE STAR

BRITAIN'S LIVELIEST DAILY   TUESDAY, NOVEMBER 11, 1986   18p (28p Eire) ★

A MESSAGE FOR MYRA HINDLEY

Hindley . . . no remorse

You will stay in jail

EXCLUSIVE: MOORS KILLER GETS A SHOCK
—See Page 2

Diana Sheiks a leg!

POP SOCKS SURPRISE

☆ TRENDY Princess Diana flew out of Brize Norton RAF base for Oman yesterday wearing this cheeky pair of calf-length popsox. But what did she have on when she arrived? She certainly couldn't be showing a leg to the Arabs.
FULL STORY: PAGE THREE

243

INSIDE Weather 2, World Wide 10, Femail 12, Diary 19, TV Guide 22, 23, Strips and Stars 28, City 30, 31, Go Ahead Girl 32, 33, Letters 33, Sport 35–36

244

DAILY MIRROR, Friday, September 2, 1988
WORLD EXCLUSIVE
SPLIT SECOND OF DEATH
Moment of impact as jet aces crash
IT'S the tragic split-second that horrified the world . . . captured in one of the most extraordinary pictures ever taken.
The photograph is so finely detailed that you can see the cockpit of a jet being ripped off — as it collides with two others, scattering debris from all three planes.
Amateur photographer Laurent Benardon saw the aerobatic jets closing on a collision course at 1000 mph — and faced a nightmare decision. Should he run for safety to nearby trees — or stand his ground and take a picture?
He chose to stay — and came up with this stunning image.
Laurent, 26, was on a hill overlooking the Ramstein air show in West Germany at the weekend when he lined up his five-year-old Leica for a routine shot.
Plunged
He has visited many air shows on the Continent and he reckoned from his vantage point 100 yards away there was a good shot in the making.
Laurent, a top Paris chef, said yesterday: "I suddenly realised what was going to happen. I thought 'Shall I stay or run and save myself?'"
"Something told me to stay and I ended up with this shot in a million.
"But I hope never to take anything like it again."

245

THE WAY TO GRAND SLAM
DAILY MIRROR, Monday, February 9, 1987
BOTHAM
Stunner for Hill
HAZARD EXPECTS HE AXE
By NIGEL CLARKE
Hoo-Ray
SUMMARY
LITTLEWOODS CUP
TONIGHT'S SOCCER
RUGBY LEAGUE
TOP DOGS BEST
CLIVE AID
DIXON GOING
Zola fear
NOT GUILTY

246

DAILY EXPRESS Monday September 22 1986
THE NEW MILD MARVIN
And how his second wife Pam helped to work the miracle
PAM MARVIN
REPORT: DAVID WIGG PICTURE: DAVID STEEN
THE face is still as tough as old boots . . . the muscles taut and steely.
But this is not the hell-raising, hard-punching Lee Marvin of old. "I'm a tamed man," he said in London yesterday.
25,000 volt shock for 'show off' boy
Mellow
More meat back on the menu
Welsh TV plan may put £1 on licences
Maggie's 'No' to twins plea
FEAR OF THE SACK 'MAKES SICK WORK ON'
A REVOLUTIONARY CONCEPT IN FITTED BEDROOMS
PLANNED FREE BY EXPERTS
SEND FOR COLOUR BROCHURE
Dreamline

244. Big pictures still make news, often in full colour too, as in this remarkable picture of a split-second disaster at the Ramstein air show in West Germany. The photograph is so finely detailed that you can see a jet's cockpit being ripped off as it collides with two others.

245 and 246. The best cut-outs or steps in picture treatments are those designed for the benefit of the page or picture, rather than to ease the job of filling a page. Figure 245 shows an unobtrusive cut-out which gives greater depth to the picture than would have been possible. The cut-out in Figure 246 is made by the fact that Lee Marvin seems to be taking a rest on the advertisement.

247 and 248. Two pictures worth a thousand words of argument . . . Figure 247 is an excellent example of tight cropping but Figure 248 says much more about this meeting of two church leaders.

THE INDEPENDENT

No 7 — TUESDAY 14 OCTOBER 1986 — Published in London 25p

President told to 'get his act together'

Reagan flies into space defence row

From Peter Pringle
in Washington

HERBIE KNOTT

Dr Robert Runcie and Cardinal Basil Hume at Lambeth Palace yesterday where they announced they will pray for peace in Assisi on 27 October. They had been invited by the Pope along with leaders of almost all world religions and Christian denominations.

Mitterrand may stand down at next election

From Patrick Marnham
in Paris

Trading record for TSB

By Patrick Donovan

INSIDE

NOBEL PEACE PRIZE
Searching for
a worthy winner
Page 11

HOSPITAL QUEUES
The long wait
for treatment
17

WHAT NEXT
FOR ARMS
TALKS?
19

NEIL WILSON on
Birmingham's
bid for

247

THE INDEPENDENT

No 7 — TUESDAY 14 OCTOBER 1986 — Published in London 25p

Senator tells President: 'Get your act together'

Reagan flies home to space defence row

From Peter Pringle
in Washington

HERBIE KNOTT

Dr Robert Runcie and Cardinal Basil Hume at Lambeth Palace yesterday where they announced they will pray for peace in Assisi on 27 October. They had been invited by the Pope along with leaders of almost all world religions and Christian denominations.

Mitterrand hints he may bow out in 1988

From Patrick Marnham
in Paris

Trading record for TSB

INSIDE

NOBEL PEACE PRIZE
Searching for
a worthy winner
Page 11

HOSPITAL QUEUES
The long
miserable wait
for treatment
17

WHAT NEXT
FOR ARMS
TALKS?
19

NEIL WILSON on
Birmingham's
bid for the

248

Durham Advertiser

6603   Founded 1814   FRIDAY, SEPTEMBER 10, 1982   Tel. Durham 42261   15p

Memories of a condemned cell

A FORMER Methodist chaplain at Durham Prison who many years ago ministered to a woman in the condemned cell will tomorrow celebrate his 100th birthday at a family get-together.

The Rev. George Kirtley Fawell (left), now a resident in St. Margaret's Hospital in Durham City, will be at the home of his eldest son, Mr John K. Fawell in Westcott Drive, Durham, when members of the family meet together — some for the first time in many years — to enjoy a buffet.

Cards have been flooding in, including one from someone Mr Fawell has not seen for about 50 years.

After the eventual reprieve of the prisoner in the condemned cell and after the end of her prison sentence she visited Mr Fawell regularly.

The Minister also has memories of attending the funeral of King Edward VII.

Mr Fawell was ordained in 1903 and is now the oldest Minister of the Methodist Church in the country. He was born at Seaton, near Seaham, and trained as a teacher and taught at Ryhope before going into the Ministry.

At the turn of the century he travelled extensively in Egypt, Germany and Russia, before the Revolution, witnessing the slaughter

of people at the Winter Palace in St. Petersburg.

After his ordination he served in Methodist circuits at Swindon, Hull, Bury, Stanhope, Eston, Stokesley, Hebburn, Willington, Wingate, Seaham and Durham.

After he retired in 1952 he still carried on with his work and was responsible for founding the Methodist Church in Peterlee New Town. It was there in 1960 that he was presented to the Queen.

He was married in 1915 and he and his wife, Alison, who died in 1964 had four sons.

He has been in St. Margaret's for about two years and has eight grandchildren and seven great grandchildren.

249   **250**   **251**

249 and 250. Design is part of the journalism but not a thing in itself. The 'projection' of journalism includes the difficult-to-define differences between these two versions of the same story.

Figure 249 may be a neat piece of make-up but Figure 250 is a far better story for the *Sunday Sun*, Newcastle.

251. There is a touch of over-kill in this page where eye-breaks become ornaments out of all proportion to the relatively minor problem of reading a slab of text. Technically, they are functional in being narrower than the measure so that the reader can pass through, in mid-sentence, without hazard.

252 and 253. Just who was talking to whom? There are four people in the conversation shown by the *Daily Express* picture, Figure 253, although only Prince Charles, Princess Diana, and actress Joan Collins are named. One member of the quartet has been removed from *The Sun* version which changes the conversation altogether.

THE UNION JACK TRIUMPHANT ON THE NILE AND AT CANDIA.

READ THIS WEEK'S "P.I.P."

THE SIRDAR'S NEW NILE COUP ON TO FASHODA TO CHECKMATE MARCHAND.

254

254–268. There are three basic forms of communicating in print, by words, photographs, and by non-photographic illustration; that's where information graphics come in. Graphics are in vogue but they are, of course, as old as newspapers themselves and a lot older than photographs. Drawing a picture has always been an effective way of telling a story and one with some licence for emphasis or even exaggeration as in caricature. Figure 254, taken, from the *Penny Illustrated Paper,* imparts a swashbuckling atmosphere that would be difficult to encapsulate in a photograph.

So information graphics are not new. We have merely rediscovered an art form, made much easier by the advent of the computer.

A good graphic is a good piece of journalism rather than a good piece of art. It depends on our knowing the best way to tell a story, be it through words, photographs, drawings, or a

combination of any two or all three with any element being the dominant factor.

Try to describe in words how one might tie a knot in a piece of string and see how difficult it is. Taking a series of photographs in illustration of a step-by-step guide is hardly much easier and yet much more expensive in terms of time, effort, and space, as well as cost. Do it in diagramatic form, with words as a commentary, and you have the perfect illustration, easy to understand and emulate.

As with all forms of journalism, the reader comes first. We are not describing things to ourselves so much as imparting information to a reader in a way that that reader will find interesting as well as useful.

A simple table of temperatures is enough to tell a traveller how cold or warm it is in London or Moscow. Adding a map with drawings of clouds, snowstorms, or sunshine, may add interest or even amusement but it does not increase the information. If the emphasis of the artwork is wrong, or overdone, it may decrease or devalue the information.

Figure 255 shows a simple chart, easily generated by a computer, to illustrate what has happened to the *Financial Times*/Stock Exchange share price index over a 13-month period and, inset, the position over the last week. It is illustrative but not entirely realistic in that the chart presents only that portion between 1500 and 2,400 at a vertical scale of roughly half a centimetre per 100 points. Had the scale begun at nought the graphic would have been twice as deep and the ups and downs at the top would have seemed less dramatic. Had the lateral scale been roughly half a centimetre per week rather than per month the graphic would have been four times its present width and the rises and falls would have seemed much less steep.

255

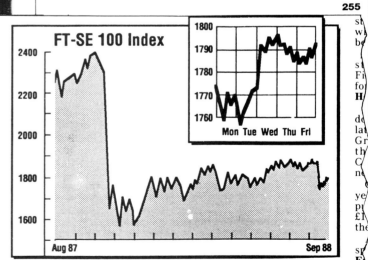

retail specialist to run the Gateway chain.

Among the engineers

Ricardo's profits slipped from £1·37m to £1·09m in the year to June 30 last, but are expected to

A simple list of facts enables a reader to compare any one with any other. Figures 256 and 257 are tables showing how much average householders pay for water and sewerage in different areas of the country and to cover every possible comparison in the form of a commentary would take many hundreds of words. The lists enable readers to make their own comparisons. Take the matter a stage further by incorporating the tables into an illustration using a running tap and a plug hole to show where the

256

WHAT YOU PAY FOR WATER

Water authority	Average household (£)	% inc on 1979
Anglian	37.93	72
North West	31.70	53
Northumbrian	39.80	113
Severn Trent	31.40	69
South West	42.70	55
Southern	35.60	78
Thames	36.46	80
Welsh	47.76	81
Wessex	40.10	38
Yorkshire	38.08	67

(Retail price index up 63% in same period)

257

WHAT YOU PAY FOR SEWAGE

Water authority	Average household (£)	% inc on 1979
Anglian	56.03	109
North West	36.55	112
Northumbrian	35.42	131
Severn Trent	36.48	66
South West	50.78	87
Southern	46.70	96
Thames	36.95	99
Welsh	45.01	93
Wessex	45.49	61
Yorkshire	34.56	108

(Retail price index up 63% in same period)

258

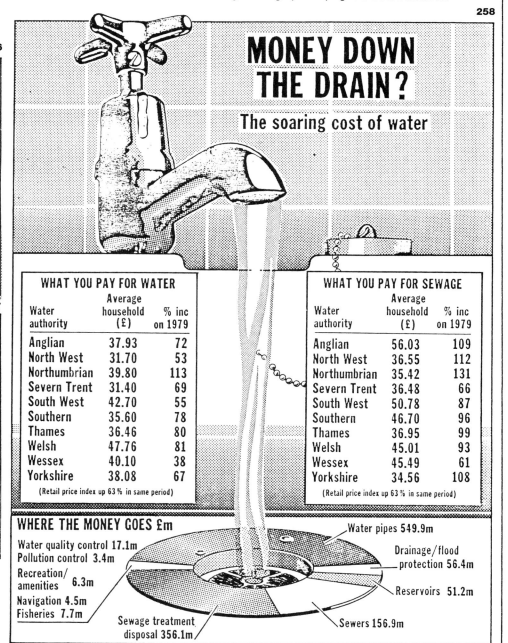

MONEY DOWN THE DRAIN?

The soaring cost of water

WHAT YOU PAY FOR WATER

Water authority	Average household (£)	% inc on 1979
Anglian	37.93	72
North West	31.70	53
Northumbrian	39.80	113
Severn Trent	31.40	69
South West	42.70	55
Southern	35.60	78
Thames	36.46	80
Welsh	47.76	81
Wessex	40.10	38
Yorkshire	38.08	67

(Retail price index up 63% in same period)

WHAT YOU PAY FOR SEWAGE

Water authority	Average household (£)	% inc on 1979
Anglian	56.03	109
North West	36.55	112
Northumbrian	35.42	131
Severn Trent	36.48	66
South West	50.78	87
Southern	46.70	96
Thames	36.95	99
Welsh	45.01	93
Wessex	45.49	61
Yorkshire	34.56	108

(Retail price index up 63% in same period)

WHERE THE MONEY GOES £m

Water quality control 17.1m
Pollution control 3.4m
Recreation/amenities 6.3m
Navigation 4.5m
Fisheries 7.7m
Sewage treatment disposal 356.1m
Water pipes 549.9m
Drainage/flood protection 56.4m
Reservoirs 51.2m
Sewers 156.9m

money goes in supplying our water (Figure 258) and the result is a *Sunday Times* graphic full of information, presented interestingly although with a heavy hint of comment.

The 'Executive Carrot' graphic (Figure 259), also from *The Sunday Times,* is different in that the aim is solely to lighten an unappetising list of typical salaries in a novel way. The carrot helps the headline, or vice versa, but does not assist in communication.

Many *Sunday Times* graphics show how things work, as in Figure 260 and Figure 261. Others are developments of the artist's impression, as in the sketch of a proposed new Royal Train (Figure 262), and the interesting shopping development graphic (Figure 263) from

the *Sheffield Star,* where an artist's impression has been grafted onto a photograph together with a comprehensive key. Graphics can describe news in the kind of detail few photographs could match.

259

260

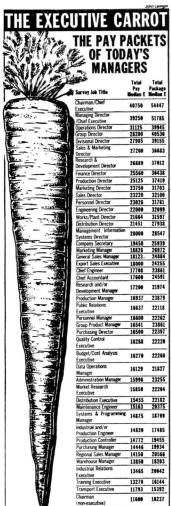

THE EXECUTIVE CARROT

John Lawson

THE PAY PACKETS OF TODAY'S MANAGERS

Survey Job Title	Total Pay Median £	Total Package Median £
Chairman/Chief Executive	40750	54447
Managing Director /Chief Executive	39250	51785
Operations Director	31125	39945
Group Director	28200	40530
Divisional Director	27985	39155
Sales & Marketing Director	27200	36683
Research & Development Director	26889	37012
Finance Director	25560	36438
Production Director	25125	37419
Marketing Director	23750	31703
Sales Director	23220	32106
Personnel Director	23026	31761
Engineering Director	22000	32099
Works/Plant Director	21664	31597
Distribution Director	21451	27938
Management Information Systems Director	20000	28547
Company Secretary	19450	25939
Marketing Manager	18826	26972
General Sales Manager	18123	24884
Export Sales Executive	18000	24255
Chief Engineer	17708	23861
Chief Accountant	17600	24591
Research and/or Development Manager	17200	21974
Production Manager	16937	23879
Public Relations Executive	16637	22118
Personnel Manager	16600	22262
Group Product Manager	16541	23861
Purchasing Director	16500	22397
Quality Control Executive	16288	22220
Budget/Cost Analysis Executive	16270	22260
Data Operations Manager	16129	21827
Administration Manager	15996	23255
Market Research Executive	15850	22264
Distribution Executive	15455	22182
Maintenance Engineer	15163	20375
Systems & Programming Manager	14875	18709
Industrial and/or Production Engineer	14820	17485
Production Controller	14772	19455
Purchasing Manager	14446	19034
Regional Sales Manager	14150	20566
Warehouse Manager	13850	18203
Industrial Relations Executive	13465	20042
Training Executive	13270	16144
Transport Executive	11793	15392
Chairman (non-executive)	11600	16237

ES 2 AUGUST 1987

MARITIME HISTORY

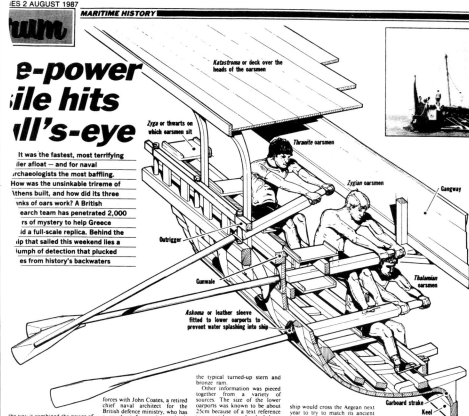

e-power ile hits ll's-eye

It was the fastest, most terrifying ler afloat — and for naval rchaeologists the most baffling. How was the unsinkable trireme of thens built, and how did its three nks of oars work? A British earch team has penetrated 2,000 rs of mystery to help Greece d a full-scale replica. Behind the ip that sailed this weekend lies a iumph of detection that plucked es from history's backwaters

Katastroma or deck over the heads of the oarsmen

Zyga or thwarts on which oarsmen sit

Thranite oarsmen

Zygian oarsmen

Gangway

Outrigger

Gunwale

Thalamian oarsmen

Askoma or leather sleeve fitted to lower oarports to prevent water splashing into ship

Garboard strake

Keel

the way it combined the power of ts 170 tightly-packed oarsmen to rive its ram into and sink emy ships.

Morrison, who prefers the cient Greek word, *trieres,* to its oman equivalent, believes the up was like a modern tank or ircraft or missile. When it emerged on the battlefield for the first time it probably helped change history, but there is no precise description available in history books.

Against the odds, however, Morrison was able to collect nough material and joined

forces with John Coates, a retired chief naval architect for the British defence ministry, who has a penchant for marine archeology.

The excavated ruins of the trireme sheds in Piraeus provided the maximum overall dimensions of the ship — 37m long and 6m broad. The dockyard's inventories offered details about the craft's length and the number of oars.

Writers, describing battles and voyages in the 5th century BC and later, spoke of the performance of the triremes, the composition of the crew and how it ran the ship. Vase paintings, bas-reliefs and coins illustrated

the typical turned-up stern and bronze ram.

Other information was pieced together from a variety of sources. The size of the lower oarports was known to be about 25cm because of a text reference to a watchman who had been caught napping and was punished by having his head pushed through the hole.

The trireme was believed to have a ramming speed of 12 knots. Thucydides, who commanded triremes in the Peloponnesian war, told the story of an Athenian trireme that dashed across the 184 miles from Piraeus to the island of Lesbos in 24 hours.

Melina Mercouri, the Greek culture minister who last week announced plans for commissioning the trireme, also said the

ship would cross the Aegean next year to try to match its ancient speed records.

However, many questions remain unanswered. In 1975 arguments about how the oarsmen sat so their oars would not clash and the actual length of the oars stoked one of the longest exchanges of letters to The Times. This gave the initial impetus to the idea of building a trireme.

The Trireme Trust was created and its first project was to fund the building of a trial section. 25ft long and containing space for 15 oars, to prove that there were three levels of oars and the oars were all of the same size.

Coates says: "The oars were all the same length. This puzzles people. But it worked. The only shorter oars were 18 aft and fore, which had to take in the curve of the ship."

By June 1984 the Greek navy had indicated it wanted Greece to build the first reconstruction of an authentic trireme. Coates prepared the blueprints. He is confident that the fundamentals of the ship — size, weight, proportions, arrangement, stability, strength and oar propulsion — are correct.

The trireme week. And John Lawr triple-ba

The me trireme i yard at Pei of Piraeus, hull first ar frames afte old technic hold the p beechwoo ployed an copper sp fastenings.

The 2.1-m modelled o found in A the recon 440lb, a fi Ancient used when were inev instance, it now to i Mediterrane pine was u has the sa were ma antiquity: producing

The une this long s the trirem In the p double together t the deck unable tc tension in to compr a moder

The tr June by water by Perama. I week a sailors re first time their han charge of Greek na performa "She g after th boys hav seven kr

But he isation Hard wc training improvi

Is Chunnel plan fireproof?

John Lawson

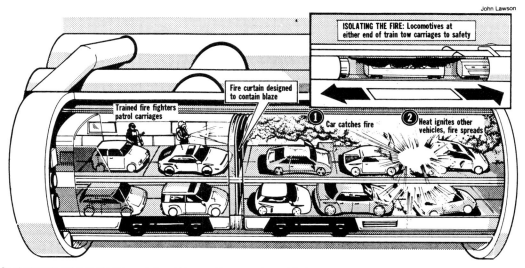

ISOLATING THE FIRE: Locomotives at either end of train tow carriages to safety

Fire curtain designed to contain blaze

Trained fire fighters patrol carriages

① Car catches fire

② Heat ignites other vehicles, fire spreads

Sparking fears: the scenario shows what could happen if a car overheated, igniting fuel, and (inset) how the tunnel could be evacuated

262

Royal dining saloon

Royal household & staff dining coaches

Catering vehicle

Royal household & staff sleeping coaches

Security coach

Generators

Princess of Wales' saloon

Queen's saloon

Prince of Wales' saloon

Royal sleeping coach

Duke of Edinburgh's saloon

Strengthened bogies

Armour plating

Armoured glass windows

Queen's saloon

Royal heavyweight: what the new train will look like – 12 tonnes of armour per coach and twice the length of an average InterCity

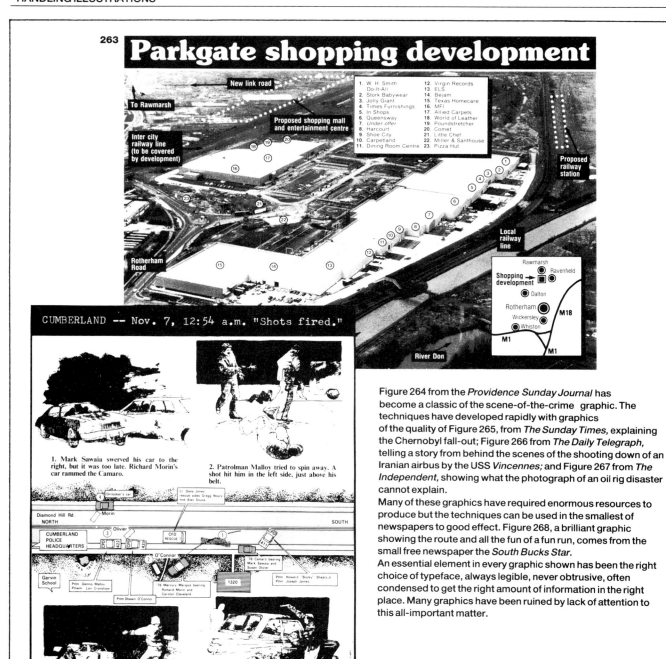

263

Parkgate shopping development

New link road

To Rawmarsh

Inter city
railway line
(to be covered
by development)

Proposed shopping mall
and entertainment centre

1.	W H Smith	12.	Virgin Records
	Do-It-All	13.	ELS
2.	Stork Babywear	14.	Bejam
3.	Jolly Giant	15.	Texas Homecare
4.	Times Furnishings	16.	MFI
5.	In Shops	17.	Allied Carpets
6.	Queensway	18.	World of Leather
7.	*Under offer*	19.	Poundstretcher
8.	Harcourt	20.	Comet
9.	Shoe City	21.	Little Chef
10.	Carpetland	22.	Miller & Santhouse
11.	Dining Room Centre	23.	Pizza Hut

Proposed
railway
station

Local
railway
line

Rotherham
Road

Rawmarsh
Ravenfield
Shopping →
development
Dalton
Rotherham
M18
Wickersley
Whiston
M1
M1

River Don

CUMBERLAND -- Nov. 7, 12:54 a.m. "Shots fired."

1. Mark Sawaia swerved his car to the right, but it was too late. Richard Morin's car rammed the Camaro.

2. Patrolman Malloy tried to spin away. A shot hit him in the left side, just above his belt.

Onlooker's car

Lt. Dana Jones
rescue aides Gregg Noury
and Alan Sousa

Diamond Hill Rd.
NORTH   SOUTH
Morin

CUMBERLAND
POLICE
HEADQUARTERS

Olivier

CFD
RESCUE

O'Connor

'76 Camaro bearing
Mark Sawaia and
Susan Olivier

Garvin
School

Ptlm Dennis Malloy
Ptlwm Lori Cromshaw

'76 Mercury Marquis bearing
Richard Morin and
Carolyn Cleveland

1320

Ptlm Howard "Bucky" Sheats Jr
Ptlm Joseph James

Ptlm Shawn O'Connor

3. Richard Morin was five feet away in a military crouch, the .38 pointed at Susan. "No!" Mark Sawaia screamed.

4. There was no time to aim. Malloy squeezed the trigger.

Journal Bulletin Graphic by BOB SELBY

264

Figure 264 from the *Providence Sunday Journal* has become a classic of the scene-of-the-crime graphic. The techniques have developed rapidly with graphics of the quality of Figure 265, from *The Sunday Times,* explaining the Chernobyl fall-out; Figure 266 from *The Daily Telegraph,* telling a story from behind the scenes of the shooting down of an Iranian airbus by the USS *Vincennes;* and Figure 267 from *The Independent,* showing what the photograph of an oil rig disaster cannot explain.

Many of these graphics have required enormous resources to produce but the techniques can be used in the smallest of newspapers to good effect. Figure 268, a brilliant graphic showing the route and all the fun of a fun run, comes from the small free newspaper the *South Bucks Star.*

An essential element in every graphic shown has been the right choice of typeface, always legible, never obtrusive, often condensed to get the right amount of information in the right place. Many graphics have been ruined by lack of attention to this all-important matter.

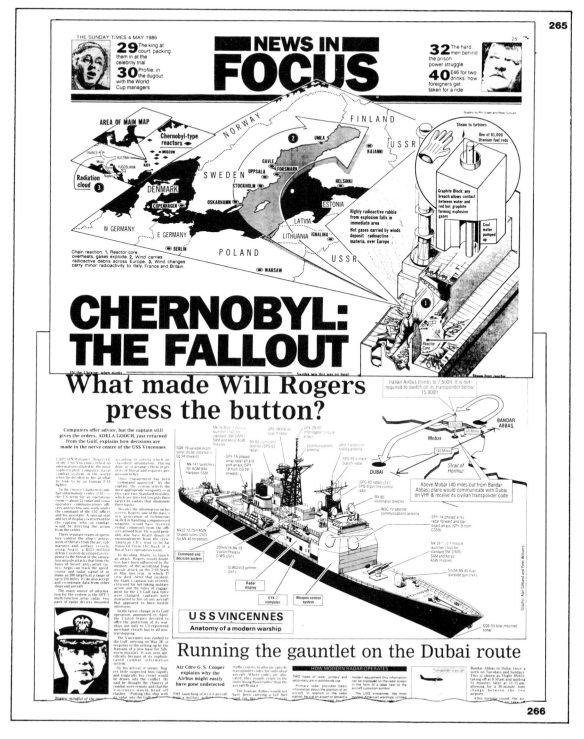

THE INDEPENDENT

No 544   FRIDAY 8 JULY 1988   .... Published in London   30p

SUMMARY

Tougher curb on BT prices

BRITISH TELECOM has agreed to a tough new formula for controlling prices which will at the very least freeze most inland charges for five years if inflation keeps at its present level.

Under the deal with Oftel, the telecommunications watchdog, there will also be a low-user scheme giving subscribers at least 40 per cent off telephone rentals if the telephone is rarely used ... **Page 18**
Outlook, page 19

TOMORROW
TRAVEL: Mark Lawson in LA
PROPERTY: House prices — the future
MOTORING: New series on second-hand cars
UNIVERSITY RESULTS
Four-page special

Ulster blast death
A man aged 23 died after a bomb exploded in Belfast. A 60-year-old woman was critically injured, and four other people were hurt .... **Page 2**

Council spending
Councils in England and Wales will be allowed to increase next year's spending just ahead of the expected inflation rate. They will receive an extra £110m to prepare for introducing poll tax .... **Page 2**

Bullion 'Chancellor'
A London solicitor, described as the "Chancellor of the Exchequer" of an operation to launder part of the £26m proceeds of the Brink's-Mat gold

Oil field 'atom bomb' kills 160

'We saw fellows waving frantically on the heli-deck. I think they got blown off. There was a massive explosion. There was a big ball of fire and we didn't see them again.'

By Mark Douglas Home and Phil Reeves
in Aberdeen

Gas leak blamed for first explosion

A GAS ESCAPE appears to have caused the first explosion on the Piper Alpha platform, *Mark Douglas Home* writes. It set off a chain reaction of other explosions and fires and wrecked the 34,000-tonne structure, its operator, Occidental, said last night.

John Brading, chairman of Occidental International Oil, told a press conference at the company's North Sea headquarters near Aberdeen: "It's going to be a matter of not hours, not days, but weeks and possibly months before people are satisfied they have got to the truth of this matter.

[diagram labels: Drilling derrick; Possible source of gas explosion; Helideck; Quarters; Diesel module; Mud module; Switchgear & control; Drill floor; Drillwater tanks; Pedestal crane; Lifeboats (6); Production modules; D Power generation; C; B Gas compression; A Oil & gas separation; A Well head; Well conductors; Flare; Deck support frame; Steel jacket; Pin piles]

[map labels: SHETLAND ISLANDS; BRENT ALPHA; ORKNEY ISLANDS; Sullom Voe; PIPER ALPHA; CLAYMORE; TARTAN; Flotta; Wick; Lossiemouth; Nigg; Kinloss; Inverness; SCOTLAND; Aberdeen; 17 mile exclusion zone; 0 miles 50]

DENIS BISHOP

267   **268**

Choose your spot to cheer them on

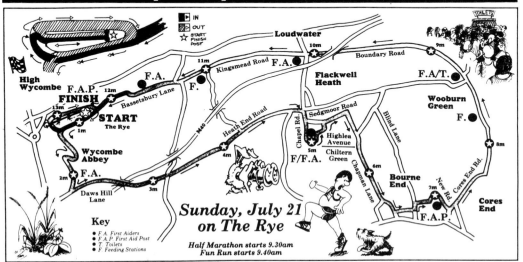

Sunday, July 21
on The Rye

Half Marathon starts 9.30am
Fun Run starts 9.40am

Key
- F.A. First Aiders
- F.A.P. First Aid Post
- T. Toilets
- F. Feeding Stations

COLOUR

THE TITLE of this chapter was originally Colour and Graphics for these two subjects are linked, almost inseparably it seems, whenever and wherever people talk about innovation in newspaper design. Yet they are not necessarily linked, nor have they much to do with innovation for there has been colour in newspapers for a great many years and the use of graphics pre-dates the newspaper photograph.

269. There are some things that you cannot do in black-and-white, such as showing the political composition of a country in the political colours of controlling parties.

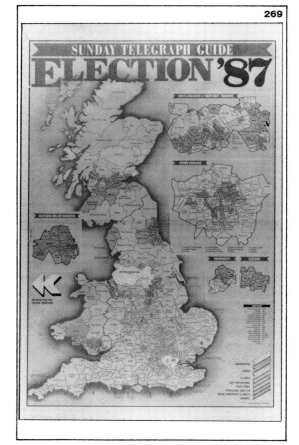

269

SUNDAY TELEGRAPH GUIDE
ELECTION '87

By themselves, colour and graphics are merely vehicles for journalism and we should not fall into the common trap of considering what is good colour, what are good graphics, without essential evaluation of the content. Colour that is technically good may be no more than that, and much the same may be said of graphics. Good colour is technically good, relevant and the best way of projecting the content. Colour that is bad, however, will always be bad and may ruin good journalism because it cannot do it justice. There is so much good colour to be seen in just about every other form of printing that colour of poor quality in a newspaper is apt to be counter-productive.

Colour in newspapers is nothing new. London's *Daily Mirror* could boast superb colour in the 1960s, printed on the run, daily, but only in its Northern Ireland editions because of the limited runs available in web-offset in those days. The *Daily Mirror*'s work in pioneering colour for national newspapers came to an untimely halt when the plant was destroyed by fire, but the expertise gained was transferred to Scotland to get the group's *Glasgow Daily Record* off to a colourful start.

Significantly, in 1988 the *Daily Mirror* turned again to full colour printing initially in some regional editions but the speed of technological advance is such that soon all editions of the paper were able to use colour daily. Most of its rivals can be expected to follow suit.

The spread of newspaper colour was steady but very slow until two or three years ago, when it became increasingly obvious to newspaper managements that the days of the black-and-white newspaper were numbered, just as those of black-and-white television were numbered once colour television fell within popular reach. A 1987 survey showed that 40 per cent of newspapers in the UK were using full colour photography; well over 90 per cent using spot colour at the very least.

Few people will be bold enough to say that colour actually sells newspapers. What evidence we have tends to suggest that the use of colour in a newspaper is beneficial in creating and encouraging the attitude among readers that here is a modern, go-ahead good-value newspaper. This in itself is a very positive attitude to be welcomed after a period when newspapers generally appeared to have lost at least something in the public esteem. The use of colour in some newspapers will also clearly arouse the need for it in others; a great many people who are used to seeing colour in the smallest of weeklies will expect to see it in their new local papers.

In this respect we may adapt the message of Stanley Morison, mentioned in our introductory chapter, that an old-fashioned layout will act like a tariff against the new readers who must be secured if the wastage of circulation by death of old readers is to be repaired. So far as a great many local newspapers are concerned, the biggest wastage of circulation will be in the movement of population; winning new readers among newcomers poses problems different from those of gaining circulation in the existing population.

There are many mistakes to be made in converting the black-and-white newspaper to one that is basically black and white but also uses colour. Most newspapers will admit to having made them all in one way or another, so there is much advice generally on offer! Newspapers going into colour for the first time are apt to take nervous steps, and that can be a mistake. Colour should not be treated as something just for use on special occasions but as something that is perfectly natural, an everyday facility to be handled with as much confidence as any other element of the paper. This is not to say that we should handle colour in the same way as we handle black and white, for that too can be a big mistake. Colour requires the same *amount* of expertise, not the same expertise.

Colour is different in that it poses different problems. There are different things to look for, different things to beware of. To begin with, we must choose colour photographs with a keen eye to tones, for what looks a good picture in the form of a photographic print or transparency will not necessarily reproduce well on newsprint, which is incapable of producing white because it is not white to begin with, and cannot produce a true black because of the inks used and the way they are absorbed into the paper.

We can use a meter to measure the tones on a scale of 30 points, 0 being pure white and 30 being true black: the more tonal values there are between those extremes the better the picture will be for printing. However, newsprint cannot handle that full range nor anything like it, and the most suitable pictures for printing purposes will have a range of tones that totals in the main around 17 or 18 of those 30 points. We do not need a meter to measure this. Imagine the tones laid out as though keys on a piano, running from left to right. You can have any sequence of 17 or 18, from one end or the other or from somewhere in the middle. Very quickly we will get to a point where we can choose the best colour pictures on a rule of thumb that says they are made up of, say, basically light tones, or

THE TIMES

TUESDAY JUNE 3 1969

FOUR PAGE RECORD OF MAN'S PURSUIT OF THE MOON

On the edge of the moon

The Apollo 10 spacecraft photographed from Snoopy, the module which carried man to within eight miles of the moon's surface

Daily Mirror

5d. (6d. in Eire) Wednesday, July 30, 1969 ★ ★ ★ ★ No. 20,401

FOOTPRINTS (AND OLD GLORY) ON THE FACE OF THE MOON

A SOLITARY flag marks man's loneliest outpost—238,840 miles from Earth. Around it, the imprints of mankind's first faltering steps on another planet.
   The Moon photographs that millions have been waiting for since the return of America's three lunar-

nauts, were released last night. This one, taken from inside the lunar module, underlines the stark emptiness of the Sea of Tranquillity.
   This is the area where Neil Armstrong and Edwin Aldrin walked alone for more than two hours.
   In its airless environment

Old Glory droops listlessly from a hidden wire, which stretches it out from the 8ft. tall, gold-coloured staff, planted firmly in the lunar dust. The pole in the background holds the TV camera which flashed pictures back to Earth.
The Shadow That Will Shape the Future—Page 10.

270 and 271. There has been an explosion of colour in newspapers in recent years but its use is by no means new, even in mass-selling papers.
Figures 270 and 271 show how *The Times* used pre-print for a full-page colour shot of Apollo 10 in June 1969, and the *Daily Mirror* marked the Apollo 11 moon-landing a month later with colour on the run hours after the picture was released.

light to middling, middle to heavy, or all on the darkish side. The important rule is to beware of choosing a picture just because it looks good in its original form.

Traditionally, newspapers and magazines have printed colour from transparencies rather than prints, but in the last two or three years there has been a swing towards the print. Elsewhere in the book we illustrate the front page of Bradford's *Telegraph & Argus*, with a picture of a soccer stadium blaze taking up almost the whole page. This was taken from a print, as are most of that paper's colour pictures. Handling prints is perhaps easier for a journalist who is used to black-and-white prints, but there are many who prefer transparencies, especially large transparencies, and it would be difficult to rule out one

method or the other. However, with print or transparency, it is essential to choose in the most favourable circumstances. Transparencies ought to be viewed on a light-box with standard white light and a surface mask blocking out all light except for a slight rim around the transparency; or by means of a small projector, again equipped with standard light and with a magnification of no more than four or five times the original size. Prints ought to be viewed in a box or cupboard containing standard light.

The question of the right light must be stressed. Viewed under different forms of electric lighting a transparency will appear to change its colours and will do so even in daylight according to the time of day. Anyone who has taken a tie, a suit or a dress to a shop doorway to see how it looks in daylight must readily accept the same sort of need in choosing colour pictures.

The colour handler must be adept at recognising colour casts. With modern scanning equipment these can easily be removed, but they have first to be recognised; a cast left untreated will deteriorate seriously in the printing process. We need reality in colour pictures – traffic lights must show the right colours. Pictures that have the washed-out look of over-exposure or de-saturation, are to be avoided, as are pictures lacking sharpness. We might get away with a black-and-white picture that is slightly out of focus; but not in colour.

Getting the size right is crucial in colour, for the over-sized picture can kill a news page stone dead. We know from advertising studies that even a single touch of spot colour can greatly increase the attention paid to an advertisement – the reader's eye is that much more likely to be drawn to the colour above all else. In editorial terms, when the eye is drawn to a colour picture first it may interfere seriously with news values. This can be tested quite easily by showing someone, very briefly, a front page containing a large colour picture and then asking them what was the lead headline, the second lead, etc. Most people will remember the picture, having looked at it first, and had perhaps no time to look at anything else. This is less likely to happen with a page where there are perhaps two or three items in colour and none is so big that it dominates the page. The big picture is at its best in the one-subject page, like that soccer stadium fire picture just mentioned and in lots of other blockbuster stories. It works too in the feature treatments where, again, there is no interference with the priorities accorded in a page of unrelated items.

Confident cropping is a necessity. Too many colour pictures are used full-frame or nearly so through lack of ease in dealing with small transparencies. The answer here is to have a quick and rough black-and-white 'proof' print made from the transparency or for a rough sketch to be made so that cropping marks can be indicated with some accuracy.

Some of the worst mistakes in use of colour are caused by lack of thought in choosing spot colour or multi-spot colour, especially when it is used in association with full-colour photography.

Just a little thought is usually enough (for most people know a good deal more about colour than they are inclined to think) when confronted for the first time with the problems of planning a page with colour. Do we not put this knowledge to good use, almost subconsciously, when we decorate a kitchen or a bedroom, choose matching clothing or plan a flower garden with colours that sometimes contrast and sometimes blend? We live in a world of colour, without much apparent thought about it, even when we use colourful phrases in everyday speech and talk about colours that are cheerful or drab, warm or cool. Everyone who reaches for the tuning knobs on a television set is exercising a form of colour choice and control. In all of these things we succeed when we achieve what we say is just right – in other words, natural or real.

It will help our study of colour if we think about what we know already and at the same time take up a few technical terms that describe what we know. For instance, there are three primary hues – yellow, red, and blue – that cannot be made by mixing other colours. Mix the three primaries together and a muted muddy grey results. Mix any two of the primary colours and we get a secondary hue. Yellow and red together will produce orange. Yellow and blue will give us green. Blue and red turn into violet. Between the primary and secondary colours we can mix different shades or intermediate hues, a yellowy-orange or a red-orange, a pinkish-violet or a blue-violet, green that has a bluish look or green which has a lot of yellow in it. With disciplined colour mixing we can achieve a myriad of hues. Colours that share a pigment, as with yellow and orange, red and orange, yellow and green, blue and green, blue and violet, red and violet, etc., can be described as blending or harmonising colours; colours that do not share a pigment can be described as contrasting colours.

The question now is one of knowing when we want colours to blend and when we want them to contrast.

Think of a shop window displaying the new season's fashions and the art of the window-dresser in harmonising the colours of clothes and accessories. Think of a floral display where spikes of deep purple lupins stand out against a bed of yellow pansies. Clearly there are parallels in newspapers. The front page 'goodies box' or blurb may be promoting a series of linked items, so a choice of blending colours will help project the package as a whole. On another day the blurb may be a series of unrelated and competing items – a tremendous news story on page three, a feature on page four, competitions on page five, a pull-out leisure guide in the middle and a whole collection of 'goodies' in the sports pages; the use of contrasting colours here will demand attention and promote the idea that the paper is full of excitement and importance.

We wish to set a picture-and-caption story, or a series of pictures, against a colour tint background. Do we wish the colours to blend? Or to contrast? As we said, it takes just a little thought to realise that we all know a good deal about colour and its function.

Let us move on a little to what the more scholastic among colour-conscious people would call 'luminosity values' and the interaction of one colour with another. Our purple lupins stood out brilliantly against the yellow pansies, providing a contrast difficult to achieve with some other colours – but why? Goethe gave us a simple table of luminosity, according a value of 10 to white and 0 to black. Black-on-white and white-on-black we know to provide perfect contrast. If yellow is the next brightest colour to white, with a luminosity value of 2, and purple is the nearest thing to true black, with a value of 9, they too will contrast splendidly. If we give a value to all the other main colours – orange 3, pink 4, red 5, green 6, blue 7, violet 8 – and say that the greater the contrast the greater the difference in numbers, it may at long last make sense of those rules of thumb we were given as children, that red and green, or blue and green, should never be seen. The modern equivalent of white chalk and a blackboard at school might be yellow chalk on a purple board.

It is not accidental that motorway signs have white or yellow lettering on dark green or dark blue backgrounds. Legibility is also achieved with a sans-serif face, usually in lower case, and this too offers food for thought in newspapers. The tint chosen to stand behind text should be far removed in luminosity value from the text itself, black against a brightly luminous or pale pastel shade, perhaps, and a sans-

272 and 273. If there was a prize for the most remarkable achievement in the use of colour in newspapers, *The Register,* of Orange County, California, might well win it for the quality and volume of coverage of the 1984 Olympic Games, symbolised by this page. During the two weeks of the Games, *The Register* published 187 colour pictures in addition to more than 100 non-Olympics colour pictures. The prize for a one-picture front-page might well belong to Bradford's *Telegraph & Argus* for its soccer stadium fire treatment.

serif face will cut a more legible image into the chosen background.

One of the more useful books about colour, in an artistic rather than a newspaper context, is *Theory and Use of Colour* by Luigina De Grandis, a well-known Italian artist. As well as discussing Goethe's scale of luminosity, the author argues that in order to obtain a harmonic balance the surface area of two fundamental colours should be in inverse proportion to their respective luminosities. In other words, we will achieve equilibrium, perhaps even floral perfec-tion, if those purple lupins cover three or four times the area of the yellow pansies.

Some colours may be brighter than others, but we cannot escape from the fact that black is the strongest colour of all. The black headline will always be stronger than one in, say, blue, or red, although a headline in colour at the present time may have a novelty value that commands attention.

Good colour, indeed, demands a good deal in the way of thought, knowledge, and expertise. Success is not achieved without such things.

THE CHANGING SCENE

WHEN historians look back on the development of the English-language newspaper in the twentieth century, they will pay particular attention to the 1980s as one of the most influential decades in newspaper history. They will look to the rise of new newspapers and the fall of old ones, the arrival of new techniques and the revival of old ones. Few newspapers have remained unchanged in an era to be remembered for the sudden advance of technological innovation after years of economic retreat. These two things have not always been linked, although quite often one has been an apparent consequence of the other. In the United Kingdom especially, a change in the industrial climate brought about the end of resistance to the much misunderstood and utterly misnamed 'new' technology. What became known as the 'Shah revolution' spawned the new newspaper *Today*, and this, with the even more significant move of the Murdoch titles away from Fleet Street, to set up anew in Wapping, lit the bonfires of antiquated working practices. The newspaper industry moved almost en masse into the twentieth century, albeit a little late. Fleet Street, the traditional home of the British Press, was left almost deserted. The oldest newspaper industry was catching up with the rest of the world.

The 1987 report of the Newspaper Design Awards described the effects:

The introduction in many newspaper offices of what is variously called electronic editing or direct input has aroused a general excitement in which new and perhaps greater than ever attention is being directed towards editorial quality. There is a powerful enthusiasm for doing things which are new or which were hitherto difficult to achieve for various reasons, not least among them antiquated working practices and resistance to change. When innovation succeeds, as it appears to be doing so, it exercises great influence on all of us.

This influence is clearly apparent in the swift transformation of a great many newspapers, sweeping aside the tired old look of hot-metal newspapers which had per-

274

sisted in some cases long after the hot metal had gone. New newspapers have arisen, not all of them successful, it's true, but the arrival of competition with the possibility of even more to follow has given even greater impetus to the need for change. Old newspapers have been revitalised and some have gone under but again this has added to the thrust to modernise.

Modernisation, in newspaper terms, means more than investment in new and more efficient equipment, vital though this is. It means producing newspapers which reflect the needs and requirements of a potential readership which includes a generation of young people who have not been brought up to read newspapers as a matter of course. This in turn puts so great an emphasis on marketing skills that it becomes blindingly obvious, to some people at least, that there is an essential marriage between promotional activity and editorial projection; indeed they are part and parcel of the same thing.

274 and 275. There are close to a thousand free newspapers in the UK and it may appear to be condescending to observe that many of them are superb newspapers in both content and appearance. Birmingham's *Daily News* won a major design award in 1987 when the judges said: It is a free newspaper which demonstrates quality journalism, first-class news treatments, and excellent picture spreads, and these things stand above the resources employed. They also show why so many 'paid for' newspapers look worriedly over their shoulders in fear that this sort of free newspaper might haunt them. Figures 274 and 275 show two small-town free newspapers which are equally impressive, especially in their choice of typefaces. The *Mirror*, from Milton Keynes, scores with a powerful lower-case titlepiece in Clarendon (spot red) above a powerful sans headline combination of Futura Extra Bold for the lead and Univers of different weights for minor headlines. The *Bedford & Kempston Express* has an equally strong title in Rockwell Extra Bold, topping an all-Univers display.

This 'essential marriage' of editorial and marketing skills was not very evident in some of the new ventures. *Today* struggled for survival through three ownerships; Robert Maxwell's experiment with a 24-hour newspaper, the *London Daily News*, was expensive and short-lived; the controversial resurrection of the *London Evening News* proved to be a fleeting re-appearance; and some other new titles fought on against heavy odds. If a newspaper truly can be regarded as a consumer product, with all that implies in the marketing operation, it was seen at its best in the launch of *The Independent*, which set out to be a quality product for a clearly defined market.

In the United States there was no revolution, retrenchment, retreat or even anything defensive in the birth of *USA Today*, arguably the most expensive launch in history. In its first five years it had operating losses of $457 million (reduced to $233 million after tax). The figures were quoted in the paper's own columns, worn as a badge of pride by the founding fathers in the Gannett Corporation who, on the paper's fifth birthday, could point to the first profits. Much more important than the first surplus was the fact that the USA's first national general-interest daily newspaper (to distinguish it from the *Wall Street Journal*) had established an average daily readership of 5,541,000 people.

From its inception, *USA Today* became the most talked about newspaper in the world, and the most mimicked too, with enormous influence on newspapers the world over. When people talked of colour, they pointed to *USA Today*. When talk turned to graphics, they pointed to *USA Today*. The paper may not have been the best exponent of colour or graphics, but it was the innovating influence that set the fashion in these and other fields. The design of a newspaper could be seen to incorporate the dual function of marketing and editorial projection. *USA Today*'s influence was felt on both sides of the Atlantic. Who could have dreamed that within half of this decade of change the majority of the UK's daily papers would enjoy not only the fruits of direct input but also boast full colour, on the run, and many of them right through the paper? Everyone had to catch up, including the weeklies and the frees.

The design of *USA Today* is worth detailed study, for it is a *news* newspaper, where the aim is to give the content the projection it deserves; this is different from what might be called the *magazine* newspaper, where all too often the layout comes first. There is a strong emphasis on news briefs, well-written, well-edited, and well-read too, despite all those jokes about 'investigative paragraphs' and 'fast-food journalism'. The high story count has played an enormous part in the success of *USA Today*, and here again the paper has worked like a beacon to guide others along the same route. The new paper did not blaze a trail as far as type dress is concerned but followed a well-tried formula of Times Roman and Times Bold with Helvetica to provide contrast in various weights and widths. Text is in very readable sizes of the highly dependable Imperial, a typeface so compact that it reads well in 9pt over a narrow 10-em measure even though it is much better suited to a measure of 15 ems or more.

A good many afternoon papers converted to morning paper production during the 1980s. The trend was best exemplified in Florida's *The Ledger*, which underwent design and 'editionising' changes as well, and went on to win major awards for substantial and sustained circulation increases in each of several successive years. *The Ledger* exploited the old techniques of geographical editions coupled with the new idea of a later, newsier, 'sunrise' edition which could be put on sale on news stands everywhere. It was a brilliant idea, designed to overcome the problems

275

276

277

278

279

276–279. Two newspapers with the interesting marketing strategy of broadsheet editions in midweek with tabloid issues on Saturdays.
The Royal Souvenir edition of Bradford's *Telegraph & Argus* (Figure 277), created something of a record for the paper's daily colour reproduction. It was on the streets with a four-page wrap-around less than two hours after Prince Charles arrived in the city.
Nottingham's *Evening Post* employs two different cover prices as described in a line under the titlepiece, 19p for casual sales but only 16p for regular home-delivered copies.

associated with readers who like the local news of a geographical edition and those who prefer the broader and later coverage of a more general newspaper. Take that concept one stage further, to arrange home delivery of the 'local' or geographical edition, but put the general or 'sunrise' edition on sale at the news stands, and you get the best of both worlds – some families will buy both newspapers.

In many respects *The Ledger* is typical of the modern broadsheet, not so broad as once was usual but still maintaining the distinction from the tabloid page that goes much deeper than mere size. Formality adds to the distinction, with wide measure for editorial, slightly less wide for run-of-paper display advertising, and a positively narrow column for classified advertising. There is enormous skill in designing pages to allow for a basic format of, say, six columns for editorial, eight for display advertising and nine for classified advertising, or even ten or eleven as in some UK broadsheets. That skill becomes all the greater when it allows news values to dictate story lengths and picture sizes, and greater still when accommodating rather than dictating advertisement shapes. Not for nothing do we advocate the abilities of journalist and designer in one dual function rather than in separate disciplines.

Developments in the UK during the changing 1980s have been dominated by three main happenings: the sudden change to direct input methods, the mass conversion of a great many broadsheets into tabloids, and the remarkable rise of the free newspaper. Let us look at these in turn.

The UK's national newspapers had lagged behind the regional press in the introduction of new methods. The regional newspapers, large and small, had pioneered the introduction of photocomposition, web-offset printing and use of colour, while the techniques of national newspaper production remained rooted in the past. It was a Fleet Street joke, with some truth, that if Caxton returned he would find that very little had changed. Although the provinces set the lead only one title of note, the *Nottingham Evening Post*, had managed to introduce direct input methods and this after a lengthy and bitter trade union dispute. With most of the other leading papers linked in ownership with national newspapers, there seemed little chance of a major breakthrough – not until Eddie Shah came to London, fresh from a long struggle with the printing unions in the provinces and full of fight and enthusiasm for the new newspaper that became *Today*. It was an appropriate name for

the first national newspaper to be produced by today's technology, although inevitably it invited comparison with *USA Today*. As things turned out, critics were soon to say that it owed rather a lot to just about any newspaper you could think of. This was a pointed reference to the fact that in little over a year it had three owners, three editors, and more changes in direction and presentation than some newspapers experience in a lifetime. Very little was to remain from the original paper apart, perhaps, from its emphasis on colour.

The titlepiece itself seemed to epitomise the paper's problems. It was appropriate and patriotic, presenting a fresh and bold image in white out of blue, bordered top and bottom by red. But 'Today' is a short word to stand alone, and it was allowed to float around the top of the page in various positions and sizes as though no one knew what to do with it until, under Editor No. 3, it changed to an italicised version of more manageable width – which only seemed to increase the paper's identity crisis by giving it the appearance of the popular tabloid. Time alone can tell us whether the paper will settle into a place in the market where it can successfully exploit all that technology offered and yet failed to fulfil in its first eighteen months. The paper could point to design awards for its features and sport sections, but media watchers were to be more concerned with circulation figures.

Robert Maxwell's 24-hour *London Daily News* failed spectacularly to find any kind of niche in the market. It too appeared to have great difficulty in deciding which way to go, a problem summed up in an article in the trade journal *Printing World* a few days before the paper's demise:

Clearly the *Daily News* must have done an enormous amount of research in the long build-up to its launch but much depends on the way this is interpreted and communicated to the front-line journalists who win circulation battles. It would not be the first time that a newspaper suffered from contradictions in policy and practice.

And contradictions there are in plenty. On one level it comes in the quickest 'quick' crossword imaginable – the three-letter word is predominant – but inside there's a cryptic crossword of scholarly standard. Catering for all tastes, you might say, but does all that fine writing about opera, music, art, literature sit happily in a paper where the mystery-probe-drama-riddle-blast-blaze headline rules OK in heavyweight sizes? It's a bit like wrapping *The Guardian*'s art pages inside the *Daily Mirror*; readers of those two newspapers may have something in common, but it's not the newspaper they read.

The most surprising thing about the launch of the *London Daily News* was that the paper did not contrast sharply with the appearance of the long-established London *Evening Standard*. Observers had expected a bright and breezy approach with, above all things, a sans serif headline style in opposition to the Century serif of the *Evening Standard*. Instead the paper chose Bookman, giving it a bookish look that was heavily criticised as being slow and ponderous and not at all in keeping with the paper's pop headline style. Changes came, somewhat late, but in these the paper moved even closer to the *Evening Standard* look by opting for the rather elegant look and feel of Century Schoolbook and Schoolbook Bold, which did not sit happily alongside a contrasting Franklin Gothic.

Inside the paper there was further contradiction. Again we quote the article published in *Printing World* in the week the paper died:

> There is elegance and style in the Metro section, currently vying to be one of the best things in British journalism, and the typographical treatments really are superb. The Rockwell theme for headlines, Helvetica for listings, the perfect wedding of legibility sans and readability serif in the TV guide, these are the things that suggest that journalists are becoming the masters of type and not its traditional servants.
>
> The choice of Nimrod for text is a good one although, alas, Nimrod Bold, size for size, doesn't make an equal partner. The City section is first-rate, and sport too, especially racing (except for the big mistake of not listing the also rans and their starting prices!). Picture treatments are above the average for Fleet Street and almost as good as *The Independent*'s and that's no mean compliment. The new titlepiece is a lot better than the first poor effort.

The short life of the *London Daily News* offers scope for fertile study of the editorial/marketing marriage we have referred to. No doubt the lessons to be learned from it were aired at the private autopsy that followed the death.

Racing Post, another of the UK's new national newspapers, faced a mighty task against the long-standing racing favourite *Sporting Life*. A racing paper must stand or fall by the quality of its information. Coupled with content is the need for high legibility so that the punters can actually read the small print necessary to pack in the fine detail of racing information. *Racing Post*'s choice of typefaces was a winner in itself, for the paper won the Allen Hutt Award in the 1987 Newspaper Design Awards. This award is given each year in recognition of some special contribution to newspaper design, and the new

280, 281 and 282. Award-winning pages from the *Birmingham Daily News*, Britain's first free daily and as good as, if not better than, many a paid-for paper. These show the undoubted design strengths of three leading free weeklies.

283 and 284. The *Birmingham Daily News* took on more of a quality look in adopting a serif dress in a new design in 1988.

paper gained it for its type dress. The judges' citation said:

Every paper undergoing the kind of changes we have talked about in this report must tackle quite serious problems concerned with choosing text and display faces which will best meet the demands of readability and legibility. The very nature of *Racing Post* puts emphasis on the need for legibility in such matters as race-cards, form guides, betting forecasts, etc, and we could not fault the typefaces Calvert and Helvetica to serve these ends. Helvetica was perhaps an easy choice for it is the world's most used sans face but *Racing Post* is the first newspaper in the world to choose the new slab serif Calvert and use it well for main headlines and form guides. In addition, the paper chose the relatively new Nimrod as its readability face for the body of the paper. We salute their choices.

Calvert is a truly remarkable typeface, designed by Margaret Calvert primarily for use on platform signs on Tyneside's new metro railway system. There is a lot of difference between lettering intended to stand several feet high as it does on the Tyne and Wear rail stations and one that can be used in the small text and headlines of a newspaper. Common to both, of course, is the need for legibility. If Calvert was the find of the year as a newspaper typeface, Nimrod must run close to being the find of the decade for the main body text of a newspaper. *Racing Post* was just one of a large number of papers choosing Nimrod which is

discussed and illustrated in detail on page 55.

The Independent may prove to be the most notable of this new generation of national newspapers and makes a ready case study for anyone else planning to produce a new title. Its planning was meticulous and included a month of full-scale dummy runs for every department, from the commissioning and carrying out of reporting assignments to the printing of the paper itself. The reward was a first-class product on the day.

Typographically, *The Independent* showed great courage in returning to the standards of yesteryear, including the truly broad broadsheet, wider than any of its main rivals, those other broadsheets, *The Times*, *Daily Telegraph*, *The Guardian*, and *Financial Times*. Its slightly wider columns and slightly condensed typeface, the eminently readable Dutch Roman, adds to the 'feel' of a good solid read. Headline dress is in Century Bold and Century Expanded (which must not be confused with the widened Century Extended). A minimum of contrast is provided by a light and bold Gothic sans serif used for the front-page summary and various items of house information, and there is a relieving touch in employing the elegant Latin Roman for standing heads.

The Independent figured strongly in various awards lists in its first year. In the Newspaper Design Awards it was adjudged overall winner among national newspapers and it also won the award for sports pages. Again we quote the judges' report:

> Instinctively we all liked *The Independent*. It was our idea of what that sort of paper should look like; a real newspaper, reassuring, authoritative. Its picture treatments are marvellous, so much so that someone actually criticised them for being too good in looking more like works of art than newspaper pix. The type-dress is impressive with Dutch Roman text, slightly condensed to suit the basic measure, an extra half point between the lines, and with headings in Century, the bold, light, and expanded versions.

The noticeable trend of converting afternoon papers in North America to morning paper publication has yet to reach the UK (if, in fact, it ever does). The presence of so many national newspapers and strong regional morning newspapers perhaps militates against such a move, although no doubt there are gaps in the market. So many 'evening' papers have such early deadlines – the bulk of paging being handled on an overnight basis – that conversion to morning publication may merely give a longer shelf life to the same material.

The biggest change of the decade among UK evening papers has been the conversion of a great many broadsheets to tabloids, a trend that has concerned newspapers of all kinds, although the heaviest rate of conversion seems to have been among evening papers. The fashion (for that is what it has become) can be traced in large part to the thin paging of the 1970s, brought on by lack of advertising during recession. Turning tabloid and, in theory, doubling the number of pages was thought to make the paper bulk better in the reader's hands and make it seem better value for money. Later it simply became the thing to do because so many broadsheets had gone that way before, and various readership research projects were interpreted as suggesting that small was indeed beautiful, and much handier, for consumers.

Clearly there are pros and cons in the question of whether to convert. Some newspapers have made significant gains from the change; others have not. One thing can be regarded as certain, though: turning tabloid is not in itself a panacea for all ills. The change is unlikely to succeed if it is not tackling the right problem.

Although, as we said, turning tabloid may double the number of pages, 'in theory' it can of course result in a heavy reduction of space. After all, a broadsheet page turned into two tabloid pages now has a wide

285

286

285 and 286. *Racing Post,* set up in 1986, won the coveted Allen Hutt Award for newspaper design in its first year. The award was given for its choice of typefaces and the judges' citation said:

The very nature of *Racing Post* puts emphasis on the need for legibility in such matters as race-cards, form guides, betting forecasts, etc, and we could not fault the partnership of the typefaces Calvert and Helvetica to serve those ends. Helvetica was perhaps an easy choice for it is the world's most used sans face but *Racing Post* is the first newspaper in the world to choose the new slab serif Calvert and use it well for main headlines and form guides. In addition, the paper chose the relatively new Nimrod as its readability face for the body of the paper. We salute their choices. Figure 285 shows *Racing Post* with its award-winning typefaces in use for headlines and text. Figure 286 illustrates the mix of Calvert and Helvetica in a typical race-card.

287 and 288. Changing shape and changing character, which presumably was the aim in this tabloid revamp of *The Irish Press.*

289. 'Now, where have they put the weather?' asks the headline-writer, poking gentle fun about the redesign of *The Advertiser,* Adelaide. It was in fact a significant change from narrow columns to broad measures and the new look included a much-praised digest column across the foot of the page.

287

288

289

gutter running across its middle, and over the paper as a whole this can be a significant loss not only for editorial matter but also in advertising. A broadsheet page of classified advertisements will obviously take up more than two tabloid pages for the same reasons. The only way to claw back such a loss of space must lie in such areas as tight writing, tight editing, smaller headlines and smaller pictures. If the story count suffers on conversion from broadsheet to tabloid it can be taken as a danger signal.

Headline sizes are quite easily reduced for tabloid publication. Whereas there is a need for shading down type sizes in a broadsheet page, as part of the process of guiding the reader through the menu, there is much less of a need for such a guide in the small page, where the reader is unlikely to lose his place or fail to see some of the elements.

Interestingly, two major evening papers, Bradford's *Telegraph & Argus* and the *Nottingham Evening Post*, converted to tabloid publication for their Saturday editions only. The Bradford paper has since gone the whole hog and turned tabloid altogether. It will be interesting to chart its progress.

Relatively fewer of Britain's regional morning papers have turned into tabloids. The top three in the circulation league table are all broadsheets.

The third large-scale development in the UK scene has been the phenomenal growth of the free newspaper. Two decades ago the free newspaper was unheard of and the early 'free sheets' bore little resemblance to paid-for newspapers other than in carrying the same sort of advertisements. By the end of 1987, however, free newspapers counted for something over 45 per cent of the 90 million or so copies of regional newspapers published each week. It would be patronising to say that many of them are indistinguishable from their paid-for counterparts; many of them are, indeed, better than a number of their paid-for counterparts.

At the time of writing there is one free *daily* although others are said to be in the planning stage. The *Birmingham Daily News*, to be strictly accurate, is published four times a week, distributing some 340,000 copies each time. Now in its fourth year, it is reported to be nearing its first profit. The paper won the 1987 Newspaper Design Award for free newspapers. The citation said:

In some respects it may seem unfair that the *Birmingham Daily News* should take the overall award and that for the news pages when it is clearly in a class of its own as a daily with resources to match. However, it is a free newspaper

290

291

290–294. A series of
titlepiece changes from
Today.

which demonstrates quality journalism, first-class news treatments, excellent picture usage, and these things stand above the resources employed. They also show why so many paid-for newspapers look worriedly over their shoulders in fear that this sort of free newspaper might haunt them.

Many paid-for newspapers are already tormented by such papers. Other free paper winners on the awards list were the *Bromsgrove Advertiser*, an 80-page tabloid, and the *Bognor Regis Observer*, a 52-page broadsheet, 'both super bundles to drop on anyone's doormat for free,' said the judges. Two more frees shortlisted came from the same city: the *Oxford Journal* and *Oxford Star*.

A year later there was a new crop of frees among the 1988 Design Award winners. Manchester's *Metro News*, the UK's biggest free, dominated the awards list. A lot has happened in the changing 1980s.

295

LAUNCH ISSUE **LONDON** GOLD TOP
DAILY ◆ NEWS
TUESDAY FEBRUARY 24 1987 No.0001 20p

Exclusive: Patient is infected in skin graft
operation–and now surgeon is at risk too

New London
Aids danger

IT'S HERE: A CAPITAL PAPER FOR A CAPITAL CITY

by CELIA HALL, Medical Correspondent

A LONDON man has become the world's first known victim of Aids contracted through a skin graft

INSIDE

London soccer
clubs to merge

296

LAUNCH ISSUE **LONDON** MIDDAY SPECIAL
DAILY ◆ NEWS
TUESDAY FEBRUARY 24 1987 No.0001 20p

The Daily
News is
off to a
cracking
start

by BOB GRAHAM

Rate-capped council draws up plans
for £150million deal to avert cuts

Hackney
Marshes
for sale

–Star's flight at the opera–

A RATECAPPED council is considering selling Hackney Marshes, one of the largest open spaces in London

INSIDE

THE TOP
LONDON
NEWS
TODAY

End of the
Fulham era

Video war on
graffiti vandals

EXCLUSIVE

by CHRISTIAN WOLMAR
London Government
Correspondent

Father's fight
to halt abortion

New riot wagons
for the Met

Will hotel replace
ICI's Millbank HQ?

297

LAUNCH ISSUE **LONDON** LATE EXTRA
DAILY ◆ NEWS
TUESDAY FEBRUARY 24 1987 No.0001 20p

The Daily
News is
off to a
cracking
start

by BOB GRAHAM

Legislation planned to outlaw closed
shop and make leaders face election

New Tory
assault
on unions

–Star saves day–

THE GOVERNMENT today announced plans to outlaw the closed shop and make trade unions more accountable to their members.

INSIDE

End of the
Fulham era

Video war on
graffiti vandals

Marshes going
up for sale

Baby appeal fails

New riot wagons
for the Met

HQ sale could
net ICI £65m

WEATHER 9, DIARY 21, TV 35, SHORT STORY 39, STARS 40, CROSSWORD 40, CITY PRICES 56 ● FULL INDEX 3 ▶

295–301. There was a battle between rival evening papers in London during 1987 following the launch of the ill-fated *London Daily News* as Britain's first 24-hour newspaper. Figures 295, 296 and 297 show three editions of the first day's issue with a fussy titlepiece which at least one critic described as being reminiscent of the Pathe Gazette Newsreel or Movietone News. There was also much criticism of the heavy Bookman headline face being too slow for slick news pages.

Both the titlepiece and the typographical livery changed during the paper's short life (the Grand Finale in Figure 298) but changes did little good. The basic reason for a spectacular failure was said to be in not identifying the likely audience, with the result that the paper often had an upmarket look but a downmarket feel. It was caught between the established *Evening Standard* (Figure 299) at the top of the market and, at the bottom, the resurrected and half-price *Evening News* (Figure 300) which the *Evening Standard*'s proprietors brought out of retirement in what was clearly recognised as a spoiling operation.

At the end of the day the *Evening Standard* reigned supreme and the *Evening News* went back into hibernation.

Ironically there were some superbly designed elements in the failed *Daily News*, notably the elegant and decidedly quality Metro guide to arts and entertainment (Figure 301), elements of which set a fashion and a standard for a good many newspapers to follow.

298

THE LONDON
DAILY NEWS

FRIDAY JULY 24 1987   No.0126   20p

MORNING ★ GOLD TOP

Judge Caulfield reviews the cast of the Archer show

GRAND FINALE

by EILEEN MacDONALD and PAUL CHESTON

THE JUDGE in the Jeffrey Archer libel trial summed up the main characters yesterday as the court-room drama neared its end.

Mr Justice Caulfield arriving, stern-faced, at court yesterday

299

300

Evening News

TUESDAY 24 FEBRUARY 1987   15p   No. 30,600   TONIGHT'S WEATHER: COLD

Opera star Lynne flies in to save the show

To the rescue!

BY DIANE CHANTEAU

LYNNE, the high-speed soprano, who jetted 600 miles to save last night's Covent Garden opera performance with just ten minutes to spare, was off again this morning back to Milan.

Flying Saviour: Lynne Strow Piccolo had ten minutes to spare before curtain-up.

Abortion dad loses appeal

301

TONIGHT'S WEATHER SHOWERS   **WEST END FINAL**

Evening Standard

LONDON THURSDAY 11 JULY 1988   20p

The big wait for Wacko Jacko

A MILLION OFF DOLE QUEUES

BRITAIN'S booming economy has brought unemployment down by more than a million since its peak two and a half years ago, Government figures showed today.

86,085 drop is 23rd monthly fall in a row

Hurtling by train to Paris at 180 mph

FULL REPORT—P14

●TV Sir David Attenborough as snake charmer ●Rock Big Audio
Dynamite's late explosion ●Cinema Exploring the Jewish heritage

TV PAGE 28

MetroWeekend

LONDON'S ONLY DAILY INDEPENDENT GUIDE TO THE ARTS AND ENTERTAINMENT

Clive Davis meets a soldier turned rising pop sensation

D'ARBY DAY

303

303–307. *USA TODAY* has been one of the most influential papers of the decade as far as other newspapers are concerned, for it is by far the most mimicked. Its use of colour and graphics, epitomised in its full-page weather cover, has been copied quite blatantly by newspapers the world over. It has also had a considerable influence in reviving the forgotten arts of tight-writing and tight-editing so necessary to bolster story-count. Interestingly, the paper breaks a few typographical rules and

302

snubs even more conventions but there is a thin dividing line between idiosyncrasy and individual style and *USA TODAY* seems destined to be a setter rather than a follower of fashion. One feature to be admired most is the use of the text face Imperial, set rather large at 9.5pt on a slightly bigger body to a measure of 10.3 pica ems. Typographically speaking, it is one of the most readable newspapers in the United States. Headline dress is idiosyncratic, an equal mix of Times Bold and

304

sometimes a mix with either for the headline and the other for the text.

USA TODAY is cited whenever and wherever there is talk of colour in newspapers and yet here the mimicry often fails. *USA TODAY* rarely uses big pictures in colour, their spread being restricted in the main to one, two, and three-column treatments. Colour is treated as a natural ingredient of the page, occurring on all pages and in any column with the result that it takes its

305

Helvetica Medium and Bold, but within a tight framework. Major heads, running across the page, are in Times Bold, as are run-of-the-mill single-column heads but down-page doubles are in Helvetica Bold with subsidiary decks, set rather strangely in the first leg, in Helvetica Medium. The sans Helvetica is more legible than the serif Times on colour backgrounds, for headlines and text, but surprisingly both are used indiscriminately, sometimes all serif, sometimes all sans,

place in the scale of events and neither dominates nor detracts from the news itself.

Figure 304 shows a front page which is special – celebrating the paper's fifth birthday – and yet typical for there is little difference in practice or philosophy from those of Figures 302 and 303. Figures 305, 306 and 307 show the same basic ground rules at work in Sports, Life, and Money sections.

308–310. Neater shapes and neater type-dress in a redesign (Figure 308) of the broadsheet *Bromley Times,* with a titlepiece in matching style which is a big improvement on the untidy sans title in Figure 309. Figures 310, 311 and 312 show the new design adopted as the corporate livery for other papers in the Kentish Times group.

311 and 312. The story taken a stage further when the redesign is adapted to tabloid format.

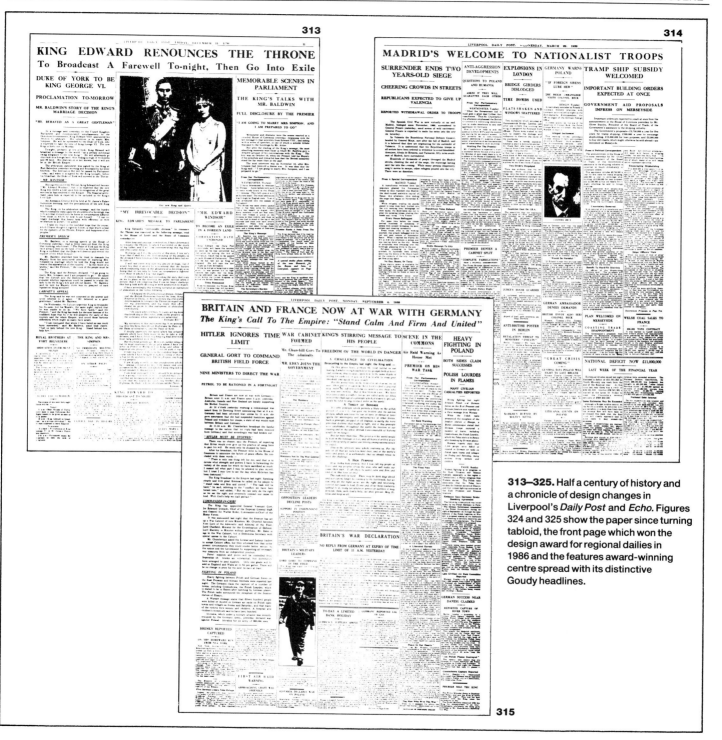

313–325. Half a century of history and a chronicle of design changes in Liverpool's *Daily Post* and *Echo*. Figures 324 and 325 show the paper since turning tabloid, the front page which won the design award for regional dailies in 1986 and the features award-winning centre spread with its distinctive Goudy headlines.

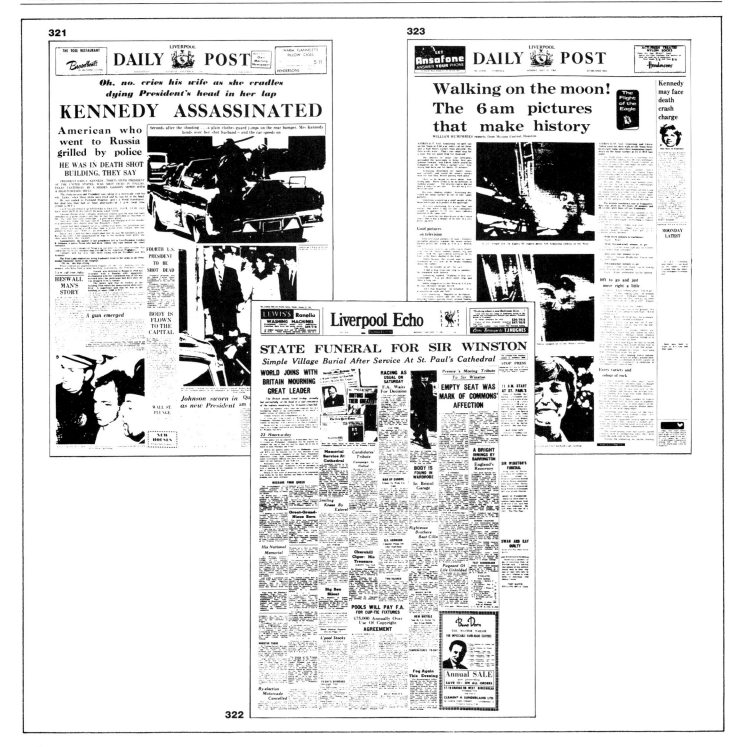

324

325

326

327

326 and 327. Varying measure in the *Oxford Mail,* a ten-column broadsheet with a basic measure of little more than 8 ems, seen in column one.
Figure 327 shows the same paper as a tabloid.

328–331. Two of the many regional newspapers which have turned tabloid in recent years. The *Evening Echo,* Basildon, and the *Western Daily Press,* Bristol, are regular winners in the UK Newspaper Design Awards.

328

Evening Echo

Tuesday, June 11, 1974   No. 1199

Experts probe blast at Army camp

Death of the happy-go-lucky father stuns neighbours

'Blackmail' storm over soccer terror fear

How to win the World Cup TV battle

KNIFE MANIAC MURDERS CABBIE

DETECTIVES launched a massive murder hunt today after a London taxi driver was stabbed to death by a frenzied killer.

Did you see his car?

Priest at IRA march sacked

MPs press for action on IRA marchers

Forensic tests on cab and clothes

Civil servants work flat out on pensions

'Running man' search

Police warn of bogus detective

'Typhoid' river row

H. W. STONE of LEIGH

SWITCH to STONES & SAVE ON COLOR RENTAL

FERGUSON 3713 19" £5.75

ULTRA 6713 PHILIPS 320 22" £7.25

Plus — FREE COLOR TV LICENCE — FREE TV AERIAL INSTALLATION

LOW COST — FINEST SERVICE GUARANTEE

329

Evening Echo

Monday, September 24, 1984   No. 3778   15p

TRAGIC END TO A HONEYMOON

By Pat Stone

We're in fine shape

That's title-winning Jane ... AND your new-look Echo

A COUPLE who had to wait six months for their honeymoon have been airlifted home after their two-week sunshine dream trip ended in disaster.

Michael O'Reilly, a Rochford Hospital therapy worker, had a massive stroke seconds after he and his wife Diane set foot on Italian soil.

Insurance

Demo hits hospitals

£¼m school fire attack

Pit chaos vote

Hospital man found hanged

Fury over late trains

Knife raid

330

WESTERN Daily Press

FRIDAY, MAY 6, 1983   No. 40,343—Vol. 200   Price 16p   The Champion of the West

LATE CITY

Cliff-hanger as Tories snatch the lead

LABOUR LOSE BRISTOL

Still it's a guess for Maggie

Super prizes in the new Press

MONDAY 9 MAY

Liberals hold the balance of power

By Jonathan Shorney

LABOUR lost control of Bristol by a whisker early today leaving the Liberal-Social Democrat Alliance holding the balance of power.

Sky-dive rescue cripples hero Para

By John Vincent

A RED Devil parachutist was hailed a hero today as he lay in a hospital bed with a broken back after a spectacular stunt went tragically wrong.

RESULTS

The new Lord mayor is safe

10,000 mob in Paris riots

Crashed

Scraped

West poll surprises

THE ODD SPOT

Civil Service snub to Left

ELECTION RESULTS PAGE 6

Unsettled

THE QUAD 405—2

£247.00 The QUAD FM4

£199.00

331

INSIDE: Your complete 8-page Budget special

WESTERN Daily Press

The Champion of the West

LATE CITY

'2p off tax, and almost nothing goes up in 'no bribes' Chancellor's election Budget

HONEST NIGEL'S SAFE BET

By Chris Bell

What it means to you — full tax guide in our 8-page Budget pull-out

Sports palace plan for Rovers' return

By Steve Egginton

CHANCELLOR Nigel Lawson yesterday turned into Honest Nigel, the punter's friend, with a safety-first Budget that knocked 2p off income tax, without looking like an election bribe.

Budget At A Glance...

MASSIVE SAVINGS

AT FRANK VOISEY CARS

ARE YOU THINKING OF PURCHASING A

NISSAN SUNNY 1.6 SGX?   SAVE £2,400
MAZDA 626 LX   SAVE £1,500
TOYOTA 1600 GL   SAVE £2,300
VAUXHALL ASTRA 1.6 GL   SAVE £1,800
FORD ESCORT 1600 GL   SAVE £1,800

BY PURCHASING A NEW HYUNDAI PONY 1.5 GLS 3-DOOR HATCHBACK

AT £5,500 ON THE ROAD

TEL. BRISTOL 559356 / 656742
714 FISHPONDS ROAD, BRISTOL

INSIDE: Weather 2; TV 6; Mr West 7; Women 8; Grass Roots 17; Crossword 20; Sport 20-24.

332

333

332. *The Sunday Telegraph* underwent a major redesign in 1988 and brought its titlepiece into line with *The Daily Telegraph*'s.

333. An unusual titlepiece treatment providing a frame for the page and a place for some promotional detail.

334. One of the best blackletter titlepieces designed in recent years, *The Standard*, from St Catherine's, Ontario, a simplified line, set left, well-spaced, and printed in blood red.

334

335–338. The history of the *Daily Mail* is studded with design successes. Figure 335 shows an historic front page when it was a broadsheet. Figure 336 sees the paper on turning tabloid when it merged with the *Daily Sketch* (Figure 337). The paper is much changed today but the elegant titlepiece remains.

335

336

337

338

339–343. There's nothing new under the Sun, so they say, but these three tabloids have little in common apart from their almost identical titlepieces. Neither the *Fiji Sun* (Figure 339) nor the Brisbane version are as noisy as the brash version from London (Figure 341). Suns keep rising and setting all over the world. Fairly new on the horizon is the rather ornate and very colourful *Sun* from Auckland, New Zealand (Figure 343) while the once-powerful Sydney *Sun* (Figure 342) sank for the last time in March 1988.

344. A titlepiece almost lost in the bric-a-brac of headlines across the top third of the *San Francisco Examiner* front page.

345

346

Saturday

THE DENVER POST

July 5, 1986   Voice of the Rocky Mountain Empire   Final Edition\25¢

Salute to America

President and Mrs. Reagan join the crew of the battleship USS Iowa for a salute to the United States during Friday's parade of tall ships through New York Harbor

Fireworks give Lady a star-spangled sky

By The Associated Press

NEW YORK — The biggest blast of fireworks in America's history crowned an all-day birthday party for the Statue of Liberty and the nation Friday.

The bombs bursting in air over New York Harbor illuminated a fleet of majestic ships that had filled the harbor earlier in the day

for a spectacular Fourth of July parade.

"What a glorious Fourth of July! One thing America knows how to do is throw a party," said Lee Iacocca, chairman of the Statue of Liberty-Ellis Island Foundation.

There was pageantry on land, on sea and in the air, part of the four-day extravaganza marking the res-

toration of the statue and her 100th birthday.

The scene in New York Harbor recalled the splendor of a bygone era as 22 tall-masted schooners, square riggers, barks and brigantines from 18 nations glided by the Lady of the Harbor.

On the island of Manhattan, the Harbor Festival provided a giant

street fair of food and entertainment through the afternoon.

The Boston Pops led a musical tribute to the statue in an hour-and-40-minute concert in Liberty State Park in New Jersey. The United States Marine Band provided accompaniment to the fireworks with a medley of patriotic songs.

After dark, the sky was filled

with a dazzling shower of 40,000 shells fired from 41 barges in what was billed as the world's biggest pyrotechnics display.

President Reagan kicked off the 28-minute show by telling the nation and thousands of sailors aboard the aircraft carrier USS

Please see LIBERTY on 4-A

Crown makes wearer a king of High Tack

By John McGrath
Denver Post Staff Writer

NEW YORK — She was sitting behind a souvenir-store window, near the corner of Sixth Avenue and 56th Street, when she caught my attention.

"Buy me," she whispered.

Forget it, I thought.

For one, her appearance, the very essence of commercialism, cheapened the meaning of a special symbol. For another, she looked ugly. No, worse. She looked positively atrocious.

But then, I am a fool for foolishness, so I went inside and purchased The Lady of the Weekend. Actually, I purchased several. A Lady Liberty button, and a Lady Liberty pin that had "GOD BLESS AMERICA" on the top and, some what redundantly, "I LOVE THE LADY" on the bottom, and a Lady

Liberty T-shirt, and a Lady Liberty crown.

The crown intrigued me most of all. Part of it, I suppose, was made with foam rubber, but mostly it was the product of gall — gall that enables the American free-enterprise system to succeed largely because our appetite for High Tack knows no limit.

Some questions came to mind when I put Lady Liberty's green, seven-spiked crown next to the cash register.

Who would buy something as repugnant as this? (I would.)

How could anybody wear this in public? (By putting it on.)

Why would people — specifically, Fifth Avenue's chic and lofty — do when they observed a fellow pedestrian touting a foam rubber

Please see GLITZ on 6-A

Boulder rider Bruce Mueller wipes his brow after finishing the tour Friday

Cycli… is hist histor…

By Clare Martin
Denver Post Staff Writer

For weeks you clouts on the city tale yellow jersey or high five and about next year.

The 1,400 riders Civic Center Park paling memories and them.

But while The Rockies' bicycle Richard Schlosbe definitely be anot…

Friends and fa the bikers as the route from Idaho that included a m an exhilarating ri

In celebration riders stuck smal mets or bike bags one group. Te white and blue ri of their wheels, a wore a crown sur or of the statue of

WEATHER

DENVER AREA Partly sunny and turning cooler today. Fair cool overnight. Highs 85-90, lows 55-59.
Details on Page 6-C

INDEX

Classified 4D-16E
Comics 12-13B
Digest 8A
Editorials 4C
Movies 9-11B
Metro 1-6C

Obituaries 3D
People 8A
Saturday 1-16B
Sports 1-12F
Region 3C
Television 14B

SUPER BOWL XXI
PASADENA EDITION
BRONCOS vs GIANTS
SUPER SUNDAY, JANUARY 25, 1987

THE SUNDAY DENVER POST

Voice of the Rocky Mountain Empire   50 cents — Denver & suburbs / 75 cents elsewhere in Colorado

SUPER BOWL COUNTDOWN

GUIDE TO THE GAME

Super Sunday is here, and The Post's Guide to the Game will take you from the opening kickoff 'til the clock runs out. All you need to know about Super Bowl XXI is in the 56-page special section inside.

How do you watch the game on TV? See the Guide to the Game.

SPORTS

Viewpoints: Buddy Martin on why the Broncos will win; Todd Phipers on why the Giants will win; John McGrath's look at the Broncos a year from now /5C

CONTEMPORARY

You may not be able to go to Pasadena, but you can build a whole team of Broncos right here. Just find some wet snow and follow our lead. /10

WEATHER

DENVER — The Mile High City will be mostly to partly sunny and warmer Sunday. Highs near 40, lows in the upper teens.

PASADENA — Partly sunny today, low 57. Fair Sunday. Denver Post…

INDEX

Business 1-14H
Classified 1-38I
Editorials 5-7G
Federal-Military 7B
Lively Arts 1-20D
Movies 2-4D
Perspective 1-8G
Real Estate 1-14F
Sports 1-16C
Travel 1-8T

PASADENA
Partly sunny today, low 57. Fair Sunday. Denver Post…

Goofy over the Broncos

The Broncos pick up important support from the hometown crowd. Mickey and the gang at Disneyland in Anaheim come out for Denver

Where we want 'em: Giants at OK Corral

By Leon Uris

PASADENA, Calif — Big Ed glowered down the long mahogany table, his trusted aide Hogan standing a respectful step behind and within range of his Honor's good left ear.

Yes, further business?" Big Ed threatened with a voice given its meaningfulness of a Korean quarterwatch with the unexchangeable wrist bands. Hogan shifted his feet nervous-like, gulped a hard dry…

Joisey Jints, Broncles in clash of 3 worlds

By Ray Flack
Denver Post Staff Writer

PASADENA, Calif — Rain and wind and wind in wind and the rain shall meet. So said Rudyard Kipling, a keen observer of human behavior and a Pro Bowl quality war correspondent in the 19th century.

A gang of course never covered a Super Bowl, especially an event like today's date with destiny. It produces teams and rabid fans from two disparate areas, New York, New Jersey and Denver. They're clashing in a third confrontation, free-bowling culture. The sometimes sunny often snow-filled, and traffic-clogged nature of Southern California.

In terms of winning west, clouds have labeled Super Bowl XXI as a one-of-a-kind of contest because only 20,000 tickets were divided out by the two NFL teams.

Please see FANS

---

347. London's *Evening Standard* tried several new titlepieces in recent years before settling on lower-case.

348. There is no missing the almost bludgeoning titlepiece of *The Observer* or the *Sunday Telegraph*'s features supplement.

349 and 350. National pride from Scotland where the thistle motif carries the title line and is repeated in the leader-page masthead.

351. The *Australian Financial Review,* a superb titlepiece above a neat Bodoni page. The telephone numbers in the bar below the title would be more legible in a slightly bolder sans.

347

348

350

351

349

GLOSSARY

BANNER A main heading running right across the top of the page.

BOX An item enclosed on all sides by a rule or border.

BRIEFS News items of a few lines, sometimes called NIBS (news in brief).

BROADSHEET A page the full size of a rotary-press plate.

CAPTION The descriptive matter accompanying an illustration; also called a cutline.

CASTING OFF Calculating how much space will be required for a given amount of editorial matter, and vice versa.

COPY Editorial or advertising matter to be printed.

COPY-TASTING Assessing news values.

CROSSHEAD A sub-heading in text, usually centred.

CUT-OFF A rule used to separate elements on a page; also the depth of sheet of a rotary-printed page.

DECK A separate portion or section of a headline as in 'second deck' meaning a subsidiary headline of one or more lines following the main headline; often wrongly used to refer to individual lines of a headline.

DUMMY Also called plan, scheme, layout, or make-up sheet, and meaning a 'blueprint' of the intended layout, either advertising or editorial, or both.

EAR OR EAR-PIECE In editorial terms, the advertising space or spaces beside the front-page title-line.

EDITIONISING The process of producing different versions of one issue of a newspaper, sometimes determined by time, as in 'first edition', 'last edition', 'early special', 'late final', etc., and sometimes by geographical definition, as in 'City edition', 'County edition', 'North' or 'South' editions, etc.

EM Much misused term intended to mean (a) the square of the body depth of any given type size, or (b) the constant unit of area measurement, the 12pt or pica em.

EN Half an em; when referring to half of a 12pt or pica em sometimes called non-pareil or nonp or (for verbal ease) nomple.

EYE-BREAK An element more substantial than a crosshead or sub-heading, used to break up a lengthy run of type.

FLAG More often TITLEPIECE or TITLE-LINE, meaning the newspaper's name as it appears at the head of the front page; often referred to (but wrongly) as the MASTHEAD (q.v.).

FLUSH As in 'flush left' or 'flush right', meaning to line up with the edge or margin of a column or measure.

FOLIO A sheet of copy; the running headline of a page bearing title, date and page number; a tabloid (q.v.) sheet.

FOUNT Sometimes FONT, which is the

GUTTER The space between columns or facing pages.

HAMPER Relatively new term to describe a multi-column element, often enclosed in a box, placed above the main headline on a page.

HANGING INDENT These days more often referred to as REVERSE INDENT or 'nought and one', meaning the first line of each paragraph is to be set full out to the setting measure but other lines to be indented by one em; may be varied as in nought-and-two, nought-and-three, etc., as in television programme guides where the time and title of a programme may stand to the left of the descriptive matter that follows.

KICKER One of those words that change meaning as they cross the Atlantic. In Europe usually taken to mean one element of a page that contrasts by type-style with the rest of the page, i.e., the one sans-serif headline on a page of seriffed headlines. In the US a headline of a few words appearing above the main headline and at about half the typesize; in the UK this device is usually referred to as a STRAP-LINE.

LAYOUT See DUMMY.

LOGO A label or insignia, in type or artwork, that identifies a section or column such as 'Women's Page', 'Business', 'Personal finance', 'Life-style' etc; also referred to as standing head, label, page-top, etc.

MAKE-UP See DUMMY.

MASTHEAD Loosely and incorrectly used for the front-page title-line; more properly used to describe that element displaying the paper's name and other house matter above the leader column on the editorial page.

MODULAR That style of page design where all the elements form regular shapes, usually rectangles.

POINT The standard unit of type size, 12 points to a pica, the basis of print measurement.

PROCESS COLOUR Usually taken to mean full-colour reproduction achieved by colour separation on individual pieces of film.

REVERSES Those typographical elements that reverse or vary the normal use of black lettering on paper; i.e., white-on-black, black-on-tint, white-on-tint; often abbreviated to WOBs, BOTs, and WOTs.

SPLASH The main story on page one.

STANDFIRST A kind of typographical aperitif, a sentence or two presented in display fashion to introduce a news story or feature and perhaps its writer.

STRAP-LINE Subsidiary headline placed above a main headline, usually at about half of its type size.

STREAMER The main heading on a page, running across several columns but less than the full width of the page; see BANNER.

TABLOID A page half the size (the folio or single fold) of a broadsheet.

WHITE OR WHITING Generic term for space, i.e., the non-printing portion of a page.

WIDOW A lonely word making up the last line of a paragraph, to be avoided when it would fall at the top of a second or subsequent leg or column of type.

BIBLIOGRAPHY

ARNOLD, Edmund, C., *Modern newspaper design*, Harper & Row, New York, 1969.

BARNHART, Thomas F., *Weekly newspaper makeup and typography*, University of Minnesota Press/Oxford University Press, 1949.

BIGGS, John R., *An approach to type*, Blandford Press, London, 1961.

BROWN, Charles H., *News editing and display*, Harper & Brothers, New York, 1951.

CHESKIN, Louis, *Colours and what they can do*, Blandford Press, London, 1952.

CRAIG, James, *Production for the graphic designer*, Watson-Guptill, New York, 1983.

CROZIER, Michael, *The making of The Independent*, Gordon Fraser, London, 1988.

DE GRANDIS, Luigina, *Theory and use of colour*, Blandford Press, London, 1986.

EVANS, Harold, *Editing and design* series in five volumes: *Newsman's English*, 1972; *Newspaper design*, 1973; *Handling newspaper text*, 1974; *News headlines*, 1974; *Picture editing*, 1978.

—*Front page history*, Penguin Books, London 1985.

HALEY, Allan, *Phototypography*, Robert Hale, London, 1980.

HODGSON, F. W., *Modern newspaper editing and production*, Heinemann, London, 1987.

HUTT, G. Allen, *Newspaper design*, Oxford University Press 1960.

HUTT, G. Allen, *The Changing Newspaper*, Gordon Fraser, London, 1973.

BERRY, W. Turner, A. F. Johnson & W. P. Jaspert, *The encyclopaedia of type faces* (revised ed.), Blandford Press, London, 1983.

LIEBERMAN, J. Ben, *Type and typefaces*, Myriade Press, 1967.

McLEAN, Ruari, *Magazine design*, Oxford University Press, 1969.

—*The Thames and Hudson Manual of Typography*, Thames and Hudson, London, 1980.

MOEN, Daryl, R., *Newspaper layout and design*, Iowa State University Press, 1986.

MORISON, Stanley, *The English newspaper*, Cambridge University Press, 1932.

ROOKLEDGE, Gordon, and Christopher Perfect, *Rookledge's international typefinder*, Sarema Press, London, 1983.

REHE, Rolf, F., *Typography and design for newspapers*, IFRA, 1985.

SELLERS, Leslie, *Doing it in style*, Pergamon Press, Oxford, 1968.

—*The simple sub's book*, Pergamon Press, Oxford, 1968.

—*Keeping up the Style*, Pitman, London, 1975.

SMITH, Charles, *Color: study and teaching*, Van Nostrand Rheinhold, New York, 1965.

SIMON, Oliver, *Introduction to typography*, Faber & Faber, London, 1969.

SPENCER, Herbert, *The visible word: problems of legibility* (rev. ed.), Lund Humphries, London, 1969.

SULLIVAN, Peter, *Newspaper graphics*, IFRA, 1987.

TRACY, Walter, *Letters of credit*, Gordon Fraser, London, 1986.

WILLIAMS, Ian, *Newspapers of the First World War*, David & Charles, Newton Abbott, 1974.

WILLS, F. H., *Fundamentals of layout*, Dover Publications, Mineola, NY, 1965.

NEWSPAPERS ILLUSTRATED

A VAST number of newspapers were generous in the provision of illustrations – so many, in fact, that there has not been room for all of them. The scope of this help may be gauged from the following list of those individual newspapers and groups cited and the pages where they appear: *Wigan Observer* (pages 8, 9); *Bild*, Berlin (10, 11); *The Times*, London (12, 14, 18, 35, 55, 135, 152, 153, 161); *USA Today* (12, 120, 157, 159, 168, 169, 170); *The Sunday Times* (14, 15, 108, 109, 115, 122, 142, 145, 146, 147, 149); *The Northern Echo* (14, 98, 110, 111, 113); *Bexhill-on-Sea Observer* (16); *The Buckinghamshire Advertiser* (16); *The Daily Courant* (16); *The Daily Mail* (17, 123, 133, 139, 181); *The Star* (18, 125, 132, 139); *The Independent* (19, 102, 141, 146, 150, 157, 160, 161, 162); *Woman's Own* (19); *Vogue* (19); *Harper's Bazaar* (19); *Financial Times* (19, 50, 64, 95, 121, 161); *Sporting Life* (19, 160); *Die Zeit* (20); *Daily News*, New York (20, 21); *The Guardian* (22, 113, 128, 159, 161); *The Courier-Mail*, Brisbane (26, 79); *News Chronicle* (28); *Dublin Independent* (28); *New York Times* (38, 65); *Financial Post* (39); *The Observer* (40, 42, 43, 185); *Burgess Hill Leader* (42); *Sydney Morning Herald* (43); *Winnipeg Free Press* (44, 45); *Evening Standard*, London (45, 118, 128, 133, 160, 166, 167, 185); *Evening News*, London (45, 157, 166, 167); *The Globe and Mail* (46); *Today* (46, 107, 131, 132, 156, 159, 164); *The Daily Telegraph* (46, 47, 67, 115, 135, 149, 164, 180); *The Sunday Telegraph* (46, 47, 180, 185); *Stock and Land* (48); *Liverpool Echo* (49); *The Age*, Melbourne (50, 51, 97, 106); *Berita Harian* (51); *The Boston Globe* (52, 53); *Pravda* (54); *Keighley Target* (56); *The Sun*, Auckland (182, 183); *The Sun*, London (58, 100, 130, 133, 143, 182); *The Sun*, Fiji (58, 182); *The Sun*, Sydney (100, 182, 183); *The Ledger*, Lakeland (64, 157, 159), *Now!* (64); *Malton Gazette & Herald* (66); *Sunday People* (66); *The Vancouver Sun* (68); *Century Magazine* (68); *The Alabama Journal* (69); *Toronto Star* (70, 71); *Telegraph & Argus*, Bradford (71, 104, 105, 119, 128, 153, 158, 159, 164); *Daily Express* (72, 125, 132, 157, 140, 143); *The Providence Journal* (74, 75); *Daily Mirror*, London (76, 98, 119, 122, 126, 131, 132, 140, 151, 153, 159); *Daily Mirror*, Sydney (119); *The Christian Science Monitor* (76); *The Yorkshire Evening Press* (76, 77); *South China Morning Post* (79); *Darlington & Stockton Times* (80, 81); *Canberra Times* (88, 89); *Auckland Star* (90); *Waikato Times* (90, 91); *The Herald*, Melbourne (92, 93); *Chicago Tribune* (74, 95, 106, 120); *Wall Street Journal* (95, 97); *Shields Gazette* (96); *The Morning Call* (98, 99); *Manchester Evening News* (87); *Western Morning News* (87); *Los Angeles Times* (106); *Hendon Times* (122, 123); Press Association pictures (124, 126); *Evening Gazette*, Blackpool (127); *The Birmingham Post* (127, 130); *Yorkshire Evening Post* (129); *Evening Echo*, Basildon (129, 178, 179); *Evening Post*, Chatham (129); *Huddersfield Daily Examiner* (129); *Daily Record*, Glasgow (133, 151); *Evening Argus*, Brighton (136); *The Western Mail*, Perth (138); *Durham Advertiser* (142); *Sunday Sun*, Newcastle (142); *Sheffield Star* (148); *Providence Sunday Journal* (146, 148); *South Bucks Star* (150); *The Register*, Orange County (154, 155); *Milton Keynes Mirror* (156); *Birmingham Daily News* (156, 160, 161, 164); *Bedford & Kempston Express* (156, 157); *London Daily News* (157, 159, 160, 166, 167); *Nottingham Evening Post* (158, 159, 164); *Printing World* (159, 160); *Racing Post* (160, 161, 162, 163); *The Irish Press* (163); *The Advertiser*, Adelaide (163); *Bromsgrove Advertiser* (165); *Bognor Regis Observer* (165); *Oxford Journal* (165); *Oxford Star* (165); *Manchester Metro News* (165); *Bromley Times* (171); *Dartford Times* (171); *Kentish Times Group* (171, 172); *Oxford Mail* (178); *Western Daily Press* (178, 179), *The Standard*, St Catherine's (180); *The Leader*, Staines (180); *Daily Sketch* (181); *San Francisco Examiner* (183); *The Denver Post* (183); *The Scotsman* (185); *Australian Financial Review* (185).

INDEX